W9-BKW-511

75265

COMMUNAL SOCIETIES IN AMERICA
AN AMS REPRINT SERIES

SHAKERISM

ITS MEANING AND MESSAGE

AMS PRESS
NEW YORK

NO. 1. FRONTISPIECE. HOME OF THE AUTHORS.

SHAKERISM

ITS MEANING AND MESSAGE

EMBRACING

An Historical Account, Statement of Belief and
Spiritual Experience of the Church from
Its Rise to the Present Day.

BY

ANNA WHITE

AND

LEILA S. TAYLOR

(North Family of Shakers, Mount Lebanon, N. Y.)

"Let him that readeth understand."

COLUMBUS, OHIO
PRESS OF FRED. J. HEER

The Library of Congress Cataloged the Original Printing of this Title as Follows:

White, Anna, 1831-1910.
    Shakerism, its meaning and message; embracing an historical account, statement of belief and spiritual experience of the church from its rise to the present day. By Anna White and Leila S. Taylor . . . Columbus, O., Press of F. J. Heer [ᶜ1904] 417 p. front ., plates, ports. 20ᶜᵐ

    1. Shakers.   I. Taylor, Lella Sarah, joint author. II. Title.
                                                          5-3724
Library of Congress   BX9771.W5
                           [41f1]

Reprinted from the edition of 1904, Columbus
First AMS edition published in 1971
Manufactured in the United States of America

Library of Congress Catalog Card Number: 73-134421
International Standard Book Number: 0-404-08462-1

AMS PRESS INC.
NEW YORK, N.Y. 10003

PREFACE.

SHAKERISM presents a system of faith and a mode of life, which, during the past century, has solved social and religious problems and successfully established practical brotherhoods of industry, besides freeing woman from inequality and injustice. To this there must be added that it has banished from its precincts monopoly, immorality, intemperance and crime, by creating a life of purity, social freedom and altruistic industry. A system that has rendered such a service to mankind merits attention from all thoughtful people, whatever may be their position in life.

That the Shakers, through the teachings of their faith, have wrought out a practical solution of many social enigmas of the time, is admitted. It now remains to fit the principles embodied in this faith to the needs of the great world.

For a better understanding of their work and its meaning, this message, embodying the thought and word of many Shakers, is sent forth.

Mount Lebanon, N. Y., June 28, 1904.

(3)

TABLE OF CONTENTS.

(5)

LIST OF ILLUSTRATIONS.

PAGE

(9)

EXTRACT FROM ANCIENT SHAKER HYMN.

YE ARE GOD'S BUILDING.

Inspired by wisdom, in union and love,
We sing of Jerus'lem the city above,
And in the male order, Christ Jesus we own,
Her Great Master-builder and chief corner stone:
    And we'll sing alleluia! her founder is free!
    Amen! alleluia! Even so let it be.

The time being come for the house to be rear'd,
In the female order a stone was prepar'd,
A woman cut out and redeemed from the fall,
To stand in her order, the MOTHER of all:
    And we'll sing alleluia! our MOTHER is free!
    Amen! alleluia! Even so let it be.

In man and in woman, that work did begin,
Which cleanses the soul from the nature of sin;
And God has confirmed, by His promise and oath,
That His holy temple shall stand upon both:
    And we'll sing alleluia! our Parents are free!
    Amen! alleluia! Even so let it be.

Now Zion's foundation forever shall stand,
Upheld by our FATHER's omnipotent hand;
And our Blessed MOTHER shall certainly bear
All souls that shall find an inheritance there:
    And we'll sing alleluia! their children are free!
    Amen! alleluia! Even so let it be.

      Published in "Millennial Praises," Part I, 1812.

A MODERN SHAKER HYMN.

THE COMING OF THE LIGHT.

There are mighty forces gathering
  Round the standard of the right,
There are myriads appealing
  For the coming of the light,
To reveal the growing evils
  That are spreading far and wide,
Threatening to engulf the nations
  In a dark, o'erwhelming tide.

Lo! amid the great uprising
  Like the surging of the sea,
There are mighty forces working
  To uplift humanity;
Swelling waves of revolution,
  Borne upon the tide of thought,
Are precursors of the triumph
  Truth and justice have outwrought.

Sons and daughters of the Spirit,
  Filled with inspiration's power,
Speak the words of truth prophetic
  That shall meet the present hour;
And the people mass for freedom,
  Great as Israel's serried host,
For the King of Glory cometh,
  Bringing judgment to earth's coast.

Be ye lifted up, ye everlasting gates,
  Let the King of Glory enter in!
For He cometh, even now,
With the light upon His brow.
  To redeem the world from sin.

Martha J. Anderson, Mount Lebanon, 1899.

(12)

I

ORIGIN OF SHAKERISM

THE history of mankind like the history of the earth reveals the workings of a mighty Force; in rocks and stars is traced its action upon matter, in the records of racial religions is read its operation upon the soul of man. Each great movement of spiritual energy has culminated in some master mind, such as Zoroaster, Gautama, and o hers, many of whom have been forgotten, perhaps in decadent races, or on continents now slumbering beneath the sea. Again and again has a spiritual flood-tide lifted man up and its ebb brought him low. These tidal waves of divinity rose highest in Jesus of Nazareth, known to over three hundred millions of nominal followers as Jesus the Anointed. The religious history of races and peoples calling themselves Christian reveals the same record of ebb and flood.

The 17th century of our era was marked by an affluence in religious sensibility among the common people of Europe. The world of matter had not begun to veil the world of spirit. The telescope in man's hand had opened the heavens and beyond their blazing systems he saw God. The microscope was not yet in all men's hands, atom and embryo focusing his conceptions till matter became All. In this period, the Spirit of God wrought in men's hearts a deep sense of their own weakness and sin, of His might and purity, and the relation of the soul to God became a subject of intense personal interest. Christ, God manifest in flesh, victorious over sin, the Redeemer of the race,

(13)

was at hand; the end of all things was near; the world and its wicked life was to stop; heaven and hell, antipodes in the utmost of sentient, emotive existence, were believed in, and I, you, must be ready for the one, would we escape the other.

As spirit forces swept low over humanity the religious element in man's nature was stirred. The winds of God blew strong and men shook beneath their sway, bowing at the touch of God as forests bend before the electric force that precedes a mighty storm. In France, this religious upheaval took the form of remarkable psychical development and strong physical action. Trance and vision, followed by violent bodily agitation, marked the reception and utterance of inspired truth. Prophecy, mingled with warning and denunciation, aroused against the recipients of this strange influence opposition and persecution.

From Cevennes, in 1689, the exiled Camisards went forth over Europe and visited England in 1706. Here they were known as the French Prophets. Out of rhapsody and ecstatic emotion grew lives of purity and uprightness. The Quaker Church, a parallel movement, was remarkable for stillness before God till moved by the power of the Spirit. Some who were especially subject to spiritual influence upon the external being were called in derision "Shaking Quakers" or "Shakers." A society, led by James and Jane Wardley, was formed in Manchester, England, in 1747. The members gave themselves up to be led by the spirit of God and continued to increase in numbers, although suffering much from persecution. This little band became the matrix for a new influx of Deity.

Ann Lee.

In a lowly cottage in a humble lane of Manchester had been growing up a bright, active little girl. Born February 29, 1736, Ann Lee was the child of John Lee, an honest, industrious blacksmith. She had five brothers and two sisters. As a child, Ann was serious and thoughtful, subject to strong religious impressions and given to reverie and vision. There were no free schools for the children of the poor in that day, and little Ann, like others of her class, learned to work instead of to read, and at an early age was busy in the mills. Endowed with the spiritual organization which in that time sent some to the witch's gallows who today would be cherished and protected, this little factory girl told her visions of angels to the ear of an affectionate, God-fearing mother of piety and common sense, who, like another mother, "hid all these things in her heart." Intense desires for purity and holy living filled the heart of the child. As she grew older she was deeply impressed by the depravity of human nature and showed a strong repugnance to marriage. Pitiful were her pleas to her mother's love to protect her from impurity. Useless your prayers, O little Ann! Woman, in your day, had but one life before her, and at an early age Ann was married to Abraham Stanley, a blacksmith like her father, a kindly man, who loved his beef and beer, his chimney corner and seat in village tavern. Four children came and passed away. Ann Lee was a soul apart. She is pictured in mature life as of average stature, well proportioned, with blue eyes, light brown hair and regular features. With a mild, expressive countenance, she had a keen, penetrating glance and by many was called beautiful. Strong and healthy, she possessed a sound constitution and remarkable powers of mind and body.

Always has it been true that a great religious movement has started with one person. About this humble, unlettered woman centered some of the most remarkable spiritual phenomena the world has seen — electric streams from

Deity using her as transmitter of spiritual force. The usual verdicts accounting for extraordinary developments of this nature here will not serve. Too healthy for hysteria, too well balanced for insanity, too practical for visionary or self-deceiving egotist, too real and well attested in all her manifestations of power, for hypocrisy.

Soul Struggles.

Ann had been induced to marry contrary to her own feelings and conscience; her early convictions returned, increased by the repugnance due to her sensitively organized spiritual nature. Qualms of conscience troubled her; strong desires possessed her for a life of purity, for a knowledge of truth, for an understanding of the right relation of the soul to God; the sense of sin and the need of personal salvation oppressed her. These feelings intensified as time wore on. She must know the truth — how man came into his lost, helpless condition, the hidden cause of his sin and shame. Like no other woman did she travail in soul and cry to God. Burdened, not only for her own soul, but for that husband from whose physical embraces she shrank with sensitive repugnance, burdened for parents, friends, for all mankind, her prayers were unceasing for release from sin, for purity of heart. In 1758, when twenty-two years old, she had united with the society of the Wardleys and, in accordance with their custom, had confessed her sins before her leaders, but her mental struggles continued. Her own simple language, as repeated from time to time to her followers, best tells the tale: "Soon after I set out to travel in the way of God, I labored anights in the work of God. Sometimes I labored all night, continually crying to God for my own redemption; sometimes I went to bed and slept; but in the morning I could not feel that sense of the work of God which I had before I slept.

This brought me into great tribulation. Then I cried to God and promised Him that if He would give me the same sense that I had before I slept, I would labor all night. This I did many nights; and in the day time I put my hands to work and my heart to God; and when I felt weary and in need of rest, I labored for the power of God and the refreshing operations of the power of God would release me, so that I would feel able to go to my work again. Many times when I was about my work I felt my soul overwhelmed with sorrow; and I used to work as long as I could keep it concealed and then run to get out of sight, lest anyone should pity me with that pity which God did not.

"In my travail and tribulation my sufferings were so great that my flesh consumed upon my bones, bloody sweat pressed through the pores of my skin and I became as helpless as an infant. And when I was brought through and born into the spiritual kingdom, I was like an infant just brought into the world. They see colors and objects but they know not what they see; and so it was with me when I was brought into the spiritual world. But before I was twenty-four hours old I saw and I knew what I saw."

One who knew her well in these early years has testified that in these periods of mental suffering she wasted away like one in consumption and became so weak and emaciated that her friends had to feed and care for her as though she were an infant. At times her skin was covered with a bloody perspiration and her groans and cries were such as to bring dismay to all who heard her. For nine years this mental suffering and attendant physical anguish continued, with intervals when her strength would return and her heart be cheered by visions and revelations of divine light and glory.

2

There is something here worthy of consideration. Ann could not read and the sermons, the whole body of divinity, as well as the philosophy, religious and infidel, of her time, were of no use to her; she knew not even their names. Church and clergy helped her not. She turned from them, for they lacked the knowledge and power of salvation. The conditions of her problem were few and simple. She, an unlettered woman, burdened with her sins, was one of a lost race; God, the Creator, was on high and to Him she went. There was no doubt, apparently, of His being, nor of His power to grant her requests. She had no psychologic mists to befog her; there is no record of any skepticism, none of the vagueness of mental perspective that prompted the infidel's famous prayer: "O God, if there be a God, save my soul if I have a soul!" There were four elements intensely real to her — a double duality. There were Ann Lee and sin; she was sure of them. There were God and salvation; she believed in both as surely as she knew their human correlatives, and she went to work.

To one who would give herself, with such persistence and endurance, to the search for divine light, small wonder that the heavens opened and that she saw, as in a mirror, the facts about which man's fancies and interpretations had drifted like concealing clouds for centuries.

Not in one revelation, but many, in repeated openings of the unseen world, Ann, prepared by abstinence from personal indulgence of any kind, by her mighty faith, her directness of aim and her tense soul absorption, was met as such a nature must be met. She testified, in the most solemn, though humble way, over and over, both in England and America, that Jesus Christ revealed himself to her, showed her things not yet apprehended among men and anointed her, Ann Lee, blacksmith's daughter and blacksmith's wife, with the Spirit of Christ.

Among these revelations were two striking at the root of the constitution of things in church and state. One was the duality of Deity, God both Father and Mother; one in essence — one God, not two; but God who possesses the two natures, the masculine, the feminine, each distinct in function yet one in being, Co-equals in Deity. The second was that the secret of man's sin, the hidden cause of man's fall from uprightness, his loss of purity, lay in the premature and self-indulgent use of sexual union. With the story of the Garden of Eden in her mind, not as an eastern tale, but as a divinely revealed, historic fact, Ann Lee saw in vision the act of the first pair performed, not as a natural function, under divine control in a proper time and sequence, for the divinely directed purpose of propagation, but as an act of self-indulgence and therefore of sin. This symbolic vision portrays the truth that underlies humanity's actual history. The natural function, which was intended in each individual to subserve its purpose and then to be left behind as higher spiritual development was attained, became, in fact, for all humanity, a constant curse, the source of crimes of all degrees of hideousness, of wars and sufferings untold. Woman, under its sway, became in all lands and among all races, the abject slave, burdened not only with the weight of her lord's cruelties and passions, but with her own vile passions as well.

The view of the cause of man's defilement brought also in clear light the command to abstain from such indulgence. Jesus, the Revealer, was in his human life pure and undefiled; such were his early followers. Such must all become, said Ann Lee, after this revelation and anointing, who would be true followers of Jesus Christ.

As these revelations were accorded her, she told them to the society where she obeyed, as head and elders, the two guides of her youth. The latest and most complete unfold-

ings were experienced in 1770, when she was in jail at Manchester, where religious persecution had placed her. On
her release from prison she related in full the experiences
she had undergone and her story was accompanied by such
displays of the Divine presence and approval, with so much
of light and glory in her soul and person and with such
keen, searching power in discovering hidden sins and works
of darkness, that every one was filled with fear and trembling. In the language of her followers: "They saw at once
that the candle of the Lord was in her hand and that she
was able by the light thereof to search every heart and
try every soul among them. From that time she was received and acknowledged as the first visible leader of the
church of God upon earth."

Ann, by her obedience to the voice of God in her soul,
through faith and suffering had become fitted, as a pure
temple, to receive the spirit of Christ. The Christ Spirit,
emanation from, manifestation of the invisible God, Father-
Mother, had descended upon the man, Jesus of Nazareth,
who in a similar way had prepared himself, a temple fit to
receive the indwelling Spirit. This anointing by the Eternal Spirit of Christ occurred at the baptism by John and
Jesus became, henceforth, Jesus the Anointed. He became
the second Adam. It was necessary that the Christ Spirit
should come again and in a woman complete the spiritual,
as Eve had completed the natural, human creation, the
image of the Divine. This baptism, received not at the
hands of man but from the person of the risen and divine
Jesus, gave to Ann Lee the authority as well as the spirit
of the Maternal Presence — the Mother in Deity. Henceforth, Ann Lee was recognized among the humble band
of "poor in spirit," "pure in heart," who in England's hidden
by-ways were waiting for "the consolation of Israel," as the

living, visible Head, the one in whom dwelt the Divine Mother.

There is something sublime in the simplicity and directness of this unlettered woman, for whom the usual joys of womanhood had faded and fallen like autumn leaves from off the swelling buds of a new year. When she united with the society of the Wardleys, she determined to know God for herself and she strove until she found Him. Not turning away from her humble duties in any quest of a mission, but in her solitude, in the midst of toil, striving as did Jacob of old through midnight hours with the angel of mystery, gaining from the conflict recognition, truth and a name and nature filled with the Divine. From the depths of woman's secret life, bearing the untold wrongs, the unwhispered shames of all womankind, of her to whom it was said and by whom it has been bitterly fulfilled, "Thy desire shall be to thy husband and he shall rule over thee," out of the dregs of society, knowing the pangs of ignorance, the toils and burdens, the pinching poverty of the downtrodden poor, — she conquered all by her mighty reliance on God, her soul uplift for herself and all womankind.

Why was Ann Lee so unlike all the other poor women of Manchester, her neighbors in Toad Lane? Because she was called of God and obeyed the call, and thus became the Chosen, the Daughter of God, of whom it may be said, "Many daughters have done virtuously, but thou excellest them all."

Ministration — Persecution.

The life of a religious enthusiast is not easy at any time or place. The experiences of one whose ideas are so radically at variance with the established ways of mankind as were those of Ann Lee will be sure to meet with hostility, varying from the smile and shrug of contempt and indifference to more pointed expressions of disfavor and disgust, demonstrations growing in point and force as the habit of expression among a people is simple and unrepressed.

In 1770, among the English townsfolk of Manchester, brutally frank and outspoken, the fact of a woman presuming to preach and teach, and to preach and teach against the natural life, against the good old Bible command to "Multiply and replenish the earth," was cause enough for decisive action. No matter if the earth were already replenished to repletion, till annual starvation threatened themselves and their children with death, that command they would adhere to, no matter what others were broken! Ann Lee herself was as direct in her earnest zeal as her outraged neighbors and talked plainly and pointedly, to all who would listen, of the sins of the flesh and the lusts thereof.

Finally, goaded to distraction by her persistent rebukes and, perhaps, pierced by their own aroused consciences — they thought to silence her voice by prison walls, with what result we have seen. Ann Lee came forth from Manchester jail an instrument more finely attuned, keyed to a truer pitch than ever before,— a mouth-piece for the Divine voice, a presence charged with the live currents of truth, with the power of God to convict and to slay, with the love of God, also, to pardon and to heal. "I kill and I make alive, I wound and I heal."

Then followed until her death in 1784, a constant series of ministrations of this power and love to those with whom she came in contact, and also a succession of the most unrelenting persecutions history has recorded of anyone. Among her persecutors were some of her own family. A brother became so enraged as she sat singing, that he seized a stick the size of a broom handle, and beat her over the head and face, until the end of the stick was splintered.

Then he called for a drink and began again with the other end. She records that she distinctly saw and felt bright rays from God pass continually between her face and the stick, so that she did not feel the blows, and she felt her own breath as healing balsam.

At one time, a mob seized and dragged her, kicking and beating her, for two miles, when they were met by a nobleman from some distance away, who stopped their proceedings. He told her that he had felt a sudden, strong impression to go in a certain direction. So strong was the feeling, that having ordered his horse saddled, he sent a second messenger after the first and mounting, rode as rapidly as he could till he met the concourse of roughs and rescued the solitary victim.

At times she seemed protected by an invisible power. Once they tried to tie her with ropes but could not secure the knots; at another time they took her with several of her associates into a valley, prepared to stone them to death, but though the missiles were many and large not one would hit. Ann said: "I felt myself surrounded by the presence of God and my soul was filled with love. I knew they could not kill me for my work was not done." While being led down into the valley of stoning she sang this song:

"Touch not mine anointed nor do my chosen harm;
I the Lord Jehovah will shield them with My arm.
I am a God of mercy, of justice and truth;
My work of love and power shall yet spread o'er the earth;
I dwell not in a mansion that's far, far away;
Nor do I inhabit a tenement of clay;
Beyond the starry regions I do not fix my throne,
But in My church on earth I am in spirit known."

During this time Ann Lee was proving the reality of her call by the work of redemption which went on through her ministrations. The custom of the society of the Wardleys, arising from what they believed a spiritual command, both in the Bible and to their own understandings, to confess all their sins, one by one, before their leaders, was established in the greater light that came through Ann Lee. Many, by her heart searching talks, were aroused, convicted and came to her voluntarily confessing their sins. By such was experienced a soul change, real and convincing to them as to thousands who since have followed in their steps. The sins confessed were forgiven and removed from memory. Power was obtained over faults and weaknesses, and men and women daily became victors over long established sinful habits and dispositions. With the life of God flowing into the soul came gifts such as distinguished the primitive Christians of apostolic days; they saw visions, they healed diseases, they spoke in strange and unknown languages, when under the spell of a power like that felt at the Day of Pentecost. Some could not speak in their own tongue for several days but spoke in prophecy in an unknown language.

But, wonderful as were these endowments, the surest proof, then as now, of indwelling divinity was in changed lives, in hearts made pure, lips made clean, speech made gentle and lives made true. Ann Lee and her followers were everywhere spoken of as good, honest, upright and pure, and such has been the reputation of her followers to the present day. Among her peculiar gifts, which gained for her the reputation of witch and sorceress, was the power to read the mental tablets and their record of the past. Many a time did those who came into her presence quail before her clear unfolding of hidden deeds and thoughts. Lips that made but half a sacrifice, while pretending to confess all, were met, like Ananias and Sapphira of old, with the statement of the whole truth and were paralyzed with fear. It is a fact, well attested both in England and America, that while those who honestly confessed their sins and by a new life manifested their repentance and acceptance of the Gospel, as revealed through Ann Lee, became changed and grew into pure, noble characters, those, on the other hand, who rejected and opposed the light thus brought to bear on heart and conscience, soon lost even their former sense of religion, degenerated in character, became debased and hardened, and in many cases, died in misery and wretchedness. An experience common to all now who truly confess their sins to her successors, as it was then common to all who thus went to her and those with her, is that sin seems exceeding sinful; a loathing and hatred is felt for what before seemed but foibles and weakness, accompanied by power to overcome, to put them aside, to leave them behind and to arise in purity and sinlessness. This power, in its fulness, has been unknown elsewhere since the days of the apostles. These are living proofs of the reality of the claim that this work is that of Christ. They are the continual seals of her ministry and testimony.

An ancient Talmudic tale recounts that the giving of the Mosaic Law on Sinai was in a language which to the hearers became resolved into the seventy languages believed then to be spoken on the earth. The story is significant of the test to which Ann Lee was subjected. At one time, to secure her conviction and suppression, she was accused of blasphemy, and that the question might be settled, she was brought before four clergymen of the Church of England, all noted as linguistic scholars. The penalty, if convicted, was to have her tongue bored through with a red-hot iron and to be branded in the cheek. The mysterious Presence, which in a former age had said to the disciples of Jesus: "Open thy mouth wide and I will fill it," did not desert this woman of whom it has been said that she could neither read nor write. The power of God fell upon her, the gift of tongues was imparted and she discoursed to these clergymen, speaking, as they testified, in seventy-two different languages, speaking many of them, as they declared, better than they had ever heard them spoken before. They advised her persecutors to let her alone.

Not only were her naturally rare powers of intellect stimulated to action, her bodily powers also, unusually vigorous as they were, at times received increase and sustenance as well as protection from the unseen side of life. She was once imprisoned at Manchester, without legal process, by secret connivance of the jailer with her enemies, for the express purpose of starving her to death. For fourteen days she was kept without food, nor was her cell door once opened during that time. The cell was so small that she could neither stand nor sit nor even straighten herself. James Whittaker, then a young man, felt so strongly for her, that he succeeded in conveying to her nightly a small quantity of wine and milk by means of a pipe stem inserted in the keyhole of the door. This was all the nutriment she received. At the end of a fortnight her brutal captors opened the door, expecting to drag out her dead body. To their utter amazement, she arose and walked off, looking nearly as well as ever. One who afterward became a Shaker Elder was present, and said, years later, that everybody was astonished and acknowledged that she must be under the protection of some supernatural power and that it was wrong to try to injure or oppress her.

In the year 1838, an English woman visiting at Alfred, Maine, remarked that she was from Manchester. Two Shaker sisters said, "Why, that is where our Mother came from," and proceeded to give some account of Ann Lee. The woman was greatly affected, and said with emotion:

"That is the very woman I have heard my mother talk about and cry as if her heart would break; she would give anything to know what had become of that woman." Her mother had been present when Ann Lee had been let out of the stone prison. A very great multitude had assembled to see her and were much affected by her appearance. The sisters told their visitor to tell her mother, when she returned to England, that Ann Lee had come to America and that she herself had seen some of her children. The woman replied with emphasis that she should not wait for that, but should write to her mother at once about it. She also said that there had been a prophecy extant that the same work begun by Ann Lee would be there again,.but that it would come from afar.

At last, to such desperate straits had her opponents come in their struggle with this one poor woman, that a man was sent off to interview the King and obtain authority to crush and silence Ann Lee. The man died suddenly on the way, in such a manner that his death was looked upon as a judgment of God. Others of her tormentors met a similar fate and at last her opponents took counsel of events and let this strange woman alone. For two years she and her followers were free to preach and practise their religion as they would. No one presumed to persecute or interfere.

II

SHAKERISM IN AMERICA

ALTHOUGH free to work and worship, the little church could not advance in England. The stolid, conservative minds of the common people did not open readily to the new, strange doctrine and the course of its expounders was directed to the New World; to a land where speech was free, religion untrammeled and where men, unshackled by the independence of pioneer life, quickened by its emergencies, freed from precedent and custom, could think and act for themselves.

Ann Lee, ever intent on the will of God, received visions and revelations wherein a plain command was given to go to America, with a promise that there the Gospel would be accepted and a church built up which should never fail. Explicit views of places and people were seen, that were recognized at sight years after. She said: "I knew that God had a chosen people in America; I saw some of them in vision and when I met with them in America I knew them."

On the 19th of May, 1774, a band of nine set sail from Liverpool in the ship Mariah for New York. Besides Ann Lee there was her husband, Abraham Stanley, her brother, William Lee, James Whittaker, John Hocknell and his son Richard, James Shepherd, Mary Partington and Nancy Lee, a niece of Ann Lee. John Hocknell was the only one possessed of means and it was through his generosity that they were enabled to make the voyage and establish themselves

(28)

NO. 2. WATERVLIET, N. Y. MEETING HOUSE ON THE RIGHT ERECTED BY THE UNITED LABOR OF SHAKERS FROM EVERY SOCIETY IN THE U. S.

in America. The ship was an old, leaky vessel which had been condemned as unseaworthy. They were two and a half months on the voyage and narrowly escaped foundering in a storm. Mother Ann, as she had long been called by her followers, told the captain before embarking that he would have nothing of which to accuse them unless it were concerning the law of their God. On the Sabbath they came out singing and dancing in their usual manner of worship and Mother Ann spoke boldly against the wickedness of the sailors. This enraged the captain and he threatened that if they did so again he would throw them overboard. But they thought they must obey God rather than man and, nothing daunted, when next the spirit moved them to worship in song and dance on deck, out they came! The captain in great anger proceeded to put his threat in execution, but was stopped by the ship springing a leak. It was in the midst of a violent storm and everyone had to work at the pumps. The water gained fast and they expected to go to the bottom. Evening came and Mother Ann went to the captain, saying: "Captain, be of good cheer; there shall not a hair of our heads perish; we shall all arrive safe in America. I just now saw two bright angels of God standing by the mast, through whom I received this promise." She then encouraged the seamen and she with her companions worked at the pumps. Soon after, a great wave struck the ship and, it is thought, pressed into place a loose plank. The leak was stopped and after this the captain gave his strange passengers full liberty to worship as they felt right, and upon his arrival in New York he declared that but for these people he would never have reached America.

Landing in New York August 6th, 1774, the little party separated in order to earn their living. Ann worked at washing and ironing. John Hocknell and others went up the river to Albany, where they secured a piece of low, swampy land in the wilderness about seven miles northwest of Albany, at Niskeyuna, the modern Watervliet. Hocknell then returned to England to bring out his family. Stanley became very ill and Ann tenderly nursed him through a long and severe sickness, which took all her time and strength so that they had no means of support and were reduced to extreme poverty. He rewarded her after recovery by abuse and desertion. He renounced the faith, abandoned her and married another woman. Ann was often in great poverty and privation. At one time her only shelter in a cold winter was a small, bare room without fire or furniture, and once her only food was a small cruse of vinegar. She sat down on a cold stone seat, sipped her vinegar and wept. These physical ills were small to her, however, in comparison with the spiritual sufferings she endured. The struggle she had experienced in England was intensified here, as there pressed upon her the burden of her mission, the preaching of the Gospel to the people of America.

On Christmas Day, 1775, John Hocknell with his family landed in Philadelphia, in company with another Shaker, John Partington and his family. After meeting Mother Ann in New York, they went on to Albany, where in the spring Mother Ann joined them. Through the summer they worked hard on their land at Niskeyuna, clearing and preparing the soil for cultivation, erecting buildings and making provision for a permanent home. Here they all gathered in September, 1776.

Waiting in the Wilderness.

In May, 1774, this hopeful little company had left England for a strange land, without friends or supporters, relying solely on the promise of God as revealed to their leader, that in America they would find a people prepared to receive their message and a church of God should be built up through their labors. Two and one-third years had passed and they had but just gained a foothold and a bare shelter. For the first time they gathered in their own home, in a log cabin, in the autumn of 1776. Then followed weary months of toil, privation and suffering in an isolation hard to be understood at the present day. On all sides was an untrodden wilderness in the midst of primeval forest, no human beings but strangers, and they at a distance. The War of the Revolution was in progress and the country was disturbed and dangerous. With small means, without machinery or appliances for lightening labor, their own willing hands, strong hearts and earnest purpose all they had to depend upon, they yet possessed a sense of God encompassing them on every hand. Months grew into years; their toil was arduous in the extreme, their food poor and scanty; they knew cold and hunger, loneliness and suffering of mind and body. As the seasons succeeded one another, more means of sustenance were secured but not one soul appeared of the great harvest they had looked for. The tides of war swept near them and then ebbed away; their sturdy toil continued. Faithful in soul labor as in farm work, worship and devotion, prayer and fasting were continuous. But the promise which had brought them into this solitude remained unfulfilled. Their faith wavered; whose would not? Could they have been deluded? Was it all a mistake? One only did not doubt, never wavered, never faltered. Mother Ann kept her confidence in God and often encouraged her little family in words such as these: "O my dear children, hold fast and be not discouraged. God has not sent us into this land in vain, but He has sent us to bring the Gospel to this nation, who are deeply lost in sin; and there are great numbers who will embrace it and the time draws nigh."

Between the call and the work of every inspired leader lies a wilderness. It may be in Judea as for Jesus, or in Arabia as for Paul and Mohammed; it may be in a prison cell as for Bunyan, or in personal solitude in crowded city streets. To all who act for God in some special way comes a sojourn in a wilderness. The seed is buried in the earth, apparently forgotten; silent, unguessed forces, educative and preparative, are at work, unseen by all but God.

Ann Lee, endowed with the Holy Spirit, sent to reveal the Mother in Deity, commissioned to utter the message foretold seventeen centuries before, at the close of the first Christian Dispensation, — "The Spirit and the Bride say, Come! Come, for all things are now ready," — at the door, the world waiting for the message, was held in solitude and silence. For three and a half years no sign of advance appeared. But in this time the soul of Ann Lee was compassing the body of America, in which she was to implant a pure life-germ. Through her was to come the life divine to men and women in America, Europe, the World. For the coming of the Christ Spirit in woman meant opportunity for the completed work of reunion between God and man. Henceforth, whatever new degrees of revelation might be given, the foundation was complete. There could be no other way; the image of God stood in spiritual wholeness. Ann Lee as a Mediator felt the world hang about her neck, rest its weight upon her heart. The Father-Mother had made complete in manifestation the Mediatorial Order through Jesus and Ann, as representative and divinely endowed Leaders.

On Ann Lee rested a burden such as no other woman has ever borne, and no man, save Jesus. Under agony of soul she wrestled for a lost world. Once, standing by a little stream that flowed through their farm at Watervliet, she cried with an outburst of tears, in uncontrollable anguish, "O that the fishes of the sea and fowls of the air, and all things that have life and breath, yea, all the trees of the forest and grass of the fields would pray to God for me!" But she never laid down the burden nor shrank behind the shelter of weak human nature. Invincible in courage and faith to endure all that God might impose as the necessity of her commission, she never flinched from suffering. Yet in her extreme agony of soul she was often heard to cry, "O that all things would cry to God for me!" After such scenes of spiritual anguish, she would see visions of angels and receive from God such revelations of the time when this Gospel would be opened to men, that her soul would be filled with joy and triumph and she could sing in full realization of the glory to be revealed.

As the second and third years of their solitude elapsed, and sowing time succeeded wintry storms, Mother Ann counseled large preparations for the feeding of a multitude. In 1779, especially, she insisted on large crops, "for," she said, "the time is at hand when many will come and obey the Gospel." It was during this year that the patience of these saints reached the crisis of its testing and their faith felt its greatest strain. The family, through the generosity of Elder John Hocknell, had framed and built a large and convenient house to accommodate those who, they believed, would soon come to learn of the Gospel. From some unknown cause, just as it was about finished, it caught fire and burned down. Mother Ann encouraged them, exhorting them not to be discouraged but to lay up stores the best they could. It was about a year before the opening of the Gospel, and although they were reduced to only log buildings, yet, by industry and faith, looking to the blessing of God, they were prospered and provided with means beyond what naturally they could have expected.

3

One day, when her little family were particularly down-cast, Mother Ann received a special influx of divine power. She led them out into the forest west of their dwelling and they were filled by her gift with the spirit of joy and hope, brought from the altar where her own soul had its abiding place. They rejoiced with all their accustomed fervor in song and danced before the Lord in sacred joy as did David, when the ark visible was brought home to the ancient Zion. After their exercise had ceased, a wave of despondency seems to have swept over them, and William Lee, known then as Elder, and in all the after years lovingly remembered as "Father William," voiced the silent questionings of every heart. It was like the question from the weary heart of John, — "Art Thou He that should come or do we look for another?" "Mother, do you believe the Gospel will ever open to the world?"

Mother Ann had not, like Jesus, the works at hand to feed their sight and sense. Bare faith, her own inner assurance was all. Grand souls were they, in that lonely forest, facing their fourth winter of apparent defeat, to accept, believe and rely upon her simple word. "Yea, Brother William, I certainly know it will, and the time is near at hand when they will come like doves."

"Mother," was his reply, "you have often told us so, but it does not come yet." Did the supreme pang pierce that Mother heart at these words, as when, in another wood, just outside the city gates, "they all forsook Him and fled?" The woman's answer came, "Be patient, be patient, O my dear children, for I can see great numbers coming now, and you will soon see them in great numbers." It is reported of Father William that in after years he said that he had felt more condemnation for that reply than for any other sin he had ever committed.

As the harvest was gathered in, Mother Ann gave orders to store up great quantities of food, and, when they asked her what would be done with so much, she replied, "We shall have company enough before another year comes round to consume it all." During the winter, these predictions and her assertions of great numbers at their doors grew more vivid and frequent. "I see," she would say, "great numbers of people come and believe the Gospel. I see great men come and bow down their heads and confess their sins."

The Moving of the Waters.

Believers in the Gospel as revealed in the person of Ann Lee have loved to compare the work in England under the guidance of James and Jane Wardley to that preaching by John the Baptist which prepared the way for Jesus; her reception of the divine power and commission at their hands to the personal touch of John at Jordan, in the human side of the baptism of Jesus with the Christ spirit. That was a time when great multitudes went out into the wilderness of Judea, and all classes repented and forsook their sins. A similar work went on in America, during the winter when Ann Lee's family were enduring the trial that prepared them for the work and suffering yet to come.

During the winter of 1779, a movement of spiritual forces took place in their immediate vicinity which bewildered many, although clear enough to those who read in all phases of life the brooding influence and training of an ever present God. In the town of New Lebanon, N. Y., the work began, but soon spread to adjacent towns and over the surrounding country. A religious revival broke out, characterized by strange and unaccustomed features, marked by peculiar intensity of feeling and accompanied by unusual phenomena. Vivid and intense were men's convictions for sin; cries for mercy rent the air; meetings were scenes of excitement, soul anguish, realistic portrayals of penalties about to come, of fear and dread or of actual present torment, as souls stood bare in their sins before the eye of God. Not alone were the vicious and reprobate thus overtaken by the realization of God and their own sins, but men and women of responsibility and position, church members of long standing, ministers, deacons and elders; their religion had failed, they were unconverted and lost; their cries mingled with the heart-broken pleadings for salvation of those who had once been hardened revilers of goodness. Conversions were swift and powerful; joy was felt as intense as the sorrow that had preceded. Visions of angels were seen; to some the heavens seemed opened. They prophesied that the day was at hand when Christ was to appear on the earth; wars and fightings should cease; the Kingdom of Heaven was to be established among men; and they waited in full expectation of seeing the Lord descend from the skies to open a new era upon the earth. Like many before them and like many since, they saw suns rise and set, winter unfold into spring and the course of nature keep calmly on; no change appeared. Their emotions subsided; the meetings, so intense and absorbing, ceased; farmers and mechanics went about their work; the war went on without much sign of an end and "all things remained as they were from the beginning." Some were true to the emotions and revelations of the winter and persistently looked for the appearance of the Lord in whom they had believed.

In March, a few penetrated to the forest about Watervliet and met our long hidden family. Returning with their report of the strange people they had found, with their startling claims and extraordinary lives, great interest was aroused; others went out to see what it meant. The report spread far and wide and, before the spring of 1780 had passed, the little band, with Mother Ann Lee at their head, found they had company enough, and that now, in truth, had the Gospel opened in America.

Opening of the Gospel.

Wherever, in America, the preaching of Ann Lee and her disciples became known, there was the same course of events : — a period when an unusual religious condition prevailed ; a revival of great intensity of feeling and strong conviction, with acute sense of sin and danger ; mental emotion and physical excitement, accompanied with visions, prophetic afflatus and a profound conviction that the Lord Christ was soon to appear on earth. After weeks or months of these phenomena, the acute manifestations passed, the excitement subsided, leaving in every case some earnest seekers disappointed and waiting for more light.

In time came reports of a strange people leading and teaching a new life, claiming to be saved from sin, to be now living in a resurrected state, together with many garbled and invented tales, which did not arise from their own claims or teaching.

Some would go to see from motives of curiosity or love of novelty ; others honestly to investigate a matter so vital, if truth really existed in such unaccustomed guise. Honest investigation was always met in the same way. Questions received a convincing, or a thought-prompting reply. Quibbling and mockery received a quick and piercing rebuke, oftentimes in the shape of an open statement of hidden sin or crime, or of secret thought or purpose ; the soul of the trifler was read and its contents brought before his frightened gaze. The thoughtless were sobered, the thoughtful convinced. Confession of sin followed, a baptism, always

of the same general nature, was received : — a burning sense
of shame and mortification, a fiery sense of God's spirit cours-
ing through body and brain, nerve and muscle, as well as
mind and thought. A violent shaking of the whole physical
frame was sometimes followed by outbursts of inspired song,
or by visions and revelations — but always accompanied
by a power that came with the words of release and forgiveness from the Elders or from the Woman who was
their source of power and inspiration. Not their own pardon and release, but that of God, as they were bidden to
give it utterance.

The power was imparted to break old bondage of habit,
to be free and pure in thought, word and deed and to walk
upright in heart integrity. Men and women, formerly absorbed in their manual labors, their farms, children, politics or gossip, became sober, heavenly-minded, lived a serene,
holy, intensely spiritual life. Their neighbors could not
understand them nor the new language which they spoke.
Boys and girls, young men and women, went out into the
wilderness laughing and jesting, and returned like the in-
mates of a higher sphere, — all taste for dress and jewelry,
for frivolity and trifling gone forever. Earnest and zealous
they preached a new life, rebuking sin and sensuality and
talking of Mother and the Elders with a love and veneration
hard to be understood. One is impressed in reading the
records of these visits as the participants penned them in
later years. One who yielded to the influence says of his
first impressions: "Their singing seemed to reach the very
heavens. They did not appear to belong to the gross inhabitants of this earth. They appeared to me like heaven-
born souls."

They were not fanatics nor fools who went wild in the
woods, affected by hallucination and delirium. Men of
trained minds and keen intellects, acute thinkers, went out

and were confounded by the answers they received. Among the first investigators were many who could be convinced only by truth. A Baptist minister of great ability, renowned in his section of country, was one Joseph Meacham. He went accompanied by Calvin Harlow. The two, together and then separately, questioned and examined with discrimination and were convinced of the truth of the doctrines proclaimed. Meacham sent his friend a second time to propound to Mother Ann this stickler: "St. Paul commands the woman to be silent in the church. He suffers not a woman to speak. But you not only speak and preach, but you seem to be an Elder. How do you reconcile your course with Scripture?" Mother Ann replied that in the order of nature, a man and a woman, father and mother, form the Head of the family. The woman, being second, is subject to her husband. This is a type of the family of Christ. The man is the head and the woman is subject to him. But when the man is gone, the woman becomes the head and rules over the family. The minister pondered the reply, and saw that Jesus, the Head of the church, Father of the spiritual family, being gone from earth, was succeeded in authority by his representative, the woman so plainly endowed with the qualities and authority of the spirit of Christ — the right of leading and governing her spiritual children.

Joseph Meacham was among the first of Mother Ann's converts, and she called him her "first born son in America," and foretold that he would become the head of the church and gather the people together after her decease. Calvin Harlow also, she said, would be a great preacher of the truth, but he must first give himself to manual labor. This he did faithfully, until, under special direction, he was commissioned to go out as a preacher and was for many years a leader noted for eloquence, faith and spiritual power.

David Meacham, brother of Joseph, a man of wealth and prominent social position, visited the Elders at Watervliet and became a devoted worker. In spite of protestations that he could not preach, in obedience to Mother Ann's instructions he fulfilled her prophecies in his own case and became a noted preacher, the founder of one of the strongest and most devoted of the Shaker communities, in his own town, Enfield, Connecticut.

Among those who early came to Watervliet was Lucy Wright, daughter of one of the first families of Pittsfield, Massachusetts, recently married to Elizur Goodrich, who had just embraced the faith. Mother Ann on seeing the young woman said, "We must save Lucy, for it will be equal to saving a nation." Soon after, Lucy embraced the faith, was zealous and devoted in the years that Mother Ann remained on earth and after her decease succeeded her as Leader of the church.

By June of 1780, people were coming in crowds to see and hear. A company of young people from New Lebanon went on Saturday to remain over Sunday and attend the meetings. They were met with kindness and their gayety was hushed as the solemn influences of the Divine Spirit fell upon them. Many of the company became earnest Believers and followed the course of Mother Ann through persecutions and sufferings. Years after, these converts, when many were in advanced life and some were aged, related their remembrances, sometimes to refute the slanderous tales that were current in her lifetime and were retailed long years after her death, in defamation of Mother Ann's purity, chastity, temperance and honesty. They all, with one accord, speak of the impression made upon them by her noble, God-like nature, and the celestial beauty of her person and manner when in religious exercise. Her sweet,

NO. 3. WATERVLIET, N. Y. ENTRANCE TO CHURCH FAMILY.

motherly spirit, her insight into character, her melodious singing and beautiful harmony of motion charmed those who came under her influence. But the tenderness of her manner to the sincere or the simply thoughtless became lightning-like severity to the hypocrite and the wilful in unbelief.

The numbers increased. From morning until far into the night they were preaching, exercising in march and dance, shaken with the power of God, instructing young converts, agonizing in spirit, wrestling for the souls that came to them. A respite of thirty minutes at a time gave them opportunity to feed the multitudes that thronged them, to whom they had been so ardently dispensing spiritual bread. Thus they toiled, all through that harvest time of 1780. Their piercing rebukes of sin, of lust, pride and licentiousness, were as forcible as of old. As they met the eager questions of thoughtful minds, accustomed to meanings regarded as inherent in theological terms, both sides found that this new life would shape for itself new forms of expression. Old terms were used with new force. When asked why they preached such a strange manner of life, they replied that they had been laboring for years in the work of regeneration, had actually risen with Christ in resurrection and were traveling with Him. The visitors sometimes said, "If you have attained a life in God that we have not, we want to receive the same, for we desire to be saved." "If," was the reply, "you are ever saved by Jesus, it must be by walking as he walked. If you have committed sins, you must confess them to those witnesses in whom Christ has taken up His abode." To the married, Mother Ann would plainly say: "You must forsake the marriage of the flesh or you cannot be married to the Lamb, or have any share in the resurrection of Christ, for those

who are counted worthy to have any part in the resurrection
of Christ neither marry nor are given in marriage, but
are like unto the angels." Many who were church members
would plead their own experiences of conversion — the conviction and sorrow for sin, and the subsequent love and
sense of pardon. Had they not been born of God? Was
that not of Christ? Then Mother Ann and the Elders said:
"The gifts and calling of God are given to souls in nature's
darkness, not because they have repented, but they are intended to lead souls to repentance." "What is repentance?"
On this pivotal word rested the whole structure of conviction and faith. "To leave off committing sins is the only
repentance God accepts," was their answer. Then as now,
members of all the churches of Christendom know that by
all their faith and washing in the blood of Jesus, however
understood, they do not leave off sin. "This," said Mother
Ann, "no one can do, short of making an honest confession
to the faithful witnesses of Christ of all the sins he has
ever committed."

The truth of this assertion is upheld by the witness and
experience of all those who sincerely came and who persistently continued through life in faithful adherence to
this light; and it was no more real and convincing to
those who thus confessed and received power to forsake
sin, in the presence of Mother Ann's spiritually beautiful
personality in 1780, than it is in 1904, to those who do the
same work faithfully in the same way. Many today, from
Maine to Kentucky and Florida, will arise to say: "By
honest confession, by union with our Elders, through obedience, we do receive power to forsake sin and leave it behind. We have never experienced nor seen that power
outside of the Gospel as delivered to Mother Ann and
through her imparted to the Elders in the Shaker Order."

"But," inquirers asked, and ask still, "it is God alone that can forgive sins; where then is the necessity of confessing them to man?" The Elders answered, "God has established that order for all souls who have committed sins, that they must confess their sins before His chosen witnesses," and then referred them to the Scriptures. "All souls," said they, "who commit sin are lost from God and therefore do not know God. For those who know God as He is do not commit sin; for it is eternal life to know God and Jesus Christ whom He hath sent." "Those who commit sin are bound in death and are not able to come to God without help, and when they come to Christ's witnesses and honestly confess their sins before them they find a relation to them and through them they find a relation to Christ, and in this sense, these witnesses become Mediators between Christ and suffering souls. They also take the burden and loss that the soul is under and bear it till the soul has had a season to gain strength and becomes able to bear its own burden." As the light grew, seekers would ask, "Are you perfect? Do you live without sin?" Humbly and honestly, the Elders would and do say: "The power of God revealed in this day does enable souls to cease from sin and we have received that power. We have actually left off committing sin and we live in daily obedience to the will of God. Those who are in Christ are not under the law of sin, because they do not commit sin. Christ has delivered them from the law of sin and given them the law of righteousness and made them able to walk in it."

John Farrington, who shared in the work of 1779 at New Lebanon and received the faith from Mother Ann in 1780, afterward becoming an Elder in the Shaker Church, has left this strong testimony to what he then experienced: "Here I received that holy unction from Christ through

Mother Ann that fully enabled me to cease from sin. Here I found boldness and confidence before God and all men and felt my adoption into the family of Christ and among the sons of God. Here I found an entrance into the pure and peaceable Kingdom of Christ and felt my soul united to the invisible heavenly host, and filled with the quickening power of God, which gave me strength to resist all evil and to keep every sinful propensity in subjection to the law of Christ. And I felt a full assurance that by continuing in obedience to the testimony I had then embraced, I should gain a complete dominion over the powers of darkness and reign triumphant with Christ in purity and holiness. In this I have not been deceived, for I have found my faith fully verified. Indeed, it was impossible it should be otherwise; for the testimony that I received and with which I united was like a two-edged sword against all ungodliness and every appearance of evil; therefore all who are in obedience to it must certainly be saved from all ungodliness. This grace I have obtained, and this power I have received through the special ministration of Mother Ann Lee, whose piercing testimony awakened the inmost feelings of my soul and roused the sleeping faculties of my mind, which had long been bound in nature's darkness. I can testify before all men that it was through faith in Mother Ann, whom God raised up and endowed with the spirit of Christ, that I was healed from the infirmities of my spirit."

Imprisonment.

When a new work of God begins in any part of the world, the adherents of the old, established religion always lead in persecution. While the Shakers had quietly practised their faith in the wilderness, they had been unheeded.

Now that they had become a centre of attraction, were un-hesitating in their rebukes of sin and their faith was gain-ing ground, the spirit of evil awoke. Persecution broke out like a conflagration. Those who had felt the power of this new light but had closed their eyes to it not only received darkness, but in many cases seemed given over to do the works of darkness. Ministers, deacons and magistrates led or joined with mobs of the lewd and base. A pretext was not wanting. These people were English; they openly preached peace and denounced war as sin, while every patriot held it as his most sacred duty to support the war for independence then raging against England.

David Darrow of New Lebanon, although he had fought faithfully in the army of the Revolution and attained the rank of lieutenant, was the first victim of persecution. While driving sheep to Watervliet to feed the crowds that gathered there, he was seized and imprisoned and his sheep confiscated, on the plea that they were for the British. Others were then imprisoned on charge of being British emissaries and finally, Mother Ann and Father William Lee with Father James Whittaker were arrested and despatched to Albany. After a short trial, without one particle of evidence against them, they were committed to prison, on charge of treason, being confined in the Old Fort above Albany with tories and prisoners of war. But prison walls could not hush their voices nor quench the light of truth. Within the prison and through its bars they proclaimed the Gospel. Crowds assembled to hear, and, as Albany was a centre for all classes, their imprisonment served rather as a means to a wider spread of the faith. Many men of candor and good sense were indignant at such treatment of people whose only crime was their religious faith and their rebukes of the dissolute and the depraved. Many inquiring minds were by these very circumstances turned to the truth.   The falsity of the charge against them was the more apparent because Mother Ann had repeatedly asserted by prophetic power that the war would end in the separation of the colonies from Great Britain and the establishment of an independent government with religious freedom for all. She was afterward confined at Poughkeepsie for several months, but with the Elders was released by Governor De-Witt Clinton and returned to her family in December, 1780.

III

THE JOURNEY EAST

DURING the opening months of 1781 the Shakers at Watervliet, who called themselves "Believers in Christ's Second Appearing," manifested increased zeal. By the searching power of the Holy Spirit, hearts were purified, faith built up and souls were growing in susceptibility to spirit influence, as the fires of Divine purity burned out the old life and the breath of God's Mother Love imparted the new. Believers increased in spirituality and understanding and became better fitted to care for the scores and hundreds of souls that were being born into the kingdom. At last the time came when Mother Ann and the Elders were sent out on their mission to the world. Leaving Watervliet about the middle of May, 1781, they started on what proved to be the

Way of the Cross.

The faith imparted by Mother Ann and the Elders called for death — death to the carnal life of nature. No easy pleasure trip is the life of the true Believer. Deep and abiding are its joys, but stern and constant is the battle with self and the lower nature. Nor did the trumpet of the Gospel give any uncertain sound; plain and distinct was the call to a cross and a warfare. What wonder that all the powers of evil were aroused to do battle with such a spirit of righteousness? From the path that led

(47)

this spiritual Mother to find the souls she had borne upon her heart, no storm nor struggle could turn her course.

From May 1781 to August 1783, this little company traversed the states of Massachusetts and Connecticut, visiting thirty-six towns and villages, some of them several times, zealously preaching the Gospel committed to their charge. Their course was attended by great displays of God's presence and the power of the Holy Spirit. Where-ever they went, numbers accepted the revelation. Their coming to Enfield aroused the inhabitants like an inroad of pestilence. At Harvard, the vision of a mob in black warned Mother Ann of threatening danger; but two angels in white were seen to pass safely through the mob and enter the Square House, and this gave her assurance of protection. In this house, famous in Shaker annals, she made her home during the two years of her sojourn in the east, if home it could be called, where so much of violence and suffering were endured and whence she often went forth on perilous journeys.

In Petersham, in December of 1781, a dastardly attack was made upon the Shakers at the house of David Ham-mond, where the most inhuman personal abuse was inflicted upon Mother Ann and others. Father James Whittaker was believed to have been killed, but he recovered and prayed for his persecutors, "Father, forgive them, they know not what they do!" The saintly, forgiving spirit of Mother Ann so broke down these wretches that they begged forgiveness for their cruelty. Mother Ann said to them, "I hold nothing against you and I pray God to forgive you." One historian of this epoch says that, in consequence of their violation of law in this affair, the people of Peter-sham signed a written agreement that Mother Ann or any of her children might thereafter pass through the town peaceably, without any disturbance, and adds that they usually kept their word.

During the winter of 1781-2, Mother Ann and her disciples continued their labors at Harvard and other places in Massachusetts. Believers from all parts came to visit them and to be encouraged and strengthened in the faith. Mobs and personal violence were of frequent occurrence. In January, a mob drove them from Harvard, while on their second visit to Enfield a mob of two hundred were ready to meet them almost as soon as the hospitable home of David Meacham was reached, and they were ordered to leave town within an hour. They departed, and following the Connecticut River northward, visited Granby, Montague, Sunderland and Ashfield, where they found safety, and quiet for a time. On the 20th of May they left Ashfield and returned for a third visit to Harvard. Placards had been put up notifying people to meet on a certain day and drive off the Shakers.

It is hard to realize the scenes of cruelty and bloodshed that occurred only one hundred and twenty years ago in such peaceful, pleasant, rural villages as Harvard, Shirley and Bolton, Massachusetts, where Shakerism received a baptism of blood and fire. Believers began to gather at Harvard and meetings were held where the presence of spiritual force was increasingly manifest. A large and desperate mob collected, keeping their design and its date a secret. But they could not control the spirits of good nor the will of God, and to Mother Ann was revealed in vision the whole plan and the coming of those who sought her life. Mother Ann and the Elders at once departed and the next day were safe at Woburn, but the brethren and sisters at Harvard had a fiery trial to endure. On Sabbath Day they had a great meeting. The Divine power was so strong

4

that onlookers and scoffers were seized and when Believers knelt, they too were forced to their knees by a power they could not resist. The rage and malignity thus aroused cannot be described.

Before daylight on the morning of August 19th, a mob of four hundred, led, as in other places, by professors of religion and so-called respectable members of society, broke into the Square House and, dragging out the Shakers, gave them just one hour in which to get their breakfast and prepare to depart, never to show their faces in Harvard again. Some of them were more than one hundred miles from home. The sisters were allowed to mount their horses, but the brethren were compelled to walk. If any aged or infirm were unable to walk as fast as their mounted captors desired, they were kicked and beaten without mercy, and whoever presumed to utter a word of protest or prayer was beaten over head and face with a cudgel. An advance and a rear guard attended the persecuted people, and for ten miles a constant scene of pounding, cudgeling and beating went on. At Stillwater, James Shepherd, the only one of the original band from England, was brutally whipped. Among the brethren who endured these acts of violence were many battle scarred veterans of the Revolution, men who feared nothing and could fight well, but in obedience to their faith they had forever grounded arms in battles of earth and had taken up the weapons which are not carnal.

During the summer and fall, Mother Ann and the Elders visited many towns in Massachusetts and Connecticut, returning to Ashfield in November, where they remained until the last of April, 1783, when they left Ashfield and made one more tour of the towns so often visited, encouraging and strengthening Believers.

War with the Dragon.

The year 1783 seems to surpass all previous years of this wonderful life in the frequency, cruelty and intensity of the warfare with evil. It seems as though a huge spiritual dragon lay in mighty coils over that country from Harvard to Enfield, through Petersham and westward to Lebanon. And as the end drew near, more terrible grew his fiery rage. But though his blasting breath and rending fangs were never still, the precious life of Divine Truth was all unconquered and but grew stronger and more enduring. The physical life of its apostles might and did fail, but the truth they taught still lives, for truth is eternal.

On the night of June first, a mob surrounded the house of Elijah Wilds in Shirley, where Mother Ann and the Elders were staying. Mother Ann was concealed in a narrow closet beside the chimney in the hall, a chest of drawers thrust before the door concealing the entrance. This was ever after known as "Mother Ann's Closet." The house was taken down in the spring of 1902. At the suggestion of Mother Ann, the family gave a breakfast to the wolfish hordes who had raged at their doors all night, most of the throng not refusing food at the hands of those whose lives they sought. After some hours, the mob agreed to leave Mother Ann in peace, if Father William and Father James would go with them, promising that they should be kindly treated. On these conditions they went, accompanied by David Meacham and Calvin Harlow. On entering Harvard, the secret purpose of the conspirators appeared. Calvin and David were thrown to the ground and held by force. Father James was tied to a tree and scourged until the ground was wet with his blood. Father William requested that he take his whipping on his knees, and this was granted, but Father James, freed from the tree to which he had been tied, leaped upon Father William, thus shielding his brother by means of his own lacerated back. At this time Mother Ann and Hannah Kendall were standing in the garden at Shirley, seven miles away, and Mother Ann exclaimed, "The Elders are in great tribulation. I hear Elder William's soul cry to Heaven!" The mob at length retired, leaving their victims to care for themselves. Kneeling, they rejoiced and prayed, and to Father James was given a new song, which he sang upon his knees, his bruised and bleeding form just from the hands of his inhuman persecutors. Nor did he fail to pray as usual, "Father, forgive them, they know not what they do!" On returning to Shirley, his brethren and sisters wept at sight of his mangled and discolored back which was beaten to a jelly. Mother Ann looked on them with pitying eyes, and said: "This is the life of the Gospel, for without suffering there is no redemption. Where there is no persecution nor suffering there is no Gospel, no ceasing from sin. All souls that will be made perfect must go through mortification, tribulation and suffering."

It is a fact of local history that the tree to which Father James was tied in receiving the inhuman whipping soon after died. The blasted tree remained standing for many years, in silent yet eloquent testimony to the scenes it had witnessed.

While here, Mother Ann knelt, weeping, and said: "The gift of God will be kept here and many souls will look to Christ in this place. It is wicked to distrust the mercy of God, for we are not called to be lost, but to be saved. When souls set out in the way of God, the devil will raise all his forces to try and turn them aside, but if you are faithful in all things, spiritual and temporal, you will have strength according to your day." The prophecy was ful-

NO. 4. VIEW AT MOUNT LEBANON. IN THE FOREGROUND
IS AN ANCIENT BUILDING, NOW A STABLE, WHERE
MOTHER ANN USED TO PREACH WHEN AT NEW LEBA-
NON; IN THE BACKGROUND IS THE SOUTH FAMILY
RESIDENCE, SHOWING THE HILLSIDE ORCHARD AT THE
RIGHT, WHERE THE FAMOUS MEETING WAS HELD,
AUGUST 23, 1783.

filled, for a Shaker society, staunch and true, has ever since existed at Shirley, Massachusetts, and the "Shirley Shakers" are known, honored and esteemed in all that section of country.

Early in July the little band went to Petersham and from there westward, crossing the Connecticut River at Sunderland, stopping for a week at Cheshire. On July 24th, Richmond and Hancock, on the western border of the state, were reached and Believers with great joy gathered to meet their Gospel parents. Meetings were held where the same work of purification and quickening was experienced that had attended the course of Mother Ann throughout this final journey along the ways of earth. At this time, Mother Ann escaped the violence of one mob, by quietly withdrawing through a rear door, and was driven off in a carriage without being discovered; but the next night the mob gathered in great numbers and committed many acts of violence, shedding blood profusely. A warrant was issued for the arrest of Mother Ann, the Elders and some of the brethren, for disturbance of the peace. Two of the brethren were sent to Barrington jail to be tried by the county court. The three Goodriches, Nathan, Daniel and Ezekiel, had their houses filled on the next Sabbath with those who came to witness the worship.

On the 23rd of August, the party were at the house of John Bishop of New Lebanon, situated where now is the residence of the South Family of Shakers. Three years before, when Mother Ann was in prison at Albany, threatened with transportation to the British army, John had come in to see her, bowed down in grief thinking she was to be taken away and he should never see her more; she had said to him, "I shall yet visit you at your home in New Lebanon." She now went through the house, giving her blessing and singing, "Now Mother has come; Mother has

come now!" "Thus," said she, "John's soul is singing."
A meeting was held in the hillside orchard, attended by four
hundred people. There was little noise or outward demonstration, but a deep, silent work of trembling and power.
Although no food was cooked on that day, more than two
hundred people were fed, — fed by the same power that
with five barley loaves and a few small fishes satisfied the
five thousand. Mother Ann then visited families of Believers in New Lebanon; at Reuben Wight's, Father James
was led to sing under a strong spiritual influence and
Believers went forth and worshiped with great fervor.

After dinner as Mother Ann was about to leave the
house, she suddenly turned back, and kneeling, uttered these
words: "God created my soul in innocence, but by sinning
against His holy commandments I was defiled and abom-
inable in His sight. While I was in this wretched state
God was pleased to call my soul by the Gospel; I was
wrought upon by the power of the Holy Ghost to see and
feel the depth of my loss; and by the same power I was
helped to travel out of it. When I was despised and afflicted
by mine enemies, Thou, O God, didst comfort me. When
cruel persecutors rose against me and put me into prison
and dungeons, Thou didst stretch forth Thine hand for my
deliverance. I thank thee, O Father, Lord of heaven and
earth, for the revelation of Christ which showed me the
depth of man's loss and the way of recovery by the Gospel.
When I was in my native land I received a special revelation of God to come to America to bring the Gospel to this
nation, and when the time was fully come I crossed the
great waters through many perils, and by the miraculous
power of God I arrived safe in this land. Ever since I
have been here, God has supported me by His special grace
under all trials and afflictions, and has given me strength
and fortitude to stand in defence of the truth. I thank

thee, O God, for raising up so great a people in this land. Thou hast made me able to plant the Gospel in the hearts of many who are now able to glorify Thy name. I pray God to protect and strengthen Thy chosen people and keep them from all evil."

In the light of the events that followed, these words seem the complement of that wonderful prayer in the upper chamber at Jerusalem, before the agonies and betrayal of Gethsemane. Mother Ann arose and went out, followed, with singing, dancing and rejoicing, by the children she had borne in the spiritual life. The next day a number of Indians visited them and Father William, though ignorant of their language, was enabled by the gift of God to address them in their own tongue, so that they understood him. The last Sabbath of August they spent at Stephentown, where some young men and women, mocking and jesting, asked the Elders, "Do you dance to worship God?" "Yea," was the reply, "and you may worship God, too, if you will." They at once stepped in and began to dance. But the spiritual power they had mocked at seized upon them and they could not stop. The brethren and sisters gathered about them and concentrated the power, until a good shaking had been given them, the young women's dresses and hair flying in all directions. When released, they were glad to slink away, mortified enough.

Monday evening, September first, they returned to New Lebanon, Mother Ann riding in a carriage. It was a triumphal procession, Mother Ann often exclaiming, "Brethren, be joyful!" and they responding, "We will, Mother!" After halting once or twice for rest and refreshment, singing and shouting till the neighboring forests rang, they reached Isaac Harlow's in New Lebanon, eight miles from their starting point. Here they spent the night, after another service of song in the open air. Mother Ann with

two young sisters went on to George Darrow's, whose house
occupied the site of the present Shaker meeting-house.
Hardly had the day dawned, when a mob surrounded the
house.   It is believed that Eleazer Grant, the magistrate, in-
stigated the mob.   In order to get David Meacham and
George Darrow out of the way, these two were arrested
on a warrant containing an absurd charge.   Believers kept
gathering until the house was full.   The mob forced its
way in through three outside doors at once, seizing and
dragging out the brethren with great violence.   Seizing
Mother Ann by the feet, they dragged her through the
house and pitched her head first into the carriage which
stood before the door.   Hannah Kendall and Lucy Wood
followed her into the carriage.   Mother Ann said to Prudence Hammond, "Prudence, keep along with us!"   The
mob cut off both reins, and, beating off the driver, drove
on furiously themselves.   Prudence, in obedience to Mother
Ann, kept running beside the carriage.   A young man tried
to head her off and even to ride over her, but without success, for Mother Ann kept saying, "Prudence, don't let your
faith fail!"   At last the young man said to his companions:
"These people have a power that we know nothing about.
It is the power of God that carries that young woman along
in such a manner."   He then politely offered to take Prudence on behind him and carry her civilly; but Mother Ann
cautioned her, "Prudence, don't be enticed by them.   Don't
let your faith fail and you will hold out to the end."   And
she did, running close beside the carriage for the mile and
a half to the house of the magistrate, nor was she at all
weary nor out of breath.   It must have been a strangely
thrilling experience to the young girl — the mighty power
of God flowing through her being from the presence of her
beloved spiritual Mother, imparting strength and speed to
her limbs, all sense of weariness and weakness banished and

she enabled, in spite of enemies, to keep close to the side of the one whose gifts of power were saving her from sin and weakness of the flesh and spirit! Could any later trial weary the faith that had been given such a test and such a sign?

At a narrow bridge on a steep hillside, close to the present residence of the North Family of Shakers, at Mount Lebanon was a dangerous precipice. Here these emissaries of evil tried to upset the carriage; but the most active in the attempt, Thomas Law, fell down the precipice himself. It is related that the accident was averted by one of the mob seizing the wheel of the carriage and preventing its overturning. Mother Ann gave her blessing to the young man thus suddenly changed from persecutor to protector, and he, after passing the woods a little farther on, left the mob and returned to his home.

Half a mile farther, Thomas Law seized Father James and dragged him from his horse, evidently intending to dash out his brains against a rock, but one of the brethren, seizing him, broke the force of the fall. Nevertheless, he fell with such force as to fracture three of his ribs. This rock, marked with the initials J. W., is still pointed out. Father James, with the aid of his brethren, remounted and rode on. Continually the Believers were beaten and abused, the mob trying to ride them down, but without success, till they were brought to the house of the magistrate, Eleazer Grant. Here Father James asked leave to enter a complaint against Law for breaking his ribs, but Mother Ann declined, telling him to let it pass and labor to be comfortable and peaceable. Soon after, a gift of healing was imparted, so that Father James felt his strength restored and that same evening he was able to ride several miles at a full gallop.

Grant was dealing with the case of Meacham and Darrow when Mother Ann was roughly dragged from the carriage into his presence. When they were disposed of, he took up her case, but she turned upon him with reproof for allowing such disorderly and abusive mobs to afflict innocent people. The constable, in Grant's presence, had struck her severely across the face and otherwise abused her. Grant ordered him to take her away and put her under guard in his new house some distance away. The constable with two others dragged her out and along the street with great abuse, till she cried out, "Must I give up my life in your hands?" Without reply, they dragged her up the stairs of the new house and pitched her headlong into a room, where she sat down, crying like a child. With great difficulty Father William and two sisters forced their way in and went up stairs to the room where Mother Ann was. Soon they appeared at a window and sang to the Believers outside, who danced and rejoiced. Mother Ann prophesied that her people would yet worship God in that house. Meanwhile, the form of trial was gone through and the prisoners were bound over to the county court. Meacham and Darrow at once acted as bondsmen, but were not allowed to take charge of the prisoners whose bail they stood. When once more in the carriage, Grant came to the door and said to the mob, "As a magistrate of the State of New York, I desire that there be no mobs nor riots," adding repeatedly, "Lay hands suddenly on no man," with such peculiar emphasis on the last two words that the mob understood that they might with impunity lay hands on a woman, which they proceeded to do.

Keeping Believers back by cruelly beating them, with Mother Ann in the carriage, they drove with great fury for seven miles toward Watervliet, driving over all the stumps and rocks within reach, beating her often and striking her

viciously on the breast. Although they passed the houses
of several Believers and Mother Ann had eaten only a few
mouthfuls of food, which Grant's wife had given her, these
human fiends would allow her no rest nor refreshment.
About dusk they came to a tavern kept by a man named
Rany, who, hearing the noise, came out and in forcible language rebuked the mob, threatening them with the full penalty of the law if they did not desist at once. As they
were near the boundary line of the town, they now ordered
all who belonged to Niskeyuna to go on, but those from
New Lebanon to return. The brethren refused and clung to
Mother Ann. They took refuge in a little log cabin and
passed the night, Mother Ann under intense pain and suffering. In the morning, from the log cabin and an old log
barn, they crawled forth, wet and muddy, bruised and torn,
just as the mob had left them. The first thing they did
was to clear a circle in the brush and prepare for meeting.
Kneeling, they wept in sorrow. Father James said: "If
Believers should hold their peace, I believe the very stones
would cry out to God!" They then worshiped with great
zeal and power. Soon after, brethren from New Lebanon
came with provisions, which were thankfully received.
After breakfast Mother Ann showed them her wounds. She
was beaten black and blue, and the sisters affirmed that
her whole body was in that condition. "So it has been with
me," she declared, "ever since I left Niskeyuna, day and
night, day and night, I have been like a dying creature!"
Years after, Prudence Hammond wrote of that day's proceedings: "Through all the violent and abusive actions of
that day Mother remained firm and composed, and, though
she was shamefully abused and treated with savage cruelty,
she bore it with patience." Later in the day they returned
to Nathan Farrington's, but soon left New Lebanon for the

last time, not, however, without more abuse from mobs which followed them almost to Albany.

Home Again.

For more than two years of constant journeyings through a rough, unsettled country, over poor roads or none at all, suffering continually in body and mind, weighed down by a constant burden of soul, at every step haunted by mobs whose venomous spirit found expression in bitter cruelty, enduring a series of barbarous persecutions with personal violence so brutal that death would have been preferable, this little band had sacrificed life in the effort to reach and save the souls of men and women. They returned to Watervliet literally worn out. In histories of this period are given many tales of persecution and suffering, with instances of divine protection, as rehearsed by eye witnesses.

When, free at last from the hands of their persecutors, the tortured little company arrived at the ferry opposite Albany, a band of Indians met them. On seeing Mother Ann they cried out in joy, "The good woman is come! The good woman is come!" and manifested the greatest delight at seeing Mother Ann and the Elders. Crossing the river, they entered the forest and, after resting awhile in peace, resumed their journey through the wilderness, reaching Niskeyuna or Watervliet at eleven o'clock on the night of September 4th, 1783, after an absence of two years and four months. What that meeting must have been, between Mother Ann and the Elders and their spiritual children so long left alone, can be better imagined than described. No one, so far as we know, has ever attempted to describe it.

More than one hundred years later, one of Mother Ann's followers wrote thus of the place and the circumstances connected with what is known as

Father James's Rock.

The long years of trial and conflict
    Had faded away,
And night, crowned with stars at its darkest,
    Burst forth into day;
The riches of August lay scattered
    O'er hillside and plain,
And hands warm from sword and from rifle
    Had garnered the grain.
To the sound of drum and of trumpet
    Had come a great hush;
On each hight seemed a transfiguration,
    A God in each bush.

So thought Father James, breathing deeply
    The clear mountain air,
His dark eyes aglow with life's sunshine,
    His heart with love's prayer;
For his was a nature so gentle
    The wound of sharp knives
Brought forth more richly the perfume
    To sweeten the lives
Of those who had wielded the weapon,
    To fill his with pain.
He recked not of sorrow's great burden
    Could others have gain.

In his English home, once a vision
    Dawned fair on his sight,
Of a tree in the wide Land of Freedom,
    Each leaf made of light,
And though bigotry's hand had been heavy
    Through many a year,
And his heart had been torn by its arrows
    This vision burned clear;
So when on the bright August morning
    'Mid the twitter of birds,
The shout of gay, innocent children,
    And lowing of herds,

There came to his ear the harsh discords
  Of hatred and spite,
And wrong seemed uplifted, triumphant,
  O'er mercy and right,
He was calm; — e'en when strong hands seized him
  With laughter and mock,
Ah, here is the place! — over yonder
  Lies still the gray rock
Where his body was flung in wild tumult
  By men in red rage,—
A shadow, a stain grim and lurid
  On nature's sweet page!

For nature is here at her fairest,
  Soft hight beyond hight,
While skies breathe their sweet benedictions
  Of color and light.
Years have gone; the Elder is teaching
  His grand truths today
In a land where the true light is quenchless,
  And none say him nay.
Years have passed and brought for the people
  This faith glowing thought,
So live Christ, and be Christ, is better
  Than all creeds have taught.

As years come and go, the brave Elder
  Looks down from the hight,
And lo! the great tree of his vision
  Bursts clear on his sight!
Its leaves for the healing of nations,
  Its fruit lofty deeds,
It flashes a light o'er the ocean
  To souls in their needs,
Still the rock, grim and gray in the twilight,
  Looks up to the hills,
And the hills whisper down, "Keep good courage!
  God righteth all ills."

Grace Ada Brown, Mount Lebanon, 1896.

IV

THE CEDARS OF LEBANON

FATHER WILLIAM was the first to pass away. William Lee, the fourth son of John Lee, was born about 1740 and was brought up in his father's trade. He married and had one son. At one time he served in a regiment known as the "Oxford Blues," the King's body guard. Of commanding figure and strong constitution, large and muscular, with a bold and open countenance, he had hair and eyes like his sister's and possessed a rich, powerful voice. Undaunted by mobs and persecutions, he often averted danger by his courage and heroism. One brave man, filled with the power of the Holy Spirit, was more than a match for many such cowardly wretches as he daily had to face. He has told his own story of his embracing the Gospel. As a young man he was proud and haughty, fond of gay living and fine dress. At length he went to visit his sister Ann, who was then a member of the society of the Wardleys. She pointedly rebuked him for his pride and frivolity. He experienced a deep conviction for sin, at once stripped off his silks and ruffles, put on plain garb, went to work at manual labor and began to strive for forgiveness and a new life. He said: "After I had confessed my sins, I cried to God day and night till I heard an audible voice from Heaven say, — 'William, thy sins are forgiven!'" He would often say of his sister, "Mother is the Lord's anointed!" and he always bore to her the attitude of a son in the Gospel. When Mother Ann took

(63)

her decided stand against the natural life of the world and bore her testimony against the "lusts of the flesh," as in their plain speech they termed the marriage relation, he stood firmly in her defence, although his neighbors opposed and persecuted him. A mob of enraged men attacked him in his father's shop, striking him over the head with a fire-hook and fracturing his skull. He recovered, however, and continued boldly to reprove them for their wickedness.

He was not gifted in public speaking, his mission seemed to be silent, secret burden bearing. Remarkable for tenderness of heart, he often wept like a child for the distresses of God's people and often in outbursts of gratitude for the common blessings of life, as food and water. He once said to some of the brethren: "I feel you are not as thankful as you ought to be for the good things God provides for you, but you will eat and drink of these precious things and not consider from whence they come. The sin of ingratitude is a great sin ; see that you are not guilty of it." He would sometimes reprove Believers for walking about in a careless manner, and would say, "You ought to pass each other like angels." To some who spoke of their crosses, he would say: "You should turn great crosses into little ones and little ones into none at all." "Wars will never cease," he once remarked, "until God has finished His work with the nations of the earth," and again, "The same sword that persecutes the people of God, will be turned into the world among themselves and never will be sheathed until it has done its work." He continued in labor and sorrow of heart to the end. He seemed not to die of disease, but to give up his life in suffering and anguish of soul. He breathed his last July 21st, 1784, at the age of forty-four years. Thus early passed this strong and robust man, giving his life as surely as any victim slain by the sword, but giving it in voluntary heartbreak over the condition and for the redemption of souls.

The funeral procession, a double file of brothers on the right and of sisters on the left, was marked by a song given on the spot to Father James. Believers all united in it and its power and harmony were said to be wonderful. Father James said of him: "He has been the most violent man against sin that my eyes ever beheld, and if such a one is not saved, I do not know who can be." The next to go was

Mother Ann Lee.

The passing of Father William, who had been her strongest supporter and closest friend, brought heavy sorrow and increased burden upon Mother Ann. Through the years in which she had labored for souls her sufferings had been unutterable. Sometimes she spoke of knowing that Believers were coming to the church who were sorely bruised and weary with their journey, for, she would say, "I feel them coming." Her own body felt sore and bruised. "When people come to the church under condemnation of sin," she often said, "it brings such suffering upon me as almost takes my life." The weight of care of the body of Believers, now brought solely upon her, affected her so that she began to fail rapidly in strength. She knew that her work was nearly done and began to prepare her spiritual children for her departure. Repeatedly she warned them to be faithful. Often she spoke of hearing her brother William call her. Soon after he had breathed his last, she remarked, "Brother William is gone and it will soon be said of me that I am gone, too." She was often heard to say, "Well, I am coming soon!" and "Yea, Brother William, I shall come soon." Weaker she grew in body but with no sign of disease and on the eighth of September, just one month and eighteen days after her beloved brother had left her side, she exclaimed,— "I see Brother William coming in a golden

5

chariot to take me home!" and passed in triumph to the spirit world.

Many years after, one of the first of her rescued children bore this witness to her work: "We know and can bear witness that Mother did effect a work of righteousness which no earthly power, no human spirit, ever did or could effect. That spirit which she administered to us has turned many souls from darkness to light and from the power of Satan unto God. It has caused the dishonest, the knavish and the fraudulent to become honest and upright. It has caused the thief to restore his stolen property and pursue an honest calling for his support. It has caused the idle to become industrious, the prodigal to be prudent, the covetous to be liberal, the false to speak the truth, the proud and haughty to be meek and humble, the contentious and quarrelsome to become peace-makers, the glutton and the drunkard to become temperate and the lewd and wanton to become chaste. In short, it has caused the wicked to forsake his way and the unrighteous their thoughts and to turn to the Lord who has had mercy on them and to God who has forgiven them."

It is said by one who was much with her, that while Father James and Father William would labor in worship with great power and zeal, Mother Ann seemed to possess within herself an inexhaustible fountain of that power which she would often communicate to others by a song or by the motion of her hands. She was the supporter of their gifts and the centre of their influence. A little before her departure Mother Ann said to Elizabeth Chase: "A ministration to this people will cease and then you will see peaceable times; then you may worship God under your own vines and fig trees and none of the wicked will make you afraid. You will not need then to teach one another to know the Lord for all the faithful will know Him." This was realized. Ministration did cease and persecution also, and, gathered in "Community Homes," "under their own vines and fig trees," they lived in peace and comfort and the Gospel which each had gathered into his own soul became an abiding substance. Many of the ways and words of Mother Ann Lee in daily intercourse with her spiritual children are preserved in publications devoted to her history.

Father James Whittaker.

At the funeral of Mother Ann, Father James, weeping as if heart broken, said: "Here lie my two friends, God help me! As ever a man desires to eat who is hungry, I desire to lie here with them. They are a part of myself. They are gone to that treasure which is my only interest, and I should desire to depart and to lie here with them were it not for your sakes. But I forbear! There is not a man in America able to keep the Gospel without help. I say the will of God be done! I desire to do the will of God. This is the greatest gift that any soul can obtain."

James Whittaker was a native of Oldham, near Manchester; his mother was a distant relative of Ann Lee and bore the same name. She, too, was a member of the society of James and Jane Wardley, and her son in early life attended their meetings with her and was remarkably obedient to the faith. While still young he was placed under Mother Ann's care and instruction, and he said of his early experiences: "I was brought up in the way of God by my Mother and I knew no unclean thing; yet, when my soul was waked up, I found myself a child of wrath. I then cried mightily to God. I do not think I spoke more than five words in a day and I verily thought that the earth trembled under me for the space of a whole year. At this time I saw by vision my own soul with Mother's in America, and I heard all the conversation that passed between us and the men that put us in prison at Albany. One day as I was walking with Mother, I felt the heavens open; such flows of the heavenly manifestations and givings of God fell upon me in so marvelous a manner that my soul was filled with inexpressible glory, and I felt such overflowing of love to Mother that I cried ou*,— 'As the Lord liveth, and as my soul liveth, I will never leave thee nor forsake thee!' Mother then and there prophesied that I should succeed her to the ministry." After the funeral of Mother Ann, he addressed the people, "My two friends and Elders are gone, I pray God to help me." He then urged his brethren and sisters to pray for him and help him to keep the way of God, urging the necessity of being more watchful and faithful than they had been, for those who had the greatest gift for their protection were gone. So solemn and impressive were his words, delivered with many tears, that all were deeply affected. It was plainly seen that the mantle of their beloved Mother had fallen upon him, and Elders Joseph Meacham, Calvin Harlow and John Hocknell came forward and acknowledged him as their Elder, that the gift of God for their protection rested upon him. Father James was under great sorrow until the morning of the third day, when he called the people together, and, seeming to be filled with the power of the Holy Spirit, said to them: "I feel like ten thousand mountains of righteousness. Now I remember the promise of God by Mother, that I should never be without a host of angels to guard me."

For three years he watched over Believers, scattered though they were over such great distances, traveling up and down in his work of the Ministry. Many of his sayings have become proverbs,— words of wisdom and truth to the household of faith. In 1786, Believers in Mount Lebanon erected a new meeting-house, and Father James spoke at the first assembly, words of solemn warning as well as cheer and encouragement. In January of 1787, he called on Believers to assemble at the meeting-house and with tears told them that he was about to leave them. With solemn words of farewell, he addressed the Elders, charging them to be faithful in their care of the people. "Do by the brethren and sisters as I have done by you." He made one last visit to Lebanon and Hancock, "breaking the bread of life from house to house," and made one more tour through the towns so often visited with his beloved Mother and brother. Returning to Enfield, Connecticut, he foretold a great increase after his departure, encouraged and strengthened Believers who came to see him, exhorting them to hold on to the faith and endure to the end. On July 20th, 1787, he departed. His funeral services on the following day were attended by great numbers of Believers who mourned for him as their Elder and Father, the last of that faithful band who had brought the Gospel to this country and had imparted it so zealously through suffering and persecution.

Elder Calvin Harlow and Elder Joseph Meacham addressed the audience, and for a time Elder Joseph felt the silent opposition of the people of the place who were in attendance. The oppression was so great that at the grave he shook and trembled from head to foot, and then spoke under the influence of the Spirit with such power that even Believers marveled. He declared that the work of God would increase and the power of God would overcome all things. After Mother Ann's death, the faith of all had been tried, few knowing on whom the gift of leadership would fall. The American brethren clung to Father James, and most of the people believed him to be the chosen leader. But the two who had come from England, James Shepherd and John Partington, would not submit to him and lost all relation to the work of God. This was concealed as a matter of prudence from the body of Believers, until told by Father James himself, after he had done all in his power to effect a reconciliation. Daniel Goodrich writes: "In all his visits with us the word of the Lord flowed from him like a mighty river. But he often warned us of a day near at hand when there would be a famine, not of bread nor of water, but of hearing the word of the Lord, which has come to pass, for we would, as he said, be glad to go any distance to hear it as we did then."

Father James is described as a strong, vigorous, active man, tall and well formed, with fair complexion, black eyes and dark hair, his countenance placid, grave and pleasant. His voice was clear and pleasing, and it was a common remark,— "I love to hear that James Whittaker speak." Of a gentle, forbearing temper, amiable in deportment and winning in manners, he was greatly beloved by all who knew him. He possessed great meekness, was simple, tender-hearted and charitable, and his soul was filled with heavenly love.

Elder John Hocknell.

About this heroic figure imagination loves to linger. Well over seventy when he came to America, to his zeal, generosity and devoted labors was due in great measure the success of Mother Ann Lee's Gospel work. A Shaker historian has well said: "It was a gigantic undertaking for a man over seventy, still burdened with family cares, to leave his native land and emigrate to a new world three thousand miles distant and make a new home in the wilderness, comparatively distant from human society, waiting and working in faith for the development of principles which should introduce upon earth an order of the Kingdom of Heaven, but the growth of which he did not survive to witness. In this man's life we have a sample of consecration to God of life, time and treasure, greatly to be admired and honored, but equaled by few. His heroism and godliness merit an imperishable record in the memory of all the followers of Ann Lee till time shall end." Elder Hocknell was remarkable for meekness of disposition and for special gifts in vision and the power of healing disease. He passed away February 27th, 1779, at the age of seventy-six.

Gathering into Order.

The missionary journey, during which converts were made in the states of Massachusetts and Connecticut, ended in September, 1783. Within eighteen months, Mother Ann and Father William Lee had passed away. After the death of Father James, Believers were left in double orphanhood, scattered up and down the land like sheep without a shepherd. Many, who had relied upon the strong personality of Mother Ann and Father James and had not a deep sense of God in their own souls, became discouraged. This had been foreseen and many warnings had been uttered by their Gospel parents, that unwary souls might not be caught in the undertow of sorrow; nevertheless, many were swept away. Mother Ann's prophetic vision had seen the coming needs, and she had frequently spoken of the time when the scattered families of Believers would be gathered into an Order; but it was not to be her work nor in her time, and as often had she named Joseph Meacham as the one through whom the work was to be established. To the people at large there seemed no preeminence among the three leading spirits, Joseph and David Meacham and Calvin Harlow; all had been sent as ministers among the clusters of Believers and all alike were loved and honored. But, as already mentioned, at the funeral of Father James, the presence of the Spirit descended in pentecostal power upon Father Joseph. The three elders at first acted jointly in the conduct of affairs. In the early part of 1788, Elders David and Calvin went on a tour of visitation among Believers in the east, leaving Father Joseph at headquarters in Mount Lebanon, where he devoted himself to the work of purifying and upbuilding the church. So potent for good were his labors, such an increase of understanding in the work of God was manifest among the people, that when the two Elders returned they clearly saw that the anointing of the Lord was upon him for the lead of his people and they came forward and acknowledged him as their Elder. The union of Believers in this appointment was hearty and spontaneous.

Father Joseph had felt the assurance that he was destined to be a leader and protector of the people, and had faithfully labored to become fitted for the work that awaited him. It is related that while the Elders were waiting in silence and prayer for a manifestation of the Divine will, the voice of Elder Job Bishop was heard, calm and decided, declaring, with a power that left not a shadow of doubt in any mind present, that Joseph Meacham was the anointed of God to lead His people. Elder John Hocknell then knelt in prayer, saying only, "Blessed be God!" It is told of these reverent children of God that they were so overshadowed by the Divine presence that they fell upon their knees and the floor was wet with their tears.

Father Joseph now patiently trod the path worn by the feet of the sainted Leaders and days and nights were passed in wrestling and soul absorption in the great work of the Gospel. When the time drew near for the next step to be taken he was divinely instructed. As Moses met the God of Israel on Sinai's desolate peaks and received the vast object lesson of Israel's tabernacle, rites of worship and the law, whose minute directions covered every part of man's physical existence, so to Joseph Meacham was revealed, in

NO. 5. SOUTH FAMILY RESIDENCE. THE EXTREME RIGHT WAS THE HOUSE OF JOHN BISHOP, WHERE MOTHER ANN WAS ENTERTAINED.

this the fulness of times, the reality, of which the Mosaic dispensation was but type and figure. As Solomon had seen in vision the details of the first great Jewish temple, now that the second, the Spiritual Gospel Temple, was to be founded, the divinely directed architect was shown the plan and its meaning and received the commission to carry on the work. The revelation was made known to Believers and, like the Israelites of old, they were willing, prepared of heart and ready to act promptly.

In September, 1787, word was sent out that those who desired could gather to a home in Mount Lebanon, N. Y. Those disposed to do so parted with their possessions as rapidly as they could to advantage and began to collect at Mount Lebanon in December. Great care was taken in the selection of members for the Church, or the central family of the new order. Unmarried persons were selected, free from all obligations, of good health, exemplary in character and sound in the faith; also some children, with the consent of their parents. The lands which formed the nucleus of the extensive estates, now the property of the Shakers, had been dedicated by several, among whom are named Hezekiah Hammond, Jonathan Walker and David Darrow. The buildings were small and poor for the accommodation of the one hundred persons who formed the first family. All inconveniences were patiently borne, until suitable provision could be made. On Christmas Day, 1787, all for the first time sat down together at the table. No sacrifice was too great for faithful souls desiring to receive the privilege of an inheritance in the spiritual Order recognized as flowing from the heavenly world. Such outward signs of the presence and power of God rested upon all which Father Joseph said and did, such inward conviction and satisfaction filled the hearts of those who were obedient to his word, that all felt an assurance that Father Joseph was the anointed Visible Head of the Order. Here is the real proof of the abiding of the Divine Presence in the Order of Believers. Through faith and obedience, it becomes apparent to the spiritual vision, a reality to the spiritual sense. It is a work which is, indeed, to the world, foolishness, no more to be apprehended than is the atmosphere with its visions of starry firmaments, or the earth with its flower-gemmed fields to be understood by fishes dwelling in the denser realms of water.

Mother Ann had already pointed out on whom the Mother Gift was to abide. Father Joseph saw in his turn, and soon all acknowledged that Lucy Wright was the chosen leader among the sisters. It is related that although Father Joseph was settled in his own mind, he set other leading minds at work on the problem of who should be the mother spirit. Childs Hamlin, one of the leaders and very close to Father Joseph, at length announced that it was revealed to him that Lucy Wright was the chosen one of the sisters. Father Joseph replied, "That is the same gift made known to me!" It is told of Father Joseph that he was about starting on a journey to visit Believers at the east, when he was so wrought upon that he turned his course to Watervliet, where Lucy Wright was then staying with the other sisters, and announced that there was a lot and place for sisters as well as for brethren.

Laying the Foundations.

The first thing to be done was to provide buildings for the people who were gathering for entrance to a Gospel Home. During the first year, 1788, a drought cut off the grain crop and great privations were endured. These were borne with rejoicing. A little eight year old boy, Calvin Green, who was born after his mother had become a Shaker, experienced the difficulties and has recounted his remembrances of the time. He says: "We had very little bread, not much milk, scarcely any pie, butter or cheese. We had to live on meat, such fish as we could get, porridge, salt meat, broth and potatoes. For a time potatoes were our chief food. In short, we labored hard, lived poor and had crowded, poor accommodations for shelter. They tried to do as well by the children as their knowledge and means would permit. The children in general partook of the same zeal in support of the cause as the grown members. They worked hard and were not overfed. I was hungry all the time. Mother Lucy possessed great love for children and did much to improve their condition and give them comfortable support. It was several years before the Church were well accommodated and had plenty of food and clothing." All toiled together and the buildings were put up as rapidly as possible.

So intense was the toil that it could hardly have been endured but for the spiritual inspiration that came in constant baptisms of power and grace. For this people did not think it enough for the body to endure a long, hard day of toil, from early morning till late evening, with poor and insufficient food; but early in the morning meetings were held, and far into the night the Gospel fire was burning, and spiritual labors, expressed in bodily exercises, were vigorously engaged in. Father Joseph preached to the people morning and evening and sometimes after dinner. The work was all done by voluntary service, no hired labor being employed. Six families besides the Church were organized. The first buildings were of logs; the first framed house was a plain, gambrel-roofed structure, standing on the premises of John Bishop, where is now the residence of the South Family. The frame of the Church dwelling was erected August 27th, 1788, and the family began to occupy it at

Christmas. Gradually, the rough, misshapen mass took to itself form and comeliness; the various parts of the spiritual body began to cleave atom to atom, and law, order and union of component parts was secured as the life principle permeated the whole. At first all headship was recognized as resting in Father Joseph and Mother Lucy. But as the new buildings were erected and families gathered into them, as the members became known, their capabilities understood and the leadings of the Spirit apprehended, the Gospel plan developed.

The Spiritual Temple.

They loved to think of their work as the founding of a temple for the indwelling of the Divine Spirit. After the order of the typical Jewish temple with its three courts, was established this temple of a Gospel Community. The Church was composed of three orders or families, the First Order corresponding to the temple proper, the Second and Third Orders corresponding to the two outer courts. These were subdivided into departments for the furtherance of the work of the time. The First Order or Family was composed largely of merchants and trades-people, whose work was chiefly within doors. This was said to be regarded as the most spiritual in degree. The Second Order, made up mostly of young people, attended to outdoor matters, farming, teaming, and the like, while the Third Order, sometimes called the Office Family, was chiefly of elderly people, who had charge of the transaction of all business with the outer world. Buying and selling were to be conducted here and not in either the First or Second Order. This division served as a pattern for all other societies, for which the Church at Mount Lebanon was the centre of union. Bishops and ministers were sent out by appointment of

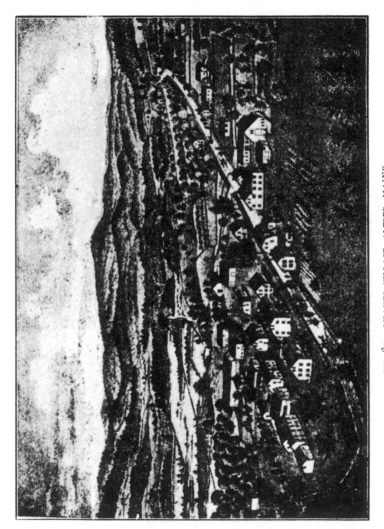

NO. 6a. SHAKER VILLAGE, ALFRED, MAINE.

Father Joseph and Mother Lucy to the different settlements. Mount Lebanon thus became the spiritual Mount Zion, whence the Law and the Gospel went forth to Believers, who, like the tribes of Israel, received "the law from Zion and the word of the Lord from Jerusalem."

Plan of Government.

In each family at Mount Lebanon, as in all other places where Believers were gathered into community homes, there was a Spiritual Head — two Elders and two Eldresses, who had the spiritual life of the people in charge. They were the Shepherds of the flock, the Parents of the family. While not directly in control of temporal affairs, they were the final authority in all things, and their consent or "union," as the phrase is, was essential in every important particular. An order of Deacons was established, two of each sex in every family, in whom was vested control, direction and guidance in all temporal matters. There was also an order of Trustees to hold the property of the society, the real and personal estate, and to care for the legal protection and management of all property. At the head of all was the Ministry, in the direct line of spiritual influx and revelation, between the Divine Parents and the visible earthly parents — Elders of the Elders. Through them came and comes now the call to go forward, the guidance and direction of the Parents in the Heavens. To their Ministry and Elders, Shakers look for direction, guidance and protection, as their predecessors, from 1787 to 1795, looked to Father Joseph Meacham and Mother Lucy Wright.

Period of Development.

It was a time fraught with peculiar difficulties,— the coming together into one family of so many, whose inter-

ests had heretofore been entirely unconnected, each centered
in himself and a small circle of relatives, each controlling
his own affairs, directing his own movements, connected
with others by outward ties of business relations or social
courtesy, but with the greater inner realm of life interest and
thought, his own. Now, all temperaments and dispositions
were brought into the close contact of family life, and a
family whose very existence depends on the self-renuncia-
tion of all and the devotion of each member to the welfare
of all the rest.

It is not easy to give up control of one's affairs, planning
of one's work, occupation of one's time; to move at another's bidding, to think, to act and speak according to the
higher law of spiritual control as embodied in orders and
regulations coming through authority. There is difficulty
in adaptation when members enter, one by one, into these
community homes where all are settled and confirmed in
long tested ways and are ready to welcome, love and assist
the newcomer; are almost uniformly forbearing, patient and
considerate toward the disposition and temperament of the
convert, doing all in their power to smooth rough places
to the feet that must stumble in the strange and unaccustomed way. But, in those days, when the ways were untrodden and the stumbling blocks were to be found by the
tripping of unwary feet, when all alike were strange to one
another, new and untried in their relation to the whole,
where every member had the same battle to fight at the same
time with old, familiar ways and ideas, each one's ins and
outs of disposition unknown as yet even to himself,— no
wonder they needed much plain and pointed teaching and
testimony! It is today a common experience for the in-
comer to find in the stress and close quarters of community
life and by the light of the indwelling Spirit that he or she
had no idea of possessing so much of selfishness and naugh-

tiness. It was certainly no less true of the people of 1790. "They were learning," we are told, "that they must make a full consecration of soul and body to God and for the blessing of his people." Nothing but the constant inflowing of divine power, the ever present gifts of love and union and the constant exercise of the spiritual faculties could have overcome the tension and the inertia of temperaments and conditions. They lived heroically, and gloriously did they conquer themselves and the difficulties of that day and time, laying broad and deep the foundations of the house of the Spirit's building, where their latest successors find rescue, blessing, home and salvation. Well may we bless those heroic souls, who, from 1787 through the early years of the nineteenth century, toiled and struggled and conquered the world within and without and left so glorious an inheritance!

In 1790, families began to gather in other places; four bishoprics were established, the seniors in the ministry in each case being sent from Mount Lebanon. These Ministers visited the home church every year. In May, 1792, a house was erected at Mount Lebanon for the accommodation of the children and youth, each order living under its own Elders. From this time the Central Ministry withdrew from temporal affairs, devoting themselves to the spiritual work of the Order. They presided also over the society at Watervliet. In 1793, Elders were appointed over that society. By-laws and orders, growing out of the demands of the time, had very early been adopted but were not committed to writing. They were designed to protect the members and to aid in confirming them in a life of purity and love, of absolute sincerity, justice and truth in all relations with one another and with the world. In 1793, several farms were purchased and added to the possessions of the Mount Lebanon Church. During these years the Central

Ministry lived in apartments in the meeting-house; in the same building dwelt several others, appointed to the place by the Ministry, to be more especially under their eye and enjoying their care and training. They were intended for Elders and Ministry in the newly formed societies. In the same year Union Meetings were established. The necessities of the business side of communistic life required the cooperation of brethren and sisters, and, the life being that of a Gospel home and not of a nunnery or monastery, social friendliness was desirable. A spiritual union of brethren and sisters was always sought. Union meetings were held in a brother's or a sister's room, a small number, equally men and women, meeting together. The brethren sat in a row, facing a row of sisters, who sat opposite, distant a few feet. They could converse on any subject connected with their home and religious life. There was usually a director to see that Gospel principles of order were maintained. Father Joseph made these meetings a means of grace and a stimulus to spiritual faithfulness, by teaching the brethren that no brother was fit to meet the sisters in union meeting who cherished hard feelings or was at odds with his brethren. These meetings were so orderly and such a source of intellectual and spiritual satisfaction, that they were continued for over a century.

V

THE FIRST SOCIETIES

A PECULIAR prophecy often referred to by Shaker historians is found in the seventy-second Psalm: "There shall be a handful of corn in the earth upon the top of the mountains, the fruit thereof shall shake like Lebanon, and they of the city shall flourish like grass of the earth." This handful of corn in the top of the mountains is to the spiritual eye of the Shaker beautifully fulfilled in the handful of true Believers at Mount Lebanon, the seed from which is to spring the harvest of redeemed humanity. "The seed of the Gospel sown by the Bride," says one of the early writers, "took deepest root in the living earth — in man; sons and daughters of God have sprung up; by their united labor have built up the beginning of the Holy City, wherein no man's labor shall be able to stand."

Early in 1795, the oral covenant which had been voluntarily entered into by the members of the Church Order was committed to writing and became a legal instrument for their protection and a visible bond of union. Such devotion of body, soul and spirit was exercised by these brethren and sisters living in the harmonious relation of a united interest, a Heavenly Kingdom, so rapidly did they accomplish the upbuilding of the visible City of Zion, that in seven years, from 1788 to 1795, the appearance of the village was completely transformed.

6 (81)

Watervliet

has always been regarded with special affection as the place where the Mother Spirit was particularly manifest. Thither the woman of revelation fled from the dragon of persecuting tyranny, there she found refuge and support, there appeared the first opening of the Gospel in America, there have ever been realized the activities of Mother's Gospel and thence ascended Mother Ann, Father William, Mother Lucy and many a saint and hero of later years.

The spot chosen for the first settlement is said to have been selected by spirit agency. Elder John Hocknell told one of the Believers that he started from Albany to purchase land and while on the way his hand was forcibly stretched out in the direction of Watervliet. It remained in that position, resisting all efforts to draw it in, until, at the spot afterwards called by Believers "Wisdom's Valley," his hand fell to his side and ·he knew it was the place appointed for the work to begin. Mother Ann told the same person that they often sat up at night to clear the land and burn the brush. When weary, they would sit on a log and sing praises to God. The land was low and swampy and has been literally redeemed by patient, persistent toil.

Hancock.

The community at Hancock, Massachusetts, was founded in 1790. Three messengers, of whom Henry Clough was the youngest, were sent by Father Joseph to bring the people into a state for further order. A meeting was called and the two oldest of the commission addressed the people, expounding the principles of the Gospel and the need of an advance and an increase in the work of faith. Then they asked Elder Henry if he had anything to say. He replied, Nay! The next meeting was similar, nothing could be accomplished and it was plain there was some obstruction, but what, did not appear. Meanwhile, Elder Henry had been a careful observer; his labors were directed toward the discovery of the evil.

A third meeting was held, and after the leaders had once more spoken, they for the third time asked Elder Henry if he had aught to say. He replied, "I believe I do feel a few words," and set before the people the fact that there was sin among them unrepented of, which must be searched out and confessed before they could receive any further blessing. The people dispersed and his seniors reproved Henry for his severity, fearing he would discourage the people. While they were speaking a brother came requesting the privilege of opening his mind. This was granted. Here was the difficulty, and after the confession and repentance of this one, the gift of confession and cleansing from sin prevailed in such manner as had never before been known among them. This gathered the feelings of the people to Henry Clough and he felt that he must be their Elder. He returned and opened the matter to Father Joseph, who replied: "Well, if you can find no one who can take the feeling from you, then you will have to go and take the charge, but if you can, then he is the one to take it." Accordingly, Elder Henry spoke to several upon the subject but found no relief until he conversed with Calvin Harlow. Then the burden left him and by this sign he knew that Calvin was the one to take charge of Hancock. Calvin Harlow had been for more than a year engaged in manual labor as a private member. When Father Joseph was told, he said at once, "Calvin is the one!" and appointed him bishop over Hancock and Enfield, Conn. Sarah Harrison was appointed senior in the Ministry over the sisters.

A striking feature of the village of Hancock is a round stone barn, which, says one observer, "reminds one in its solid massiveness, as it rises from a rocky eminence of grim Castle William in New York Harbor; but no frowning guns look out from its embrasures and a peaceful weather vane takes the place of the proud stars and stripes." The circular wall of this structure remains from the original barn, built from a design of his own by Daniel Goodrich, one of the famous twelve brothers and owner of the farm on which the society was located. The East Family were at one time engaged in shipping iron ore from a mine on their farm to the furnace at Chatham, twenty miles distant. Shaker Mills on a tributary of the Housatonic still does a large business. Many noble souls have lived at Hancock and here is still preserved the spirit of simple devotion to right that actuated the true-hearted Henry Clough, who first gathered the hearts of its people to communal organization.

Harvard and Shirley, Mass.

In June, 1791, Elder Henry Clough was sent to establish Eleazer Rand as Father of these two societies and soon after Hannah Kendall was chosen as Mother. She had traveled with and attended upon Mother Ann more than any other woman, and in more than ordinary degree seemed to assimilate the spirit and receive the energy of her great predecessor, while her own baptism with the unction of the Maternal Spirit seemed second only to Mother Ann's. For her brave, unflinching spirit, she was named by the first Elders, "Valiant." Father James on a visit at Harvard after Mother Ann's decease had exclaimed in a vision, "Pull off the shoes from your feet for the place where ye stand is holy!" On this spot the church was afterward erected. Eldress Ruth Landon, successor of Mother Lucy, said that Father Eleazer Rand and Mother Hannah Kendall laid the foundation here for souls to build upon and it would stand and could never be overthrown. "You must build upon it," she said, "for you can never have any other to build upon that God will own."

The Square House at Harvard, so called from the shape of its roof, had been built for a peculiar individual named Shadrach Ireland, who had been a follower of George Whitefield, but had separated from him, and, promulgating strange ideas, had been driven out of Boston. Coming to Harvard, this house was erected by his followers. It was raised in silence and secrecy in one night, and here his adherents came often to see him. While professing to live a pure life, he is said to have had a woman companion concealed in the house. He died before Mother Ann came to Harvard, but the public indignation against him and his secret practices was doubtless one cause of the virulence of the persecution vented upon the innocent Shakers. His followers remained and some of them, who had maintained their integrity and were looking for more light, united with the Shakers. The house was finished by the Elders. Before Mother Ann and the Elders left Harvard for the last time, Father James spoke to the heads of families, many of whom like Zaccheus Stevens and Jeremiah Willard, were men of means, and said: "This is a barren land and hard to get a living on. There is Aaron Jewett, he takes in all the needy, and how charitable he is to them! You must be kind to him and help him and God will bless you and God will bless this place."

A society was organized at Shirley in October, 1793. In the previous summer, the heads of a number of families in Shirley, twelve in Lancaster and one in Harvard had united in asking Father Joseph for his counsel and encouragement in building a meeting house. He favored the project and sent them a covenant such as Believers at Mount Lebanon had adopted. Work was begun in August and on the last night of October, 1792, silently, lest their opposers should hinder them, the frame was erected. The first service was held October 17th, 1793. The land for the society at Shirley was the gift of Elijah Wilds and others. The names of Nathan Willard, Oliver Burt, Amos Buttrick and Ivory Wilds are prominent at this time. Forty-four adults and twenty-two young people formed the first household which has since gathered hundreds into its fold.

These twin sisters in the faith nestle amid their pines and orchards, simple and strong-hearted as of yore, the spirit of peace breathing from their very fields upon the air of the townships where they hold their ancient sites. Here, Father James Whittaker, Mother Hannah Kendall and a host beside of godlike souls seem lingering, watching over the consecrated soil. Here lived Eldress Eliza Babbitt, whose days, because of righteousness, were long in the land; Elder William Leonard, theologian, preacher, genial, eccentric, a Shaker of Shakers; Eunice Bathrick, seer and visionist, whose deeply spiritual life still sends its pulsations throughout Zion.

Four bishoprics cover the history of Harvard and Shirley. Father Eleazer Rand was succeeded in 1808 by John Warner. In 1828, Grove B. Blanchard was called to the position and on the failure of his health in 1871, John Whiteley entered the office. The venerable form of this Shaker Elder is familiar all through eastern Massachusetts.

Enfield, Conn.

This society has existed since the first visit of Mother Ann in her famous eastern journey of 1781, when at the home of David Meacham she encountered the opposition that afterwards developed into bitter persecution at the hands of orthodox Christians and their ruffianly allies. It was established in organized form in 1790. Among heads

NO. 6. CHURCH FAMILY DWELLING, ENFIELD, CONN.

of families who joined the Order in those years were the Meachams, Samuel Eaton, Samuel Parker, Eliphalet Comstock, Nathan Tiffany and Justus Markham. The first Shaker in the town was Samuel Eaton, who united with the society in 1780. They were bitterly opposed by their unbelieving neighbors for several years. In 1782, twelve of the leading members were annoyed by having overseers appointed without just cause by the selectmen of Enfield and Somers, to take care of all their business and financial affairs, under the accusation that they were squandering their property. Later, an appeal to the Superior Court at Hartford secured their release. The petition for that purpose, dated August 24th, 1875, has been preserved among the Church records.

The gathering of members into large families began at David Meacham's house in 1790, under the ministration of Calvin Harlow and Sarah Harrison. The Church Family was settled on David Meacham's farm and his house, standing until within a few years, was often pointed out, the floor boards secured by wooden pegs in lieu of nails.

The first dwelling-house was built and occupied by the Church Family in 1792, situated a few rods from the old Meacham house. The family then numbered forty-eight adult members. The first meeting-house was erected in 1786; this was afterward moved and used for workshops; the second, built in 1791, was also removed and used for other purposes. The one now standing was begun in May, 1827, and dedicated in July of the following year.

One hundred years from the erection of the first Shaker home in America — Elder John Hocknell's log cabin — in 1776, the Church Family at Enfield erected a fine, commodious brick edifice, equipped with every modern convenience and containing a beautiful library, a music room and a chapel. Enfield has always been rich in men and women of strong character and historic worth.

Amid the changes wrought by a century's ebb and flow, this little circle of six societies which had felt Mother Ann's personal ministration have remained intact, meeting the 20th century with hope, courage and energy. Among the fifteen Shaker communities, these preserve mementoes of her remarkable personality as well as the spirit and faith she inspired. Numbers may fail, lands be sold, families consolidated, — assurance is still sure that the principles of the faith are true and will abide. In these homes comfort is secured as of old by industry, prudence and frugality; none have wealth, although wealth is often unjustly ascribed to them.

Enfield, N. H.

In September, 1782, Israel Chauncey and Ebenezer Cooley were sent from Mount Lebanon by Mother Ann to preach the Gospel. They called on Zadok Wright, a Believer in Hartland, Vermont, who joined them in their journey to Enfield, N. H. Here they met James Jewett working on a bridge near North Enfield, and were invited to his house, situated on an eminence known ever since that day as "Shaker Hill." Jewett was a religious man, seeking for more light than he could find in the churches about him. He responded to their teachings and became a whole-hearted Shaker. Father James Whittaker visited the Jewett home, and it is recorded that under his testimony the hill was so shaken that the neighbors fled from their beds in terror. Among the first Enfield Shakers were the families of James Jewett, Ezekiel Stevens, whose wife, Betsey, was the first woman in New Hampshire to become a Shaker, Moses Johnson and Nathaniel Draper. In 1787, eleven families of Shakers moved into Enfield from neighboring towns and by purchase or exchange obtained farms near their brethren. It so happened that one man, living near James Jewett, owned a good farm which he refused to sell, swearing that he would not give up his farm for all the Shakers in the land. But the Shakers sang and danced by day and by night, till the farmer heard so much shouting and shaking that he thought the devil had left the Shakers and entered his house. He could stand no more, and, piling his goods upon sleds in a midwinter's night, he decamped, leaving his farm, which in due time became Shaker property.

In 1793, a community was formed upon the shore of Mascoma Lake, consisting of two families, followed in 1812 by the organization of a Novitiate Order called the North Family. A school was opened as soon as the society was organized. In 1793, the meeting house was framed by Moses Johnson, who, the year before, had framed that at Canterbury, and before that the one at Mount Lebanon. He also framed the houses of worship in the societies of Massachusetts and Connecticut. In 1837, the granite dwelling-house was built. The Enfield meeting-house was covered with pine shingles shaved by hand, and these were still sound and impervious to the weather, when the Centennial was celebrated in 1893. In 1820, the societies of Enfield and Canterbury were sufficiently prosperous to send a gift of $500 to the aid of the citizens of Troy, N. Y., when that city had been nearly destroyed by fire. After one hundred years, the South was united with the Church Family and a society meeting was held in the old home to commemorate the anniversary. The room itself, 50 by 30 feet, arched overhead, was a beautiful example of the faithful work of early Believers. It contained a floor in which not a nail head was visible and the joints between the boards were scarcely discernible.

The scenery about Enfield is magnificent. Far up on the mountain toward the west, fifteen hundred feet above the village, is a lake, apparently in the crater of an extinct volcano, which furnishes a never-failing water supply, nor is there any danger of this natural reservoir ever breaking away and destroying property. The road from Enfield to Canterbury passes many interesting points, among them the birthplace of Daniel Webster and Webster Lake.

Canterbury, N. H.

The following sketch is furnished by Elder Henry C. Blinn of the Canterbury Ministry: "This society is located on gently rising ground, overlooking most of the surrounding country, high up on the Canterbury hills, twelve miles northeast of the beautiful City of Elms — Concord, the capital of the State. The society was organized in 1792, Benjamin Whitcher having generously donated his fine farm of one hundred acres, then valued at $1250 to the society. He, with his wife, Mary Shepherd, had located at an early date on that spot in the then wilderness of Canterbury on the tract of land purchased for him by his father, Benj. Whitcher, Sr., in 1774. It was several years before they had any neighbors — none within a distance of several miles.

A spiritual awakening at the time of the Revolutionary War had led to the establishment of New Light Baptist societies in New Hampshire. At Canterbury, among others was the family of Esquire Clough, a prominent man in the town, whose son Henry became a zealous preacher of the New Light faith. In 1782, Benjamin Thompson, a pedler, became acquainted with the Shakers near Albany, and, his report greatly interesting the New Light brethren, Edward Lougee and John Shepherd were commissioned to visit Harvard and investigate. They endeavored to improve on their old faith by taking on some of the Shaker customs, such as the confession of sins, the simple language, etc. This caused a division among them. While in this state, two Shaker preachers appeared, Ebenezer Cooley and Israel Chauncey, who had been sent by Mother Ann to preach to them.

Benjamin and Mary Whitcher were led to accept the doctrine of Mother Ann Lee. The Shaker testimony was first opened at Loudon Centre in September, 1782, in the church still standing, about three miles east of the Shaker settlement. Other converts were soon added and from the Church at Mount Lebanon Father Job Bishop, Edmund Lougee, Mother Hannah Goodrich and Anna Burdick were sent to superintend the organization of a bishopric in N. H. consisting of the two societies of East Canterbury and Enfield.

The formation of the society at Canterbury commenced February 10th, 1792. At that time some forty-three persons were enjoying the hospitality of Benjamin and Mary Whitcher, who had for ten years most generously and conscientiously opened their doors in welcome to all who came to seek the truth. On the formation of the communistic relation, Benjamin Whitcher was appointed one of the presiding Elders, while his companion, Mary, was chosen one of the directors of the temporal interests of the community. She continued a faithful steward until her death in 1797. Three families were in process of time formed, at first under the names of the original owners, the Whitcher, Wiggin and and Sanborn families; later they were called the Church, Second and North Families. The Church numbered the first year of its existence not less than sixty-eight persons, thirty-four of each sex.

Gradually a communistic home was evolved by the hard labor of every able-bodied member. Sisters turned their attention to the interior of the home, while earnest-hearted brethren sought to lay out a thrifty farm for the maintenance of the new-born fraternity.   Eminently characteristic of a religious people was their zeal to erect a house for public worship, which was carried into effect, the house being completed in May, 1792.   It was 42 by 32 feet, in size, shape and color, as in all the details of finish, corresponding with the one built earlier at Mount Lebanon.   Other buildings soon followed.   The central part of the largest dwelling now standing was built in 1793, but the additions and remodelings of intervening years have kept pace so far with the needs of the day.   One historian writes that the year 1818 was the first since the establishment of the Church in which the society did not repair, enlarge or construct some of its buildings.

Associated with the early history of this society were such men as Zadok Wright and Josiah Edgerly, by whose direct management and counsel the temporal concerns were gradually and harmoniously regulated; Peter Ayres, from Mount Lebanon, who died in 1857, at the age of ninety-seven; Elder Henry Clough and John Wadleigh, the old, unpensioned Revolutionary veteran; Francis Winkley and Joseph Sanborn.   The Order of Elders was established January 1st, 1794, by the appointment of Elder Benjamin Whitcher, William Lougee, Eldress Mary Hatch and Molly Drake.   The Covenant, which constituted the membership contract, was at first oral, but in 1796 it was committed to writing and signed voluntarily by every adult in the ranks. The first signatures — thirty-seven brethren and forty-two sisters — were appended to the Covenant on the 12th and 16th of May, 1796, in the presence of all the members. Amendments were made at different times and the Constitution, revised in 1832, is still in use.

Alfred Maine.

In the year 1785, Father James Whittaker in company with the Elders had stopped at Alfred on his only visit to Maine. As they alighted from their horses, they stuck the willow withes used as whips into the ground. One hundred eleven years later, a visitor to the society describes the trees that had grown from these sticks as nearly three feet in diameter. The one planted by Father James had fallen and from its trunk were growing three or four large trees. The writer says: "Thus the root will not die out, and, as the willow trees grow on and on, so the seeds of eternal truth which Father James planted in this place will also grow."

The Gospel of Mother Ann was first brought to Alfred from Canterbury, N. H., by John Cotton, born in 1760, at Portland, Maine. He moved to Alfred about 1781. About that time a religious movement of the same nature as that in other parts of New England and New York resulted in societies of New Light Baptists. An emigration to Vermont was started. John Cotton, who had joined the New Lights, set out for the new territory, passing through Canterbury and Enfield, where he was entertained by James Jewett, who had become a Shaker from the preaching of Mount Lebanon brethren. James Jewett taught him the new doctrines and John became convinced, confessed his sins to his newly found brother and received a convincing sign of the power of the Spirit in baptism, in the involuntary exercise of his body. He was seized at the breakfast table, raised from his chair, whirled rapidly about for half an hour — through the open door into the yard, down among stones and stumps to the shore of Mascoma Lake some rods away, then back again to his chair, where he found himself seated at the place he was started from. At once a seal to his faith and a baptism of the Holy Spirit, he vowed to obey to the end of his days. Returning to his old home in Alfred, he aroused in the middle of the night his old neighbors, John Barnes and his wife Sarah. They were frightened at the uproar he made, but soon joined him in the new way, as did many more of his New Light friends.

The midnight call of John Cotton had been heard on the first of June, and one month later came three messengers from Mount Lebanon, sounding forth the trumpet call, — "Come to Judgment! Confess your sins!" Their shouts as they approached were heard at a long distance, before their forms could be seen. The people of the neighborhood rushed from their houses to meet the heralds, who were James Jewett of Enfield, Ebenezer Cooley of Mount Lebanon and Eliphalet Comstock of Harvard. These messengers went from house to house and powerful meetings were held. Others followed, and like a chain of watch fires, flashing the Gospel light from Mount Lebanon to the far east, societies were organized, connected by spirit intelligencies, a wireless telegraphy.

In August, 1784, a vessel was chartered, and a company of thirteen brethren and twelve sisters sailed from Portland to New York and up the Hudson to Watervliet, to visit Mother Ann. Having seen them in vision several days before, she was prepared to meet them, and they were made welcome in the cordial way characteristic of her little family. Mother Ann, though very feeble, gave them the privilege of seeing her. James Merrill, over seventy years of age, with long, flowing, snow-white hair, received a special blessing. On their return, they encountered a terrific storm and fully expected their little craft would go to the bottom. Dana Thombs saw in vision Mother Ann, calm and smiling, with uplifted hands, breathe peace upon the troubled waters.

All fear was taken away and, as the storm subsided and the sea grew calm, their rejoicings were expressed in song and prayer. Soon after their return the news of Mother Ann's decease reached them. Carefully comparing times, this sister found that her vision of Mother Ann occurred about six hours after her departure from earth.

The society was organized in 1793, a meeting-house was erected the following year and dwelling-houses and shops in 1795 and 1796. The first Elders were David Barnes and John Cotton, Sarah Barnes and Dana Thombs. Flax was raised and spun into cloth and beautiful kerchiefs of fine linen were spun by the sisters. These industries were followed in all the societies.

New Gloucester, Maine.

On November 14th, 1793, Nathan Merrill of New Gloucester was converted to the Gospel as proclaimed by Mother Ann Lee. "Within a fortnight," writes a noted chronicler of the State, "the neighboring families were gathered in. Much opposition was experienced as the separating fires of truth broke up old natural ties of relationship." The society was organized April 19th, 1794. In later days it has taken the name of Sabbath Day Lake Society, from the beautiful sheet of water near it. This name arose, it is said, from a party of hunters who in Indian times regularly met on its shores to hunt on the Sabbath. A family of fifty Believers was also gathered at Gorham, by Elder Elisha Pote, who was called one of the best of the "fishers of men." Although very prosperous and in a beautiful situation, after some years it was removed to Poland Hill and became the Gathering Order for New Gloucester.

Tyringham, Mass.

In 1807, a number of people came from Tyringham,
Massachusetts, to Mount Lebanon, asking to have teachers
sent to them. They seemed to have a measure of faith.
The Shakers visited them and meetings were held resulting
in the establishment of a society. On the tenth of March,
Elder Calvin Green had entered the North Family as head
of the Gathering Order, in charge of the young Believers of
Watervliet, Hancock and Tyringham. In July, a Gathering
Order was established at Watervliet, with Seth Y. Wells
as its Elder.

In the spring of this year a revival had begun in the
North Family at Mount Lebanon, which spread among Believers in other places. Powerful operations were felt —
bowing, shaking, turning and speaking in unknown tongues.
It was especially powerful at Tyringham. One of the peculiar operations is described as rolling. People would be
thrown to the floor and rolled violently across its surface
like logs. One brother at Tyringham, a physician, was a
stranger to such action of spirit force over physical nature
and began to query, mentally, as to the genuineness of the
power. An Elder came up to him and clasped his arms
about him. Instantly, the power seized him, threw him
down and rolled him with great violence, so that the rest
of the people were glad to crowd against the wall out of his
way. He was whirled along to the fire and up against the
forestick, "so swiftly that he seemed fairly to buzz," then
back again, out of harm's way, before he had time to get on
fire. The power leaving him for a moment, he was fain to
crawl up on the side of a bed; but he was seized again with
greater violence than before. Thinking that his time had
come he gave himself up to die, when the strange influence
left him, but so beaten and bruised that he thought it would

result in his death. Immediately, a powerful shock went through him completely removing all ill effects. He was effectually cured of the doubting habit and lived a good Shaker for many years. In 1808, Tyringham and the neighboring town of Cheshire were given to the care of the Elders of Hancock.

A remarkable place was chosen for this village. The country is mountainous and the mountain rises several hundred feet above the buildings, while the valley in which was found their best tillage is many hundred feet below. Some of the houses, entered from the roadway, were two stories in front and four stories in the rear, being built against the side of the mountain.

VI

FOUNDERS OF THE ORDER

Father Joseph Meacham.

JOSEPH MEACHAM was born at Enfield, Connecticut, in 1742. His father, Joseph Meacham, Sen., was a Baptist Elder. The son showed marked intellectual ability, turning to the study of philosophy and religion while yet very young. He received but little school training, but made up for the deficiency by close observation, studious reading and clear, penetrating thought. Although very diffident, he was sociable and communicative. His marked ability in argument, fervent piety and excellent powers of speaking naturally brought him forward in the Baptist connection; he became well known as a preacher and was settled in New Lebanon, N. Y. But he could not be satisfied with the doctrines or the practices, either the ground work of belief or the superstructure of works, as he found them in the church life of his time.

Laboring for an increase of light and for redemption from the power of evil, he entered the dark days of the Revolution, that time of war, when passion and frenzy seem to turn men to demons and let loose hordes of evil spirits to bear sway over mind and matter. At such times, men and women of religious nature turn in disgust from the emptiness and rottenness of society in church and state and exercise themselves toward God. Joseph Meacham became a leader among such spirits. A band of them in the vicinity of his early home at Enfield had become notorious,

(98)

NO. 7.   NORTH FAMILY DWELLING, ENFIELD, CONN.

encountering ridicule and opposition. Because of his re-markable gifts in argument and persuasion, he was sent for to overcome them. He first candidly examined, attending their meetings, watching their exercises, and, observing the Divine power that attended them, he became fully satisfied that the work was of God. Having been sent to preach to them, he took for his text the words of Balaam: "How shall *I* curse whom God hath not cursed?" and gave them his blessing and cooperation, to their delight and the disgust of their enemies.

In the extraordinary revival work that broke out in New Lebanon in 1779, Joseph Meacham was an active leader. His sensitve spiritual nature made him a good subject for the phenomena that marked the time. Many prophetic visions were accorded him of the second coming of Christ and the setting up of the Everlasting Kingdom. He first heard of the strange company of English people in the woods of Watervliet, in the spring of 1780, through two of his neighbors, Reuben Wight and Talmadge Bishop, both subjects of the revival of the previous winter. Despairing of the coming of a Heavenly Kingdom, they de-cided to invest in an earthly inheritance and had started west to buy farms. On the way, they were led to the little family of Mother Ann, and, greatly interested in all they saw and experienced, they gave up the western project and returning home, told Joseph Meacham and others of this strange people. Their neighbors of New Lebanon were so much interested that they deputed Joseph Meacham and one or two others to go and investigate. The story of his investigation and its results has been told. Mother Ann had said before the arrival of these visitors, "The first man in America is coming," and had told the sisters to prepare for him and his company. She sent Father James

Whittaker to talk with him, keeping herself in the background. Father James returned to her again and again, weeping, because, seeing what manner of man he was, he realized the importance of securing this first inquirer. The conference lasted nearly all day. At length, fully convinced, the last objection overcome, he gave his whole-hearted union to the cause to which he ever after devoted his life.

On his return to New Lebanon, he advised the people to go and see for themselves. Many of them did so and the first public opening of the Gospel occurred on the famous "dark day" of 1780, May 19th. Talmadge Bishop was the first man converted in America and Molly Allis the first woman, after the public testimony was opened, although a neighbor, Eleanor Vedder, had become convinced and had given her allegiance about two years before. Five of her grand-daughters were faithful Believers for many years. Joseph Meacham's wife and children, besides his father and many other relatives, followed him in adopting the new faith.

After Mother Ann began to send out ministers to preach the Gospel and assist Believers in different places, they were usually sent two and three together, but Joseph Meacham was sent alone, for Mother Ann said, "Joseph Meacham is able to keep the gift of God alone better than any of the others." After Mother Ann's decease he was sent almost continuously, and, separated from Father James, he had to bear his own burdens and learn by experience to keep the gift of God for himself and others. Faithful, energetic and laborious, his journeyings were constant and his efforts persistent for the upbuilding of Believers in the societies to which he was sent. He received the title of Father about the middle of the year 1788.

Father Joseph is described as being a very noble and attractive man in personal appearance, tall, erect, somewhat slender, with broad shoulders and full chest, dignified and graceful in his bearing. His complexion was dark, with chestnut brown hair and bluish gray eyes, that were quick, clear and penetrating in their glance. With a bold forehead and an open, dignified countenance, he inspired respect and confidence. He possessed a rich, powerful voice. Reserved in manner, he was gentle, affable and kindly. Persevering and inflexible in duty, he always showed great wisdom and discretion. As an Elder, he was severe in reproof of whatever would defile the temple of God, yet ever tender and charitable. He gave himself without reserve to the spiritual and temporal advancement of the cause and the upbuilding of the character of the kingdom among Believers. He is said to have been entirely lacking in natural ability for the movements and exercises employed in worship, but was so determined to gain facility in them and gave himself so utterly to them, with such an effort of mind to attain perfection, that at length he became endowed with such ability and grace that he seemed to exercise more like a spirit than a human being. The floor boards of a vacant room over a shop on the premises were said to be worn smooth by his constant practise in these exercises.

It was to Father Joseph in vision that the revelation came of the peculiar movements and exercises called among Believers "laboring." He saw the hosts of Heaven worshiping in these ways and was taught the movements, which he gave to the people. They have ever since been cherished and honored as their beautiful meanings have been fathomed; the spiritual assistance and stimulus found in their use have been realized by all who in faith and simplicity have practised them in union with the gift and leading of the Spirit.

Elder Henry Clough.

The itinerant ministers at this time were David Meacham, Calvin Harlow, David Darrow, Job Bishop, Eleazer Rand, Elizur Goodrich, Ebenezer Cooley, Israel Chauncey, John Farrington and Henry Clough. Others went with them and also some powerful singers, and from the number were appointed the first Elders and Bishops.

In 1788, Henry Clough was called to Mount Lebanon to live as Father Joseph's assistant. Elder Henry was often sent to bear Father Joseph's gift to the societies, and was remarkably endowed with wisdom and discernment to bring the people to a state where could be ministered to them the life and power of repentance. Henry Clough was from one of the first families of New Hampshire, and at the time of his meeting with Mother Ann's ministers, he was prosperous in business, owner of an extensive farm, about to be married and a leading and useful minister in the New Light Baptist Church. He sacrificed all to become heir to the richer and better inheritance of the Gospel of the Cross. He says: "I did not set out to obey the Gospel because I felt pressed with conviction for sin, nor because I was afraid of going to hell, but because the requirements of the Gospel appeared to me as reasonable. I obeyed it from choice, to do that which was evidently right. I was drawn into it and kept in it by my love for that which was right and good." "To do right for the sake of right" was his motto and the star of his life.

The first Defection.

During the latter part of Father Joseph's administration, occurred the first break, by apostasy, in the new church. Some among the members had not surrendered their self-will, but insisted on their own way. This spirit of rebellion effectually killed the life of the Gospel in these souls, as it does in all who persist in refusing to yield the full sacrifice of self to God, and of obedience to His representatives in the Order of Elders.

As an illustration of Father Joseph's power of penetration and the close relation in which he stood as a spiritual parent to the members of the Church, it is related that once during this period of sorrow and labor for these reckless spirits, he was walking in the dooryard and was suddenly stricken blind. Being led into the house, he said: "There is one soul now in the Church that is shut out from the Kingdom of Heaven; there is no more sacrifice that I know of for him." The next day, Morris Farrington, a promising young man, went away and returned to the world. Another time, returning to the house he inquired who had gone, and when they told him he sadly said, "The loss of souls is very great!" The Elders tried not to have him know when anyone went away, it caused him such suffering. About a year before the first break, Father Joseph, Mother Lucy and Elder Henry had foreseen the danger and had labored earnestly to prevent the sad catastrophe. The Elder of the Children's Order led in the apostasy, which lasted for a few months. The Youth's and Children's Orders were then combined and in the spring of 1796 were dissolved altogether, the young people being placed with the First Family. Father Joseph encouraged the faithful by the repeated assertion that if but five souls were left they would have the promise of the kingdom as revealed by Mother.

Last Days of Father Joseph.

A prophecy uttered by Father Joseph is sometimes referred to by Believers. He said that he saw by revelation a perfect church completed on earth, and he labored to gain and establish its system and order as far as possible, but could only attain to one general order and that was the United Interest as a foundation — the Community Life. He prophesied that there would be seven distinct dispensations or "travels," to use the word that means so much to Shaker thought, before the Perfect Church as he saw it could be reached. This meant that seven periods would elapse, each introduced by a fresh opening of the Gospel with new and broader revelations of truth. He claimed to see all the particulars of the first travel of Believers for sixty years, intimating that then there would be an important change. The end of the sixty years marked the period of transition, when the government and leadership passed from the first generation to the second. He further said that the full and perfect work, as he saw it, could not be accomplished for several hundred years.

His efforts for the training and development of the young were very earnest. One of them, Elder Calvin Green, affirms that he was so filled with the light, power and wisdom of God, that he would at times minister to souls in a few words according to their state and needs, and implant in all ·who would receive his gift new light and knowledge of the Gospel.

Father Joseph often spoke of having a great work to do in the further opening of the Gospel, but he was not certain whether it was to be done in the body or out. After he felt that his work on earth was nearly done, he frequently said, "When I am gone, Mother Lucy will grow better in health and will have the gift of God for you." This was realized. Mother Lucy's health, which had been in a low state, improved and she was an able and wise administrator for more than a quarter of a century. After his return from his last journey among eastern Believers, July 25th, 1796, he rapidly weakened. He could not be said to have any bodily infirmity. He seemed to live in the heavenly world. It was as if the spirit traveled out of the body; the man had become so spiritualized that the walls of clay had lost their hold upon the being once enshrined therein. "Full of love and heavenly gifts to the last, he spoke of receiving glorious and beautiful revelations and encouraged all to persevere in the good way of God, setting before them the eternal blessings of the Gospel." On the last day of his earth life he heard the sound of a trumpet. His colleague, Elder Henry, heard it also several times. Father Joseph said it was sounding to call him home, and soon after, entering into a trance, he passed in that condition to the spirit land.

Several months previous to his departure, he had in a very solemn and impressive manner resigned to Mother Lucy and the Elders the care of the work and of the youth. Mother Lucy with equal solemnity and impressiveness, had accepted the charge, "beautifully setting forth the consecrated nature of church relation, and the indispensable necessity for self devotion in order to become members of the sacred institution. 'You are not gathered into Gospel Order,' were her words, 'as servants, but as heirs of all things both spiritual and temporal that the people of God possess, if you prove yourselves worthy by a faithful fulfilment of your holy calling.' "

Mother Lucy Wright.

Pittsfield, one of the attractive, flourishing cities of the "Old Bay State," is noted through the long history of the Commonwealth for the social prestige of its people, for wealth, refinement and educational advantages, as well as for its civic status and natural beauty. Few think of it as memorable because the birthplace of a woman remarkable for strength of character, intellectual power, executive ability and spiritual endowments, who early allied herself to a small, obscure and despised people and devoted her life and her noble abilities to the upbuilding of what these so-called "fanatical religionists" termed the "Kingdom of Heaven upon Earth."

Among the beautiful Berkshire Hills, in what was then a rural village, yet possessing many of the literary and social traits distinguishing the present city of Pittsfield, in the latter part of the eighteenth century, grew up a lively, black-eyed little girl, by the name of Lucy, the daughter of John Wright, who lived about a mile and a half northeast from the present Shaker Church at Hancock. The mother's name was Mary Robbins and she died when Lucy was about eighteen years of age. Possessed of means and social position, her parents gave her all the advantages at that time accorded to girls, which were by no means extensive, as judged by modern standards. But little Lucy had the gift of observing closely, a finely balanced sense of proportion, good taste and correct judgment. Her eager mind drank in at every open fountain and she early became a good reader and a clear, correct and forcible writer. As she grew older, her natural refinement appeared in her deportment. Always modest and unassuming, her gentle manners and amiable disposition, with her quick, lively ways, made her a pleasant companion, easily winning respect and affection. She grew to womanhood tall and graceful, with a fine figure, beautiful and attractive, a social leader among the young people of her native town. Married at nineteen, her husband, Elizur Goodrich, was her equal in culture, ability and social position. About nine years her senior, he was one of a family of twelve brothers, all men of talent and influence. The Goodrich family were among the first settlers in western Massachusetts.

Elizur and his young wife settled in Richmond, Massachusetts, where he was a leading merchant. They had much of the feeling, common, a century later, to pure and refined natures, that true marriage is a nobler state, with deeper and higher meanings than licensed sensuality can realize. After a few months of this lofty ideal of married life, during which the religious instincts of both were strengthened by their mutual devotion, there broke out that wonderful revival of 1779. Both were strongly affected, and the husband, especially, was an ardent sharer in the hopes inspired by its exercises, visions and rhapsodies. Disappointed and bewildered at the apparently flat failure of the work that had promised so much, he faithfully prayed and waited to see the promised Kingdom of Christ established. In this state of mind he was well prepared to meet the currents from that spiritual dynamo at Watervliet; and almost as quickly as in the famous legend of Nathan the Wise, the seed dropped upon the soil of his heart sprang to life, and, as in an hour, grew, blossomed and bore fruit to Life Eternal. We are told in the simple annals of the people, how he confessed his sins and then was burdened for the soul of his beautiful young wife. The vision of her wealthy, high-spirited family and of her own proud, sensitive nature proved almost too strong a test of his new purpose. But, encouraged by Mother Ann and the Elders, he persevered and went home with his story. Early in the summer of 1780, they came to Watervliet together in company with several others. Lucy had a vein of cool, calculating prudence and discretion in her nature. Not rashly moved to hasty action, she deliberated, weighed and counseled with her own good sense, before she moved to any course. From childhood had she been averse to anything outre, extreme, or wanting in good taste. When she became fully convinced that Mother's Gospel was the "testimony of eternal truth," she embraced it with heart and soul, and to the day of her death remained a devoted adherent and exponent of her faith.

In Mother Ann she found a mother indeed. Her father, although never openly a Believer, was always friendly to the Shakers. Elizur and Lucy sold their possessions and devoted themselves and their property to the Gospel. Elizur was sent as preacher among the people; Lucy was gathered into the family at Watervliet as first counselor among the sisters. Faithful and efficient, during Mother Ann's long absence, she gained the confidence and esteem of all who visited at Watervliet. When Mother Ann was taken with her last illness she called Lucy to her side to care for her, and in many ways sought to center the affections and thoughts of the people upon Lucy as the one who was to succeed her in the gift of the Mother Spirit. Lucy was with Mother Ann until her death. She continued after that event to reside at Watervliet, occasionally visiting other places to counsel and aid the sisters. Near the close of 1788, she was called to Mount Lebanon to live at the meeting-house and assist in the organization of the Church. Father Joseph gathered Elizur home to live at the meeting-house in Mount Lebanon, where he died in the year 1812, at the age of sixty-one.

When, at the age of twenty-eight, Lucy Wright was appointed the spiritual head of the Church in the gift of the Divine Order, she had before her a long, laborious and delicate task to train, discipline and inspire the sisters and girls under her charge, educating them in the unfolding principles of the new spiritual Order to obedience, self control and unselfish devotion. It could not be said to anyone. Go! but, Come! and heroically did Lucy Wright lead the way in all hard and distasteful toil, lifting drudgery to duty, then to delight, as the consecrated heart gift; subduing, con-

trolling, directing by inspiration of "pure heavenly love."
Natural thoughts and feelings, old beliefs and prejudices
centuries old had to be overthrown and demolished, and
these women, conservative in their very life blood, brought
up to the standard of a New Heaven upon earth where
Woman, Daughter of God, should stand side by side in
ability, authority and responsibility with Man, Son of God.
Nobly did Lucy Wright do her difficult work; well did she
earn the title, so honored as to be applied to very few, of
"Mother."

From 1792, when the Church has been considered as
established in complete Order, the sisters were prepared to
come forward bearing their share of burden and responsibility, standing in the order of their appointment as spiritual heads in the families of the visible Church on earth.
And a long line of noble, saintly and efficient leaders can
the sisters of the Shaker faith in every society look back
upon as patterns worthy to be copied!

Time of In-Gathering.

After the spirit of rebellion had been driven from the
Church an impulse was felt for the in-gathering of souls.
For ten years not one member had been added to the
Church, and now, when the feelings of Believers began to
go out into the world, for their salvation, preparation for an
increase began. Elder Calvin Green writes of this period:
"Such an ardent and devoted unanimity of feeling to this
object as was then manifested in the Church, I have never
seen equalled. Could I now witness the same united,
earnest prayer and wrestling with the Spirit prevail among
Believers in any society, and the like self devotion to do all
in their power for the spread of the Gospel, I should feel
confident that souls would soon be prepared to gather to

them. In the following winter, small awakenings began at various places at no great distance, and some of their subjects visited us and became acquainted with Believers." It was decided to open a new family or Order, for the purpose of receiving and instructing new comers, or as such have ever since been called, "Young Believers."

At this point it may be well to explain an expression that often recurs in Shaker history, "receiving a gift." New thoughts or suggestions, new plans or exercises are recognized as coming from the Heavenly, Spiritual Church. From the Church in the Heavens come the blessings, the guidance, the love, the help needed in the Church on earth. Love sends its blessings through a thousand hands, but to the beloved children, working out by patient efforts their redemption, all comes through the Order of Anointed Leaders and the pretty, grateful, expressive term, "a gift," holds in its very sound acknowledgment and gratitude for whatever the Divine Father-Mother may appoint.

In pursuance of this gift, a new Order, called the North Family, was organized on the 8th of March, 1800, situated at the northern end of the village, occupying lands and buildings dedicated by David Darrow. A meeting room and rooms for the entertainment of visitors were added to the dwelling-house on the Darrow place. The first Elder was Ebenezer Cooley. He had been a Baptist Elder when he met Mother Ann Lee and embraced the new faith. She had at once sent him out with this commission: "Go forth and preach the Gospel and never cease until the last soul is gathered that will be gathered to the Gospel of salvation." It is said that no other agent gathered so many souls as he in the first opening. When it seemed as though all had been awakened who could be cared for in the scattered state of Believers, the conversions ceased, and for fourteen years from the year 1785, there were hardly any additions.

NO. 8.   BIRD'S EYE VIEW OF MOUNT LEBANON VILLAGE, FROM THE GREAT STONE BARN AT NORTH FAMILY.

Ebenezer Cooley then returned home, subjected himself to the family discipline, and for fourteen years, as a private member, in faithful, unselfish work and obedience lived what a historian of the time calls the "ultimate preaching of the true Gospel." Recalled to the public ministry in 1800, he had as associates in the Elder's Order, John Meacham, Elizabeth Chauncey and Lydia Matthewson.

In the year 1800, Issachar Bates came as inquirer to the Church at Watervliet. When the news reached Mount Lebanon, it is related that a young sister, who afterward became the leading Eldress, ran from room to room crying out in delight, "The Gospel has opened for a man has come!" The new comer brought a family of nine in his train, and then followed in rapid succession families numbered by sevens and fives and nines; "the noble, royal Wells family of sixteen," says one enthusiastic chronicler; in all fourteen families, aggregating ninety-six members, including one family of seven colored members. These all gathered at Watervliet in the years 1800-1804. Ten more came singly. Nearly all that were gathered remained, growing to advanced age. Among the new members appear the names of Carter, Train, Bates and Harwood. Of the Wells family the father was bitterly opposed and Abigail, the mother, remained with him for many years and cared for him till he died, when she followed her children, whom she had assisted to join the Shakers at Watervliet. Of the six sons and two daughters, all became Elders or leading and influential characters in the society. This family presented a remarkable record for longevity. The father and mother deceased at the age of eighty and eighty-five years, while of the ten children, eight lived to be over eighty, one over ninety and their average age was eighty-one. All but one were stalwart Shakers.

When the Gathering Order at Watervliet outgrew in numbers the rest of the society, the Second Family was organized. Most of the members of these two families were gathered under the efforts and care of the Gathering Order at Mount Lebanon. The growth of the society at Watervliet continued, until, at the deccase of Mother Lucy Wright in 1821, it numbered three-fold what it had at the beginning. Similar enlargement of bounds was manifest in all the societies.

Fruits of the Revival.

In 1809, Elder Calvin Green was sent out in company with Elder Daniel Goodrich, Esther Bennett and Susannah Ellis, on a tour of ministration through the eastern societies, during which journey they imparted the increasing light of the continuous revelation, preaching more fully and clearly than had been done before the principles of the new spiritual creation and the appearance of the Divine Spirit in woman, teaching Believers the manner of communicating to the world these truths from God.

Elder Calvin says: "This marked the commencement of a new era of life, light and power, flowing from the heavens to the Believers in Christ's Manifestation. The shaking work went on in the world, removing obstructions to the extension of the Kingdom of Heaven. Thus, in addition to the continued openings in the west, there was a gradual increase in the number of Believers in every eastern society and prosperity and blessing attended them in things spiritual and temporal. The respect and confidence of the better class of the world continued to increase toward Believers for many years."

VII

SHAKERISM IN THE SOUTHWEST

REPEATED prophecies had been uttered by Mother Ann Lee, that the next opening of the Gospel would be in a great level country to the southwest. The meaning was not understood, for but little was known of the region referred to, the country being a wilderness, sparsely settled and covered with roving tribes of Indians. In 1804, news reached the eastern societies of a wonderful work of God that had been in progress for several years in Ohio and Kentucky. The stories were so remarkable, the circumstances so like those known in earlier days in the east, that Believers recognized the fulfilment of the well remembered predictions. The Church at Mount Lebanon, accordingly, sent out three brethren to bear, to those who might be ready to receive it, the tidings of the establishment of what was called, in the thought of the time, "The Church of Christ's Second Appearing."

John Meacham, Benjamin S. Youngs and Issachar Bates started from Mount Lebanon at 3 A. M. on the first of January, 1805, to pursue on foot this long journey of over one thousand miles. They had one horse to carry necessary baggage. Passing through the cities of Poughkeepsie, New York, Philadelphia and Baltimore, they struck into the forest and for weeks traveled an untrodden wilderness.

Just at dusk on a cold, wintry day in the latter part of March, three men, strangely dressed, emerged on foot from the forest near the comfortable, double log cabin of Malcham

8 (113)

Worley, at Turtle Creek, between the two Miami Rivers, now known as Union Village, Ohio. They were welcomed with true pioneer hospitality and were soon seated before the fire of logs in the great fireplace. They were the Shaker embassy from Mount Lebanon, New York, who introduced themselves and their mission.

Malcham Worley was a man of large means, generous hospitality, a deep thinker on great themes, well educated, intensely and actively interested in religious matters. He summoned his pastor, the Rev. Richard McNemar, of the New Light Church at Turtle Creek. Skilled in the ancient languages, thoroughly conversant with the Hebrew and Greek Scriptures, he was no mean antagonist in debate, nor was he other than a sincere, whole-hearted man of faith. Tall, gaunt, with piercing eyes and thoughtful countenance, he listened, queried, turning his thoughtful gaze from one to another of these three, strangely attired, strongly featured, calmly assured men, who, humbly and modestly, yet clearly and convincingly, declared a new life, a new faith, a new revelation. The conference lasted through the hours of the night, by the light of the log fire in the open fireplace, while the mother and nine children sat by, watching and listening. A picture to enkindle the imagination is that scene in the Ohio cabin on that cold March night, with its group of striking personalities. At last, Malcham Worley and his wife agreed to accept the faith, stand as its first adherents and be the nucleus of a community, formed after the pattern of the one at Mount Lebanon. It is related that after the messengers had fully declared their mission and opened the testimony, Malcham arose and said: "Brethren, are you there?" They replied, "We are!" Then, taking them by the hand, he exclaimed, "All I have is yours!" His lands and possessions became the starting point of the work. Malcham asserted that God had revealed to him that men would be sent to teach him the way of God more perfectly, and in these Shaker brethren he recognized the promised teachers. He had openly prophesied that a work of God would begin at his house and spread through all the country between the two Miamis, and the general impression seemed to have been that some great work of God would appear in the year 1805.

Richard McNemar invited the strangers to preach in his pulpit at Turtle Creek on the following Sabbath. They accepted and read a letter from the Church at Mount Lebanon, signed by David Meacham, Amos Hammond and Ebenezer Cooley. The second convert is said to have been Anna Middleton, a slave. Within a few weeks a dozen families had embraced the faith, among whom the Rev. Richard McNemar was an ardent, influential convert. On May 23rd, forty members were added to the community, which in a few years had grown to number seven hundred and was the centre of union to all the societies west of New York State.

What is known as the "Kentucky Revival," as recorded in the history of the time and section, is one of the most remarkable series of events in the long history of psychological phenomena. The state of society, as regards moral purity and spirituality, was at a low ebb when the religious outbreak occurred, which, spreading like wildfire through Kentucky and the adjacent parts of Ohio and Tennessee, changed the whole face of society. Camp meetings were held in the woods, attended by great numbers of people, in one place twenty thousand being estimated in one day. In wagons, on horseback, on foot, people came, days and nights were spent in praying, preaching and exhorting, spiritual and physical operations of the most astounding character were common and many hundreds were professedly converted. The good effect on life and character is acknowledged, for though a rough, they were a simple-hearted and religiously inclined people.

Coming of the Shakers.

"At Turtle Creek," said Issachar Bates, "we found the first rest for the soles of our feet, having traveled 1233 miles in two months and twenty-two days." The first centre of civilization where the three messengers were accorded a kindly reception was a place called Paint Lick, Ky., where they were kindly entertained. From there they went to Cane Ridge, where the revival was in progress. In all places visited they addressed the people. Returning into Ohio, the work which had begun so powerfully at Turtle Creek, in March, broke out three months later at Eagle Creek, in Adams County, and in July, Elder Benjamin S. Youngs addressed a large camp meeting.

Rev. John Dunlavy, formerly a Presbyterian divine, became a Believer and twenty or thirty families united. In August, many were preaching the Shaker faith in the south of Kentucky and the work spread through several places.

On the first of July, 1805, the Church at Mount Lebanon sent out David Darrow, who had been released from his Eldership and appointed first Elder over the societies to be gathered in the west. Daniel Mosely and Solomon King went with him. In September, Issachar Bates returned on foot to Mount Lebanon, traveling the 776 miles in twenty-one days, and, after a stay of several weeks, went back with $1640 and a great treasure of Gospel love. A twenty-three days' walk brought him to the site of Union Village. He says, "The land was purchased and the next season we built a two-story frame house and moved into it." The next spring, Ruth Farrington was released from her position at Mount Lebanon to assume the arduous duties of First Eldress in the Ministry at the west. She went in company with several others, brethren and sisters, who were transferred to the western field. They had an appalling journey by wagon. In all, ten sisters and twelve brethren were sent from the eastern societies to assist in the west. Father David and his sturdy associates went back and forth through Ohio and Kentucky, preaching in the woods from stumps and logs, sleeping in log cabins or beneath forest trees, sharing the wild, rough life of the frontiersman, welcoming alike Indian, pioneer or planter, ignorant negro or learned Presbyterian divine. In January, 1807, three hundred miles on horseback formed one trip from Union Village, O., to South Union, Ky. From 1801 to 1811, Issachar Bates had traveled, mostly on foot, no less than 38,000 miles, and heard the first confessions of 1100 people.

Story of Busro, or West Union.

In January, 1809, a journey was begun by Elder Benjamin S. Youngs, Issachar Bates and Richard McNemar, of two hundred thirty-five miles to Busro, Indiana, where a great revival had been in progress, thus preparing the soil for Shakerism. Starting in a rain storm, through pathless woods, over or through swollen streams, sleeping by huge fires, which they kindled to dry clothing and blankets, eating the scanty food supplies they had carried with them, making five days' ration hold out for sixteen days, passing Indians who seldom were known to harm a Shaker, waiting for the ice to form thick enough to bear them across rivers, — arriving at their destination, they found two hundred people professing faith. As a result of this journey, it was decided, in 1810, to establish three societies, one at Busro, Indiana, one at Shawnee Run, afterward known as Pleasant Hill, Kentucky, and one at Turtle Creek, now Union Village, Ohio.

The company at Eagle Creek, Ohio, started in the early part of 1811 to make the long journey of three hundred miles, to unite with the people at Busro. One community was formed in two families, called the Upper and Lower Settlements. The country, although beautiful and productive, was very unhealthy. The newly arrived contingent was almost immediately prostrated with fever and ague, forty being sick at one time. The new community had to suffer on account of the Indians, who were threatening an uprising. Because the Shakers were kind to the red men and gave them food, the people of the surrounding country accused them of inciting the Indians to revolt, and this unjust accusation gave them much trouble. An army of 1400 men came within a mile of the Shakers and the battle of Tippecanoe was fought not far from their doors. Returning parties from this famous battle were cared for and kindly treated.

The society was in the path of the troubles growing out of the unfinished Revolutionary War, and when, on June 18, 1812, the President declared war with Great Britain, they found themselves directly on the frontier, subject to loss and annoyance of every sort. Governor, afterwards President, William Henry Harrison was exceedingly kind to the Shakers, protecting them from the violence of mobs, and, when the war made it impossible for them to remain at Busro, offering them the use of his large residence at Vincennes and as much more room as they needed, with a guard to protect them. The offer was not accepted, however, for in September a conference of the leaders with those at Union Village decided to bring the members to Union Village, Ohio. On the fifteenth of the month, they bade adieu to their home secured at such cost, and with a company of three hundred persons, with two hundred sheep and one hundred head of cattle, with fourteen large wagons, one keel boat, one canoe and one pirogue, they started in two companies, one by land, the other by water.

It would be impossible to follow this persevering people in this exodus, through storms, forest and wilderness. Eight weeks from the time they left Busro, all had reached their friends in safety, the last party arriving at Union Village on the morning of November 12th. They were warmly welcomed and entertained in the meeting-house and the families of Believers. At Union Village they suffered very much from fever and ague, twenty-one dying in one year. The society whither they were sent received these suffering people with true Gospel love, and, in the words of one of the chief actors in the tragedy, "They washed them, they fed them, they clothed them, provided them with houses to live in and supported them wherein they were not able to support themselves for almost two years."

In 1814, the war being ended, preparations were begun for a return home. One dwelling only was found fit for occupancy. A number died from the effects of so much exposure, suffering and privation. For several years the plucky little company held the ground, suffering from disasters by tornado, violent and extreme weather, sickness, robbery and incendiary fires, with malarial fever, that scourge of the new, rich western land, constantly making its inroads upon the working force. At one time, one hundred and twelve were sick, two brethren only being able to work.

In November, 1826, it was decided by the Ministry, Elders and Trustees of the societies of Ohio and Kentucky that it was best to leave Busro forever. The next spring the moving began and the society was divided among those at Union Village, South Union and Pleasant Hill.

Union Village, Ohio.

Union Village, locally known as Shakertown, is situated three miles west of Lebanon, Warren County, Ohio, in a beautiful section of country. The soil is rich, productive and under a high state of cultivation. The buildings are large and commodious, equipped with the improvements of modern times. The Centre House, a most beautiful building, finished in 1846, to accommodate two hundred people, contains one million bricks, burned on the premises. The change from log to frame buildings was effected in the time of Father David Darrow, by whom five of the subsequent eleven families were organized. Thirteen different trades were at that time represented among the brethren, and all their living, even the beverages they drank, were produced on their farms. Maple groves furnished all their sugar, one year five thousand pounds being made. The kindness of the Shakers to the Indians led to reports that they were in league with the tribes; they were also accused of living in the practice of the most secret and atrocious crimes, and in August of 1810, an armed mob five hundred strong, led by a Presbyterian minister, marched against the village, for the avowed purpose of releasing the women and children who were said to be detained there against their will. Cool-headed citizens, hearing of the threatened danger, rode hastily to the village, and Francis Dunlavy, Judge of the Court of Common Pleas, was at hand to read the Riot Act to the blustering mob, who, armed with every conceivable weapon, faced a meek, quiet company of men, women and children, less than half their own number.

To the demand that they leave the country, the Shakers replied that they were living on their own lands purchased with their own money and they were entitled to the liberties allowed by the laws of the land, liberty of conscience in-

NO. 9. TRUSTEE'S OFFICE — UNION VILLAGE, OHIO.

cluded. They invited the mob to appoint a committee from their own number to search the premises, question the children or women and satisfy themselves as to conditions. This was done, and the report was that everything was orderly, neat and attractive and every one seemed happy, contented and well cared for.

In the troubles incident to the War of 1812, this society shared with others, besides experiencing accidents by flood, fire and cyclóne. They suffered from treachery and defection of trusted members and the enmity and machinations of apostates. Suits at law were projected by descendants of early members to recover the lands dedicated to the society. In all these cases the Shakers were victorious.

A test case in the court of Cuyahoga County, Ohio, on the validity of the Shaker covenant excited a very great interest in the State. Eminent counsel was employed on both sides, Governor Reuben Wood and Judge Starkweather defending the Shakers. The latter, "in the ablest speech of his life, showed that the tree is known by its fruits, that these people called Shakers, by the simplicity and purity of their lives, by their exemption from the strife of worldly ambition and by the consecration of themselves and all they possessed to their religious faith, but imitated the example of the Christians in apostolic days more than any other people in Christendom, and that their views on the subject of matrimony were in no way variant from the teachings of the Apostle Paul. The result of this trial was a victory for the Shakers and settled a question over which they could never again be disturbed. It is but a matter of justice to Judge Starkweather to state that for the valuable services he had long rendered the Shakers as legal advisor, he never made any charge nor received any compensation, save what the society deemed best to bestow upon him."

During the famine in Ireland, 1,000 bushels of corn were sent from Union Village to the starving people, large contributions were made to the Sanitary Fair and, in the business depression of 1874, no less than 4300 meals were given to the hungry poor.

In 1867, a proposition was advanced to make the society a corporate body, introducing the voting system into the government. This was severely rebuked by the Eastern Ministry, as introducing a worldly form of government, entirely subversive of the principles of Gospel Order, thereby, they wrote, "losing sight of the only true Order of the Church of Christ. While we stand firmly on the Rock of Revelation and maintain a Covenant-consecrated whole, our sacred inheritance will remain secure from the ravages of worldly influences. Never, while reason remains with us, can we extend the least toleration as union toward permitting any society of Believers to become an incorporated body." This society has suffered severely in recent years, in company with others, from unfortunate business management.

Kentucky Societies.

South Union, or "Gasper Springs," as it was once called, is 15 miles from the southern line of Kentucky, 275 miles southwest of Union Village and 130 miles from Pleasant Hill. In 1810, an Order of Ministry was established here at whose head stood Elder Benjamin S. Youngs and Eldress Molly Goodrich. In October, the society was regularly organized and the Covenant signed. Two years later, 1400 apple trees had been planted, the foundation laid for a meeting-house and they were building a tan yard, besides a dwelling-house, 50 by 30 feet, of home-made brick and a stone building, 45 by 34 feet. An epidemic known as the "Cold Plague" broke out, silencing their industries for a time. In June, one hundred and ten were sick and thirteen died. Another visitation occurred in September.

In 1813, four families were in existence, one of ninety, one of fifty, a black family of twenty and a school family of one hundred and fifty. They had a schoolhouse of four rooms, containing a school of seventy-five boys and fifty-six girls. Eldress Molly Goodrich writes in 1813 that there were one hundred and fifty under the age of fourteen and thirty under five years of age, of whom a number were less than one year old. Sixteen adult members had the Children's Order in charge. This "Little Molly," as she was affectionately termed, on whom the burden of this society rested, weighed ninety pounds, while the head of the Ministry, Elder Benjamin S. Youngs, whose normal weight was one hundred pounds, at the time when he was editing the work entitled, "Christ's First and Second Appearing," was also reduced to only ninety pounds. If not a physical he was a spiritual giant. His friend and co-laborer, Issachar Bates, speaks of him with great affection as generally called "Little Benjamin," but always mentioned in terms of respect by both friends and foes. He says: "I was always with that little Benjamin from the beginning. I always felt safe with him, for you know he is the son of the right hand; but I always termed him the father of my right hand in all things. We traveled many thousands of miles together through tribulation and sufferings, and many were the snow banks and deep waters we waded through together, and love and union were always our staff." A brick meeting-house and a dwelling for the Ministry were built in 1818. In 1819, President Monroe and Andrew Jackson with his family visited the society. Indian raids and horse thieves were a constant source of annoyance. In common with their neighbors they suffered at the hands of some unknown miscreant in the loss of horses by poisoning, twelve

fine horses being poisoned with strychnia. In the same
year they dedicated their new meeting-house. The society
early gave attention to silk culture and in June, 1832, the
sisters are reported as gathering the first crop of the season,
137 pounds or 110,285 cocoons. The most delicate and
beautiful of silk kerchiefs are still shown, the manufacture,
by hand spinning, of Kentucky sisters. In 1835, the Asiatic
cholera raged in Kentucky and one-fortieth of the population of the neighboring town of Russelville died. In July
and August, South Union was crowded with refugees. The
Trustees' office was filled with frightened people, who were
kindly cared for, many were sick with the disease and three
died. In 1848, the people were reminded of Noah's flood
by a rain of forty days' duration. Pleasant Hill was commonly called "The topmost bough upon the tree, the cream
of Kentucky." Here, the beautiful dwelling house, built
of Kentucky marble, was erected in 1824.

North Union, Ohio.

In 1821, Ralph Russel united with the society at Union
Village, became indoctrinated with Shaker beliefs and returned to his home at North Union, near the city of Cleveland, full of zeal to form a community, dedicating his own
farm as the starting point. He relates the following vision
which he had while at Union Village: "I saw a strong,
clear ray of light proceeding from the northwest in a perfectly straight horizontal line until it reached a spot near
my log cabin. Then it arose in a strong, erect column and
became a beautiful tree. That spot is the very place where
the Centre House of the Church Family now stands."

Stands no more, for North Union has long been merged
in the City of Cleveland, part of its lands being embraced in
the park system of that beautiful city. The name alone,

"Shaker Heights," recalls the community whose ardent
hopes and devoted sacrifices from 1822 to 1889 maintained
a Gospel Home. Among many names dear to Shaker memory, connected with this home, may be mentioned Elder
Matthew Houston, a subject of the Kentucky revival, a
slave holder who subsequently freed his slaves. A man
of high standing and wide influence, a classical education
gave him the training by which to use to advantage his
superior mental endowments. A great and good man, he
was noted in the Order for his childlike simplicity, humility
and obedience.

Elder David Spinning, another leader in the Kentucky
revival and a founder of North Union, a strict vegetarian,
was a public speaker of unusual power.

Elder Richard Pelham, born in 1797, adopted by a
wealthy uncle, was to have been heir to a large property,
but abandoned all to seek a pure form of religion. A man
of great intellectual ability, he mastered Greek and Hebrew
under the tuition of Elder Matthew Houston, and translated the Bible into English. He assisted at the foundation
of the societies of North Union, Groveland and Whitewater.
He died at Union Village in 1873.

Elder James S. Prescott, a relative of the famous historian William Prescott, wrote a history of the Society at
North Union. A native of Massachusetts, he was well educated in her schools, and in 1825 was employed as a Baptist
missionary to the Indians in a school at Oneida, N. Y.
By trade a mason, he responded to a call from North Union
and assisted in laying the foundation of the Centre House.
As a result of this meeting with the Shakers and of subsequent study of their history and principles, the foundation
of the Gospel was laid in his soul and in 1826 he was admitted to the society. When, soon after, he was appointed
to the Eldership, the brethren are said to have borne him on

their shoulders around the meeting room, shouting, "The lot has fallen upon Jonah!" After sixty-two years of faithful service, he passed to the spirit land in 1888.

Watervliet, Ohio.

This society, founded in 1806 at the preaching station known as Beulah, or Beaver Creek, in Montgomery County, Ohio, renamed after the first Shaker society in the "Empire State," was also one of the fruits of the great Kentucky Revival. The first Shaker society gathered here embraced among its members "many of the most respectable people, stable and upright in their faith." The industries followed included various manufactures as well as agriculture. Issachar Bates, that indomitable missionary, is said to have been its founder.

About the year 1827, a spirit of atheism crept in at Watervliet, as in other societies, making havoc, not among the faithful, simple-hearted Believers, but among those who had not made a full surrender of themselves to God, but, in selfishness and hypocrisy had crept into the fold for the sake of the fodder. An attempt was made by such traitors within, in conjunction with apostates without, to outrank the true Believers in number and then divide the inheritance. This attempt, like similar attempts elsewhere, was foiled. The voluntary sacred Covenant was tested in the courts and its legality and binding force established. As in the case of another noted religious community, in recent days, it was found that a united interest, dedicated to the worship and service of God, could not be divided.

Watervliet presents a marked contrast to other Shaker communities in its immunity from persecution. A peculiar and interesting story is told by that historian of western Shakerism, Dr. J. P. MacLean, who tells the tale in an address before the Dayton (O.) Historical Society, printed in the *"Dayton Daily News"* of January 16th, 1904.

"The Blessing of Dayton."

"The Watervliet society from the beginning received in general the kindest treatment from the citizens of Dayton. The great difference accorded to the Shakers by the denizens of Lebanon and those of Dayton was a matter of remark among Believers. One of the Shakers at Union Village had a vision. In that vision it was revealed that the Shakers should put a curse upon Lebanon and a blessing upon Dayton. Shakers, in their early history, were ever obedient to heavenly commands. David Darrow felt that the command must be obeyed. The first messenger selected was Francis Bedle. He demurred and refused. Finally he consented, if Richard McNemar should go with him. McNemar opposed the whole scheme and thought it should be passed over; but, being obedient to higher powers, he reluctantly assented. Together the two messengers rode on horseback through the streets of Lebanon, waved their hats and pronounced woe upon all the persecutors. The same day they appeared upon the streets of Dayton, riding rapidly, waving their hats and pronouncing the blessings of God upon the town and all its inhabitants. News of the action of the Shaker missionaries, in the streets of Dayton, spread upon the wings of the wind, over the banks and hills of the Miami and Mad rivers. The farmers held the Shakers in a reverential awe. Dayton had made but slow progress. Farmers now believed that the town, having been blessed by holy men of God, would become a prosperous place. Some rented and others sold their farms and moved to the prosperous city. Of Lebanon and its enterprises, on the other hand, its local historian, in his 'Centennial Sketch,' has been forced to indite that its population has remained stationary for four decades."

The writer of so many interesting and appreciative accounts of the Shaker societies of the western states says further, that the quiet, unobtrusive people, devoted to the cause of religion, practising the Christian graces, has left something of an impress on Montgomery County and that when the history of that county shall be impartially recorded, the Shaker Community known as Watervliet will form an interesting and important chapter. In the year 1900, the society was merged with Union Village.

Whitewater, Ohio.

This society grew out of a religious work which had started among a people living on the "Plains of Darby." They were visited by Shakers from Union Village, Richard McNemar and Calvin Morrell paying the first visit in June, 1820. The leaders of the Darbyites became inoculated with Shaker beliefs, which were, in fact, an advance upon their own. In 1825, enough had been gathered to warrant the starting of a community home.

In the spring of 1823, Miriam, wife of Joseph Agnew, living on the dry fork of the White Water, visited the Church Family at Union Village. She related that a revival of religion had been in progress among the Methodists at her home. Her story of the failure of the work to accomplish what its subjects had hoped for — salvation from sin, touched the hearts of the people who were finding in their practical, daily life of faith and cross-bearing this very condition. The gospel of present salvation, as they experienced it, was preached to their guest, who eagerly entered the "open door." Soon after, Whitewater was visited by two Shaker brethren and several Believers were gained, among them, Joseph, and his brother, Brant Agnew. By fall, about thirty converts were numbered. The settlement at Darby was found to be unhealthy, the lands disputed by military claims and liable to endless litigation and the number of Believers was small. It was decided to unite the two bodies and locate at Whitewater. This arrangement was completed and sixty-five permanent Shakers were established. The people were mostly poor and

NO. 10. CHURCH FAMILY DWELLING, UNION VILLAGE, OHIO.

those from Darby had been seriously affected by malarial fever. Meat, bread and other necessaries of life were scarce. "It was Lent with them nearly all the year round," says the record. Nevertheless, in the face of discouragements and privation, they persisted in their life of faith. In 1827, at the break-up of the Wabash settlement, at West Union, the greater part of the Young Believers came to Whitewater. In that year the building of a house of worship was begun. Making their own brick, with the aid of brethren from Union Village and Watervliet, the house was finished in four months. The usual Shaker experiences were undergone of slanderous reports and troubles with State military authorities. At eleven o'clock on a February night of 1830, an alarm of fire was given in the dwelling of the School Order and in twenty minutes the three buildings were wrapped in flames. Happily, the children and their care-takers were saved. Two months later, secret enemies tore down in the night the four corners of a new building partially erected. The Millerite movement sent many into this society. Much difficulty was experienced by one of the members, in obtaining possession of his children after he had joined the society. The case found its way to the Supreme Court, which distinguished itself by the decision that, by Ohio law, a person who joined the Shakers thereby forfeited all natural right to his children. The energy, enthusiasm and devotion of the early days has marked the later life of this society and it remains one of the most prosperous of the Shaker communities.

VIII

IN ONE DECADE 1811–1821

IN the year 1811, Mother Lucy, after consultation with leading minds of the Order, effected a change in organization by which the Church should constitute the First Family or Order, and the Second Family or Order should consist of those groups which had not been part of the Church in the first gathering. These, supporting the public meeting, were now combined in a united circle, having one general head, although locally divided and arranged in minor orders. A Covenant was drawn up adapted to that circle of families and signed March 27th, 1814. In November of the same year, the North Family or Gathering Order, whose temporal affairs had been under the supervision of the Office Deacons of the Church, was given control of its own affairs and a special Covenant was drawn up for this family. The various groups at Mount Lebanon became known in after years as Second, Centre, South and East Families, each occupying a group of buildings, holding and managing its own farms and industries and more or less independent in business relations. The Centre, and later the East Family, was a branch under the special care of the Church, while the North Family had a branch at Canaan, three miles distant, where the Upper and Lower Families, started in 1813, became finally established in 1821. In November, 1814, the Office Family of the Church was named the Second Order. Among distinguished men who attended the Shaker meetings at Mount Lebanon, were Martin Van

NO. 10a. CENTER RESIDENCE, WITH GIRL'S RESIDENCE ON LEFT AND BOY'S ON RIGHT.

Buren, who afterward became President of the United States, and William Wirt, the Attorney General. The former said of an address delivered by Elder Calvin Green, that it was the ablest speech he had ever listened to, at the bar, in the pulpit or before the legislature. He was a great help to Believers in their law cases before the legislature and it was through his influence that Believers were exempted by law from muster fines. William Wirt admired the worship and said of a discourse on Shaker doctrines, "No man in reason can dispute it."

Political Troubles.

Various difficulties arose in civil and military affairs which caused the Shakers to appeal to the legislatures of the states in which their communities were situated. In the War of 1812, many Shakers were drafted and enemies, generally apostates from the Order, in several instances stirred up local officials to order arrests, seizure of property, courts martial, etc., causing much trouble to these disciples of a religion of peace, whose principles would not allow even the employment of a substitute. In 1814, a man who had been a Shaker and had abandoned his faith introduced a bill into the New York Legislature to deprive Shakers of their rights as citizens, rendering their united interest of no avail. The Shakers drew up and presented "A Brief Exposition," showing the manner of the associate relation, its justice and equity. The proposed bill was dropped. This paper was widely circulated in pamphlet form and had a good effect, enlightening people in regard to the customs, ideas and religious faith of the Shakers.

For the purpose of securing immunity from military service or fines, a Memorial was drawn up and presented to the New York Legislature by Elder Calvin Green and others.

Martin Van Buren, then in the New York Senate, was their able advocate and Elder Calvin spent about six weeks urging the justice of their claims, in public and private among the law makers of New York. A petition was also drawn up, signed by about one hundred and twenty of the most respectable people, neighbors of the Mount Lebanon and Watervliet Shakers, that they might be exempt from military duty. This end was only partially accomplished at this time.

In all work of legal processes, appeals and legislative action, Seth Y. Wells, of Watervliet and later of Mount Lebanon, was an important factor. This brother, a native of Long Island, a man of sterling integrity, intellectual ability and possessing a classical education, had been previously to his thirtieth year teacher in the public schools of Albany and instructor in Hudson Academy. Uniting with the Shakers at the age of thirty, his special ability in legal and literary matters was soon recognized.

Schools.

Mother Ann Lee, although unschooled, recognized, as does everyone who is taught of God, the necessity of training and developing the higher intellectual and spiritual faculties. Her famous maxim, "Hands to work and hearts to God," has always meant to her people work of the brain as well as the fingers. Mother Lucy Wright attained high rank as a writer and judge of literary excellence, and always trained her people in correct habits of speech and in correct and easy composition. Shakers had to think, in order to hold their own against the acutest minds of their day. Mother Lucy strongly felt the necessity of a thorough education for the children in the Shaker homes and early instituted a system of schools, in which work she was ably seconded by Seth Y. Wells, who was for several years teacher in the school at Watervliet. The Shaker schools were highly commended by the local and state authorities in all the states where they were found, for their high character and thorough training. Many noble and efficient teachers were raised up in these quiet communities who were fully abreast of their times in education of the young.

In 1821, Seth Y. Wells, who had been Elder of the Second Family at Watervliet since its formation, was released from all other burdens and appointed General Superintendent of Believers' Literature, Schools, etc. in the First Bishopric, which included Watervliet, Hancock and Mount Lebanon. In this position, he edited, after careful revision, the early publications of the societies.

Storm and Pestilence.

In the latter part of 1812, an epidemic raged with great violence. There were many deaths, twelve dying in twenty-eight days at Mount Lebanon; Hancock and Watervliet suffered in the same way, as well as societies in the south and west.

In 1814, a disastrous storm at Mount Lebanon began one night in August. In about thirty hours, six inches of rain fell; the swollen brooks brought down from the mountains mud and stones, gullied the roads, gardens, door-yards and tan-yard. The dam broke and the rushing waters carried carding shop and fulling mill down stream to the valley below. Mother Lucy gave the people advice "for all to look pleasant, speak pleasant and labor to feel so." The advice did much good. All went zealously and cheerily to work to repair damages. On the day after the flood, Mother Lucy with the Elders, accompanied by the brethren and sisters, walked out over the track of the washout, and

in the afternoon she "imparted to the sisters of both Orders
a gift to go out and assist in the repairs." This gift, the
logical outcome of Gospel sex equality, was accepted, and,
accordingly, says the historian: "They came forth, leaving
their spinning wheels for wheelbarrows, the needle for a
shovel and their brooms for a hoe and rake; and encountering the huge mass of rubbish, like a band of strong men,
with the assistance of a few brethren, the stone, gravel,
wood, timber and slabs were removed, so that before night
came on, our streets, lanes and yard appeared tolerably
decent again." The main body of the brethren, meanwhile,
were at work securing the machinery, cloth and other property that had been swept away and buried in sand and
gravel.

Fightings Within.

That Believers had an inward as well as an outward
battle to wage is evidenced in the following quaint conceit,
taken from the pages of a letter written by the Elder of
the First Order at Mount Lebanon to the Elders of the
Second Order, South Union, Ky., dated August 23rd, 1813.
The writer says: "We sometimes discover lurking about
our peaceful habitation some little tory that would wish to
betray our souls into the hands of our enemies. There are
three or four scoundrels of this grade who are very pestifer-
ous. They go by the names of old Mr. Slug, Mrs. Lounge-
about, Great I and Old Fret! It may be you have heard
of them, and as we are fully authorized, we take the liberty
to treat them with as much disrespect and neglect as we
feel to. Doubtless, the young Believers under your care
often experience much inconvenience from their intrusion,
but time and due exercise of grace will deliver from their
clutches."

Summoned Home.

In 1818, it was thought best to call home from the western societies most of those who had been sent out to do the work of organization. These societies were now believed to be strong enough and sufficiently well grounded in the principles of the Gospel to care for themselves. Of the three pioneer missionaries, John Meacham was a native of New York State, born in 1770. Returning from the west in 1818, he passed from earth in 1854. Benjamin Seth Youngs, also from the State of New York, returned from his western home in November, 1836, and passed away in March, 1855. Issachar Bates was a native of Hingham, Mass., an old hero of the Revolution. He was born January 29th, 1758. Recalled in his old age to Mount Lebanon, he withdrew with great reluctance from his hard won fields in the west, mournfully sounding his "retreat." Returning on June 9th, 1835, he passed to his heavenly home on March 17th, 1837.

A New House

was needed by the North Family and, the Church giving their aid, the frame was put up July 7th, 1818, the family taking possession in December, 1819. The new structure was dedicated as a house for the Lord to dwell in. The services were solemn and impressive, an anthem, "Be Ye Holy," being sung. The structure, with later enlargements, has served as the main dwelling to the present time.

In regard to conveniences and comforts, the historian's tale of Canterbury will apply with equal force to all the societies. He says: "Few luxuries were enjoyed in the early days either in dress or food, though by economy a sufficiency for comfort was maintained. Tables were laid with wooden and pewter plates as late as 1807. The use of imported tea was countenanced in 1808, 'liberty tea' having been previously and for years afterward served. The temperance movement in the society opened in 1802, and subsequently total abstinence took its rank as one of the standard regulations."

Mother Lucy's Spiritual Gift.

About the year 1816, Elder Calvin writes that Mother Lucy manifested a gift for Believers to labor in a further work of purification. Premonitions were felt of a further opening of the Gospel. The people had lapsed into a lukewarm state, overcharged with a natural and temporal sense. She urged them to wake up, be more spiritually-minded and feel that the increase of the Gospel was their calling and ought to be their only interest. They must first cleanse and purify their own souls from all sin and defilement before they could find any further increase from within or without.

He further adds that all the Elders administered the gift with fervency and zeal, accepting it as the revelation of God,— it was cordially and universally received, the powers of Heaven were poured out and such an honest confessing and purifying work he had never before witnessed. "Here was divine revelation of the highest order, administered in a few simple words through the Anointed Visible Head. Had it not been believed and united with, it could have had no good effect, but, being believed and obeyed, its effect for good was marvelous." Having been prepared to administer to souls of the heavenly treasure, the Bread of Life, the movement in the outer world began and the people soon realized the fulfilment of the prophecy of Mother Ann, "You shall see the people flock like doves to the windows."

Opening at Savoy.

An occurrence of curious psychic interest is narrated by those who have often heard it told by the participants. One winter day at the Second Family Office in Mount Lebanon, the sisters in charge received a call from a woman, of somewhat peculiar appearance, who asked for something to eat. Food was given her, and while she ate she told them of a wonderful revival that had been going on for some time in Savoy, Mass., a small town situated on a spur of the Green Mountain range. She said the people needed help. Throughout the interview she seemed careful that her face should not be seen and the sisters did not obtain a good look at her features. Rising at last and passing out, they watched her from the door; she walked unsteadily and suddenly, while they were looking at her, vanished from sight. They decided that they had been feeding and conversing with a spirit.

Soon after, early in January, 1817, a letter was received from Elisha Smith, an outside Shaker, relating that on a business trip he had stopped at the house of a Baptist Elder in Savoy, who had told him of a people in the north part of the town among whom a remarkable revival had been going on for some time. He with others had labored among them, but of late he could do nothing with them. He thought they were getting wild and needed help and that the Shakers could help them if anybody could. This message resulted in the sending of Morrell Baker, who was acquainted with some of the people, and Elder Calvin Green.

It was found that a work was in progress of the same nature as the Kentucky revival and that the people were in danger of falling into a worse state than before the awakening. A number of visits were made by different

Elders and members, the principles of the Gospel were thoroughly opened to the people who joyfully embraced the faith and an increase resulted, for which the Order was richer in faith and good works for many years. These Believers united in forming a society under the care of Elder Calvin Green. They had a fine situation with a good water power, but a drouth in 1820, followed by a visitation of grasshoppers, affected their lands and they were reduced to great straits. Their needs were relieved by a generous donation from other societies, and it was finally thought best to dispose of the property and transfer the family of eighty members to Mount Lebanon, Canaan and Watervliet. This was done in 1825, while from the neighboring town of Cheshire came about twenty more.

Interesting Incidents.

In October, 1817, Aaron Bill, selectman of the town of Wilmington, in the Green Mountain State, brought to the Shakers two of his sister's children. He attended meeting, became interested and desired Elder Calvin to visit him at his home. Later in the month, he returned with his wife, Silence, and a neighbor's daughter, Anna Crossman, who lived with them. The three united with the Order, but kept their faith secret at home. Rufus Bishop, a Mount Lebanon Shaker, had a married sister in that section, whose husband, Frederick Crossman, had come into a religious experience parallel to the Shaker faith and a society was gathered at his house.

Elder Calvin quaintly says, "Where these waters were thus moving, I felt that there were more Gospel fish in them that might be caught and that I was called to go and attend to it." Mother Lucy felt full union with this and at his request Brother Rufus Bishop, then Second Elder in the

First Order, was allowed to go with him. They started on June 25th, 1818. Visiting among the families, Daniel Crossman, a lad of seven or eight years, by his manner and his perfect recitation of a chapter in the Gospel of Matthew, impressed the visitors as a child of a religious turn. It will trouble no eastern Shaker to recognize the truth of this impression. A public meeting was held and the visitors preached, exhorted and counseled.

Nancy Crossman, sister of Rufus Bishop, with her husband, Frederick, became interested and the following day they came to see the two brethren and ask questions. After some discussion of Bible subjects, Nancy inquired, "What does the stretching out of the withered arm signify?" The answer was: "First, it was a historical fact that a man's withered arm, by being stretched out in obedience to the Savior's word, was healed. Second, when the spiritual arm that is withered by sin is stretched out to God, it will be healed and restored so as to be able to work the work of God."

She then said, "My arm has been withering ever since the meeting yesterday!" It was her right arm and had diminished so fast that she was unable to use it. Elder Calvin saw what forces were at work and smiling, said: "When you stretch out your arm to God it will be healed." "How shall I do that?" "By confessing your sins."

Nancy then told her husband that she felt it to be her duty to open her mind and become a Shaker. He replied: "If you feel it to be your duty, you must do it; but I would like to have you wait until tomorrow and consider the matter more." "But I must do it!" was her answer. "Well," said he, "I shan't oppose it!" She then with her brother and Elder Calvin went into an adjoining room and in the presence of these two witnesses opened her whole life in audible confession to God, with such intelligent and sincere

conviction that she hardly realized their presence. Rising
from her chair, she exclaimed, "There, my arm is healed!"
stretching out her arm. Elder Calvin remarks that the
impression of her honest gift in confession remained vividly
in his mind, although not one word she had said had he ever
remembered; and he gives the incident as illustrating the
promise, which he wishes that all who confess their sins
might by the use of the same honest gift realize,— that
"their sins might be blotted out and be remembered no
more."

The story of this family recalled a prophecy of Mother
Ann's. In 1780, Peter and Abigail Bishop, of Montague,
Mass., set out to obey the Gospel and gathered all their
children but two, Nancy and Daniel. These had been given
to Abigail's oldest sister to bring up. The sister and her
husband now refused to give them up and the mother was in
great sorrow because she could not gather them into the
Shaker faith. Mother Ann said: "You have done well in
trying to gather your children to the Gospel; it is the duty
of parents so to do; but as you have not succeeded in these
two, take no further trouble about them. Nancy and her
family will be gathered to Believers in this world, and you
will live to see it." Thirty-eight years after, Nancy, grown
up and married, with six children and her husband, set out
in the Gospel.

After uniting with Believers, Nancy and Frederick with
some of their children visited Nancy's mother, Abigail
Bishop, at Watervliet. Several sisters who had received
faith from Mother Ann were present. Abigail related the
story and the prophecy, and added, "Now I have seen it
fulfilled I can die in peace." The aged sisters were so impressed and overjoyed with this evidence of Mother's revelation, that they sprang to their feet with Abigail and began
to dance. Elder Calvin remarks, "She had proved herself

to belong to the most faithful class. Had it not been for her perseverance, it is doubtful whether any of the family would have been saved from the world."

Said Elder Frederick Evans, at the passing away of one these children, Rufus Crossman, at the age of ninety-two years:

"As one of many who inherit their life-long labors, in land, houses and conveniences of various kinds, I am their debtor. When the family united, they paid their debts, righted their wrongs, confessed their personal sins, in the light they had received, and became Christians according to the pattern shown in the Mount of Transfiguration — Mount Lebanon. Their industry was proverbial; their economy —'gathering up the fragments that nothing be lost' — I have never been exceeded. In simplicity of manners and in dress and address, they were examples to the whole Shaker Order. It was such manner of people that laid the foundation in temporal things of all the Shaker villages; and a similar class of men and women laid the foundations of many New England towns and cities."

Betsey Crossman, the last of the six children, passed away in 1892, at the age of eighty-eight.

The Bushnell Family.

In this period came the Bushnells, descendants of some of the early English settlers of Saybrook, Connecticut. The mother and six of the ten children besides a son-in-law with four children were added to the Shakers. Richard Bushnell came first. The story is told by his nephew, Elder Giles B. Avery. He says: "Richard was traveling from New York in search of a farm and came to New Lebanon. While stopping at a hotel over Saturday night in the valley below Shaker Village, he was attracted to the beautiful hamlet on the hillside, and inquired of the landlady who lived there. "Oh," said she, "that is a Shaker village." "Who are the Shakers?" asked Richard. "Why, they are the fanatical followers of Ann Lee, an old witch. Do not go there, for they will surely bewitch you," was the alarming reply.

The following morning, the Sabbath, was bright and beautiful, tempting to a long delightful walk; and as he slowly climbed the hill, in spite of the warning, in calm and pensive mood, he pursued his course through the village Everything was neat, quiet and orderly. There were no dogs, no loafers, no drinking saloons. In fact there was nobody in the streets. He was struck with a singular feeling and was in deep meditation. On his return, Elder Calvin Green of the North Family observed him and, noticing that he was serious and thoughtful, invited him in to take a little rest and get acquainted. The result was that he did not visit the famous Lebanon Springs, but remained to investigate the Shaker faith, was convinced of its truth and became a prominent member of the Community. Elder Calvin Green supplements the tale: "In October, 1817, Charles and Ira Bushnell, two of Richard's brothers, came to see him. They were on their way west, intending to buy land. There had been a religious awakening in Saybrook in which Charles had been seriously affected. He had flattering business prospects and, therefore, struggled hard to make his religion answer, as that admitted the world. He was not ready to give up all for Shakerism, for he saw that would be what it would cost. Seeing this to be the case, I labored to spoil his religion and handled it with severity, feeling sure this was the only way to take him.

"Elder Ebenezer Cooley ably assisted in this labor and Charles was convinced that no religion but Shakerism would stand the test. They continued their journey, but on their return, Charles acknowledged his faith and determination to obey it. He took the book — "Christ's Second Appearing"— and zealously preached Shaker doctrine. His sister Sally said she thought he must be inspired for he spoke so clearly and forcibly that she was astonished. He was naturally somewhat stammering in speech, but while advocating Shaker faith there was no stammer. He evidently had spiritual power as a seal to the testimony.

"In about three weeks Charles and Patty paid a visit. Charles opened his mind and set out, but it was hard for Patty to give up her old religious views, family pride and natural attachments. She became convinced of the truth of the way, but desired certain evidence. This was granted in the following manner: She wanted to write home; believing that she ought not to write until she set out in the Gospel, I felt a gift to hinder her. I went into the Elder Sister's room, where writing materials had been provided, and told her I felt it was time for her to confess her sins and set out in the way of God. She wanted to write her letter first. This I thought an excuse and said, 'Then, write!' She tried to do so, but her hand was twitched away. I said, 'Why don't you write?' 'I don't know as I can,' she replied. I said, 'Try again!' As she tried the third time, her hand was violently twitched and shaken, then she was whirled to her feet and shaken, jerked and twisted in many ways and was compelled to laugh. This operation was continued until she was thoroughly baptized and wanted no more evidence. She then opened her mind and set out in the Gospel and was a faithful sister until her decease, though she had a trial to stay and take care of her aged mother for many years.

"In this I was an agent to administer the united gift of the Eldership. They both returned home strong in the faith. Two visits were made them and after considerable labor, Martha, the mother, opened her mind and was a good, honest Believer until her death." Others started at the same time. At this visit, the family were said to have desired some sign of the Spirit as a confirmation to them, and when they were all assembled, Sally Bushnell was in great exercise of mind and was made the recipient of the power of God in her own person, being shaken very violently. The house also seemed to be shaken. This was to her convincing proof that the cause was of God. She was engaged to be married to an excellent young man, their prospects were bright for a happy and useful life, but, true to her faith, she gave up her plans and her earthly love, passing a useful life among the Shakers at Mount Lebanon.

The father of the Bushnell children was at first disposed to be friendly, but, when Shakerism broke into his family and carried off his wife and so many of his children, he turned against it, still, when he found his wife fully determined in her faith, he left her unmolested. Charles possessed considerable property and a commodious country house. He devoted the whole to the support of the Gathering Order. When Richard Bushnell was appointed Second Elder in 1827, Charles succeeded him as deacon and had charge of the trading and manufacturing interests.

Elder Richard Bushnell was a spiritual father of the purest and holiest type, beloved by his family and held in highest confidence and esteem in the whole region where his life was spent. He did much to build up the North Family, and much of the comfort and prosperity of their later years is due to the self-denying labors and economics of this noble father. In the days when the people were in poverty, he employed every means in his power to earn a livelihood, often denying himself the necessities of life for the sake of the family. It is told of him that at one time when peddling garden seeds, he was suffering with extreme hunger, but did not feel that he could afford the

NO. 11.   ELDER RICHARD BUSHNELL.

twenty-five cents that a meal would cost. Riding along, he
saw something glittering in the wheel rut. There was a
twenty-five cent piece! Taking it as a gift of God provided for his extremity, he bought and enjoyed the dinner
he so much needed. Elder Richard passed away in October, 1873, at the age of eighty-two. At his funeral, the
large meeting-house was crowded to its utmost capacity,
not only by Shakers but by citizens of the town and neighboring places, some of whom spoke of the worth and nobil-
ity of the man they had long known and honored. A leading citizen wrote to the local newspaper in a neighboring
city of the tributes of the brethren and sisters: "If these
men and women are sincere, if they speak their thoughts
in all soberness, if such love cements together the hearts of
Shakers, then is their society a paradise on earth and just
without the door of Heaven."

A child of the Bushnell family was Elder Giles B.
Avery, for many years of the Central Ministry, "one of the
most gifted in the Shaker Order, prominent in both temporal and spiritual interests. A skillful mechanic, he could
act efficiently in every department of useful work; as a
writer and orator, he had no peer in the Order."

Coming with his relatives to Mount Lebanon, when very
young, he "lived the life of the righteous and died in the
harness, full of years and honors, crowned with blessing and
everlasting love."

Strong Convictions.

About two years after the coming of Richard Bushnell,
his fellow apprentice, Joseph Adams, having finished his
time, came to see his former companion. Elder Calvin
Green says of him: "After he began to think himself proof
against Shakerism, I began to say something to him that I

10

was sure would penetrate his mind and sting withal. I clearly saw that he was providentially called to the Gospel and I determined to have him, for he was the right sort.

"The speaking in public meeting was adapted to his state, and on Monday I asked him an arrow-like question. By this time he felt so awakened that he answered, 'I see what you are at. I would rather see a man with a pistol pointed at my breast than to see you.' I then felt sure of the prize. Soon after, he came to me and said, 'I must confess my sins!' I replied, 'Perhaps you had better wait longer and labor upon it. Be fully determined to be honest before you attempt to do it, and then set out to be faithful forever.' He answered, 'O, but I must do it now, or I shall certainly die, and if it kills me, I can but die!'" I said, 'Well, if you feel prepared and are honestly determined, you may.' He did open his mind as honestly and intelligently as I ever heard a person in all my experience. He set out with integrity and he has been a faithful Believer and a kind and faithful brother.

"He had committed no felonious crime nor any uncommon sin to cause him to feel such heavy conviction, but had been of a thoughtful, moral cast. By the operation of the Gospel spirit, and seeing the contrast between the life of Christ and the life of the world, sin and a sinful nature appeared exceedingly sinful. I would that all who come among Believers, or are now among them, might have such conviction and be thus powerfully wrought upon. Even those who are gathered when children need this convicting power and honestly to obey it, if they ever make solid Shakers. And from all my experience I am confident that a soul who gains this conviction and faithfully improves its honest work will certainly endure to the end of the faith and will secure salvation. All may gain this by sincere and prayerful labor, and I earnestly desire that all the young and rising generation may gain this inestimable blessing." And this ministration of the fervent Elder may well be received, nearly a century later, by those who enjoy the protection of the homes he helped to establish.

Proctor Sampson.

Early in February, 1814, Proctor Sampson, from Marshfield, Mass., came to the North House, on his way to visit his boy and girl at the Friends' School, to which denomination he belonged.

Having seen a history of the Kentucky Revival, he thought it gave account of a more substantial religion than he had ever found, and, writing to the author of the book for further information, had been referred to this place. Earnestly desiring to find a saving Gospel, he had come to see whether the people had that light and power. Like other Friends who have investigated the two, he saw in Shakerism a fuller development and superior light to that of the Quaker Church; he united with the society, placing his children under the care of the Shakers.

Proctor Sampson was a man of large means for that time, and after uniting with Believers, he dedicated his property to the Gospel cause. He aided in purchasing the George Darrow place and afterwards bought more land for the Gathering Order. He gave his children's shares of his property to the Church Family, where they resided. He assisted Believers at Savoy and also at Groveland and was much interested in the publication of Shaker literature, giving liberally for that purpose. For fourteen years he was Elder in various parts of the Gathering Order. In one of his public addresses, he said:

"When I received faith in this Gospel and saw what it would cost me, if I could have believed it would have answered the same purpose to lay my head upon a block and have it cut off, I would rather have done it, the cross seemed so great. But I saw that according to the words of the Savior, I must give up all and my own natural life also, or I never could find that life eternal in Christ which is more valuable than all things else. Therefore, I freely chose to die the death of the cross. I can testify that my soul overflows with thankfulness to God at every recollection, for the blessing and happiness His Holy Spirit has bestowed upon me. All the sacrifices I have made to obtain this unspeakable gift of justification and peace toward God sink into insignificance in comparison. I realize the promise of a hundred-fold reward for all I have given up."

Mother Lucy's Last Days.

As the time drew near for the societies to lose their beloved Mother Lucy, the feelings of anxiety grew intense among those who so strongly leaned upon her wisdom and counsel. Her motherly tenderness was the comfort and stay of every toiler in the remote fields of the vineyard.

Father David Darrow writes: "I have not forgotten the day in the North House, nor the lovely voice that directed my weary steps. I well remember that early Tuesday morning, when, going down the hill from the North House, I had a great mind to throw away my staff. Poor little staff! It is worn quite smooth — it has taken me over many a hill and brook of water, and through many a flooded marsh and wilderness swamp — and I walk with it yet, sometimes, and it puts me in mind of many things. O, I think if I could have the liberty of going up the hill to the North House, how differently I would feel from what I did when going down to leave my precious Parent and those whom I esteemed more than all things on earth beside, to go to a strange land and a strange people."

A pleasant incident is related of Mother Lucy, in connection with the lion-hearted hero of the west, Elder Richard McNemar. Greatly desiring a personal interview, in order that she might obtain from him the facts about the great Kentucky Revival, Mother Lucy summoned him to Mount Lebanon. He made the journey, and, in a long conversation, during which she questioned and catechized him in every possible way, she sought to obtain the truth about the far away field. At last, leaning back, she exclaimed, "Brother Richard, I name you Eleazer, for you are right!" He promptly replied, "Mother Lucy, I will accept the name, if you will permit me to spell right with a W." She consented, and from that time he signed his name Eleazer Wright.

In the year 1819, Mother Lucy had a brief but severe illness and, although restored to comparative health, she realized that the end of her pilgrimage was fast approaching. In 1816, she had made the last of her many visits east, giving the societies her counsel, encouragement and motherly blessing. In January, 1821, in accordance with a strong desire to end her days at Watervliet, she went thither, accompanied by the rest of the Ministry. Some changes were made in the heads of families.

On February second, a letter was received at Mount Lebanon saying that Mother Lucy was ill, and at midnight of the fifth, the Church Family was aroused by a messenger with a call for Brother Eliab Harlow, the physician, to start at once for Watervliet. He with Elder John Farrington started as soon as possible, arriving at nine o'clock the next morning. All efforts were unavailing, and at three in the afternoon of the same day, Mother Lucy gently breathed her last, having two days before passed her sixty-first birthday.

News of her departure caused great sorrow through all the societies. The funeral service was attended by about two hundred Believers. It is said that notwithstanding the grief pervading all hearts, "a remarkably calm, serene and peaceful feeling was diffused. It was very evident that Mother Lucy's peaceful spirit was present, laboring to cheer and comfort her sorrowing children."

Memories of Mother Lucy.

The appreciative hand of Elder Calvin Green penned Mother Lucy's biography and has left this picture of her:

"Slightly above the medium height, well proportioned, her well-formed shoulders seemed as if built for strength and endurance and her solid arms as if they were fitted for labor and accustomed thereto; dark brown hair, slightly gray; face fair and symmetrical; forehead rather full, indicating deep penetration and understanding; eyes black, clear and penetrating but mild and placid. Her countenance ever wore a pleasant smile — the most beautiful smile I ever beheld. She was called handsome by the children of the world, and it cannot be denied that she was naturally handsome. But there is no beauty to be compared with that light shining forth of the Spiritual Glory of Innocence, Purity and Love.

"Her whole soul was devoted to build up the United Interest and render it efficient; to promote the happiness of its subjects and extend its blessings to others. She was inflexible in practising whatever she believed and taught as principle. She was strictly punctual to observe and keep all rules, orders and regulations of Gospel Order. She always spoke as she meant and meant as she spoke and always to the purpose. She was a shining example to all her children, teaching us that it was sacrilege to waste any of the good things with which we were blessed.

"For if we were true Believers, our persons, time and faculties, with all that we possessed were consecrated to God, and we were only stewards upon God's heritage. Therefore, if we were extravagant or wasted any useful thing, it was a loss to the Consecrated interest and in proportion to its value would prove a spiritual loss to our souls.

"Her industry was equal to her prudence. Her literary ability was remarkable and she was an excellent literary critic. Through her efforts, the simple style of Gospel language became established as the universal custom of Believers. She had a fervent anxiety. that Believers should keep their own Order; the children of this world and the children of Christ and of Mother were two distinct and separate orders of people. In the administration of Mother Lucy, she proved herself a Mother indeed."

Many of her sayings and addresses have been preserved by careful hands.

Other Leaders

passed away, Eldress Ruth Farrington, the first in the Western Ministry, departing on October 28th, 1821, — "a lovely woman of God!" writes one of her contemporaries. Eldress Ruth had been a gifted woman and a faithful, zealous Shaker ever since the first opening, when, a young girl in her father's home, she became with her family an ardent follower of Mother Ann. Father David Darrow followed her to the spirit world on June 27th, 1825, at the age of seventy-five.

John Farrington had been appointed to succeed David Darrow as Elder at Mount Lebanon in 1805, and Rachel Spencer as Elder Sister in place of Ruth Farrington. Elder John, who since the age of twenty had been a faithful disciple of Mother Ann, was one of the foremost to devote his all to the work. Strong in spirit as in body, capable and reliable, he was an excellent leader, gathering the feelings of all and keeping life and energy among Believers. Rachel Spencer had been brought up in the Darrow family and was a noble and useful sister, finishing her earthly course at the age of eighty-eight in the year 1852.

Twenty years from the organization of the western bishopric, in the year 1825, there were one thousand eight hundred Believers in the west,— eight hundred under the direct care of the Ministry at Union Village, five hundred at Pleasant Hill, three hundred at South Union and a small number at West Union. During the same time one thousand six hundred had been gathered into the eastern societies.

NO. 12. STREET IN MOUNT LEBANON. ON THE RIGHT: OLD MEETING HOUSE ERECTED IN 1786; MEETING HOUSE ERECTED IN 1824; RESIDENCE OF THE CHURCH FAMILY. ON THE LEFT: OFFICE, FORMERLY SECOND ORDER, AND INFIRMARY.

IX

FORTY YEARS OF GROWTH 1821-1861

MOTHER LUCY WRIGHT appointed as her successor Elder Ebenezer Bishop, with Eldress Ruth Landon first of the Sisters in the Ministry. People of the world were drawn to the meetings in great numbers. On the twentieth of June, 1824, the society at Mount Lebanon dedicated a new meeting-house.

It had been raised one year previously and the work of construction had all been done by Shakers, none but consecrated labor having been employed. About one thousand visitors attended the first service besides representatives from other Shaker societies.

Elder Ebenezer Bishop and Elder Calvin Green addressed the audience. Elder Calvin referred to the promise of Father James Whittaker at the dedication of the first house on the same site, that if this people would obey the voice of the Lord their God and keep strictly to these religious principles which God had revealed to them, they would always be protected. They would be blessed in their basket and their store, they would not be dependent upon the world but the world would be dependent upon them, and people should come from the east, west, north and south and from all nations and hear the word of God in that house.

Elder Calvin testified that to his knowledge this had been literally fulfilled, some from nearly every real nation of the earth and from all classes of people having attended meeting and heard the testimony in the former house. The next Sabbath a larger concourse assembled, estimated at two thousand. The same structure is standing today, although since 1890, the society has worshiped in the meeting room of the Church Family's Dwelling.

The story is told of the building of the first meeting-house, that different views were held by the members as to the appropriate site, and each in love and union waived his choice for another's decision. At last, John Farrington drove up with a load of fine lumber and depositing it exclaimed emphatically, "There! that is for the meeting-house." This was taken for a sign, and on the spot where the load lay the building was erected. This ancient building is still pointed out.

Missionary Work.

In 1825, came a call from Lyons, in western New York, for instruction in the principles of Shakerism, and a company of Elders, Calvin Green, Jeremiah Talcott, Betsy Hastings and Molly Williams, were sent out. Starting on the first of August, traveling partly by canal, in five days they reached their destination.

Elder Calvin tells a pretty story of the opening of their mission. At ten o'clock on Saturday night they reached the house of Joseph Pelham, the man who had sent for aid. On the Sabbath the Shakers attended meeting and the next day visited the people and looked into conditions. On Tuesday morning, Elder Calvin, burdened in spirit, went into the woods and kneeling prayed for light and guidance and to know if here were a people ready to obey the Gospel. Feeling relief, he rose from his knees, when a young quail came up to him so close that he picked it up. It was not at all afraid and the old birds near by showed no signs of alarm. He admired it for a little while and then let it go. A spirit impression said, "You will know before night what the little quail means, and today will souls in this vicinity begin to embrace the Gospel." Soon after, a flock of these shy birds alighted on Joseph Pelham's house. This incident was taken to signify the flock of Shakers that would gather there. Before night a young girl came, saying that she wanted to be a Shaker and her parents were willing. "Here was the little quail!" The "little quail girl" was the forerunner of a gathering of souls of whom the first were her own father and mother.

Urged on every side to hold meetings, the little company remained, going from place to place in poor conveyances, or on foot, preaching, visiting from house to house, confuting their opponents, everywhere meeting those who were hungry for the Gospel as well as those who hated and derided it.

The Elders visited Sodus Bay and found it a beautiful sheet of water, with level, rolling lands of a deep, rich soil on the southern shore. A quarter of a century before, Elder Calvin had read an attractive description of the place, and now, from the ripe, luscious blackberries that grew in great profusion in the clearings, to the beautiful bay, all seemed especially adapted to a Shaker settlement. The missionaries thoroughly canvassed every available location to be secured about the bay, holding meetings, constantly beset by zealous and argumentative Methodists, ministers and class-leaders, and in more than one case finding latent faith hidden in the heart of a one time Shaker, who was glad of a chance to return to the fold.

Elder Calvin soon made a second visit, with instructions to purchase lands for a new society. On the way, he was present at the celebration of the opening of the Erie Canal. He mentions Syracuse and other places in Central New York, as "villages which may be said to grow literally out of salt." This second trip was full of missionary labors among the people. After traveling about two hundred miles in search of a suitable location, the one first selected on the shore of Sodus Bay was chosen.

A little girl, not quite eight years old, of a well-to-do family where the party stopped on their return, wished to go home with them and become a Shaker. Her parents gave their consent, Elder Calvin adopted the little Shaker as his own charge and with the child they resumed their journey on November 25th, 1825. The canals were clogged with ice and the journey was cold and disagreeable. That night they refused to put up at a tavern, as "the boatmen were thick as frogs in a frog pond and were an ungainly set to be with." Having been ferried across the Mohawk, they took their baggage and, "on a clear, moonlight night, accompanied by the ferryman and several others, in various costumes, each carrying bag or sack, with the little girl trudging along with her tin pail and without making the least fuss, — altogether we made a grotesque group," writes Elder Calvin, who seemed to get enjoyment of one kind or another out of every situation in his varied and picturesque career. The last stage of their journey, when within two and one-half miles of Watervliet, the indefatigable Elder shortened the distance one mile by a vigorous push in a bee line across lots, through snow, over fences, reaching the Second Order at seven o'clock in the evening. "Our brave little girl trudged along without a whimper or complaint. Although we helped her all we could, she must have been extremely tired. I thought she was about the bravest and most spunky little one I ever saw and one worth having," comments Elder Calvin. They were cordially welcomed at Watervliet, and on the second of December reached their North Family home.

The little girl adopted by Elder Calvin on this journey was Polly Reed, for many years Eldress in the First Order, afterward serving in the Central Ministry. For many years Eldress Polly Reed was teacher of the Shaker School and a most excellent instructor, — "a finished scholar, a beautiful speaker and a most loveable associate." Her penmanship and map drawing were remarkable. A map of the Holy Land, including parts of Egypt and surrounding sections, a map of the Hemispheres and other work of like character are still shown, the work of Eldress Polly Reed, every stroke done with the pen. It is hard to believe that the perfect map before the eye is the work of the hand and pen and not the product of the engraver's art.

The New Community.

Other visits were made to western New York, and in 1828 a society had become established in a beautiful situation on Sodus Bay. Joseph Pelham was the first to occupy the newly purchased home in March, 1826. Ten years afterwards a canal was projected, whose terminus was on the premises of Believers. The property was sold and a new site was purchased at Groveland, Livingston County, about eighty miles distant. This society was also known by the name of Sonyea, where, many years later, Elder Calvin wrote his entertaining memoirs.

One Hundred and Twenty Years Old.

In May, 1827, a funeral service was held at Mount Lebanon for a colored sister, Melinda Welch, who passed away at the ripe age of one hundred and twenty years. Her age was determined by her recollections of the great

snow storm in New England in 1717. She was a slave in
the family of a son of a New Hampshire Governor, and
was sold at the time that she was ten years old.

She received the Shaker faith in the days of Mother
Ann, and had been purchased by Enoch Goodrich, the
youngest of the twelve Goodrich brothers. Although not
himself a Believer, he paid for her $100, the equivalent of
$1,000 in later times, and then set her at liberty, that she
might unite herself to the people of God as she had greatly
desired to do.

The Philadelphia Mission.

In the years 1826 and 1827, there was a movement
started in Philadelphia growing out of the communistic impulse that came with Robert Dale Owen, George H. Evans
and others from England. Among the leaders was Abel
Knight, a descendant of a primitive English Quaker who
had accompanied William Penn to America. A community
of about three hundred people was started at Valley Forge,
the famous winter camp of Washington in the War of the
Revolution. The community did not prove a success. One
May evening in 1827, there arrived at Mount Lebanon, a
party of seven from Valley Forge, desiring to see the Shakers and learn from them the secret of successful communism.
They were kindly received and were given every opportunity to observe the workings of the community.

In August, Clauson Middleton arrived, bearing a letter
from the Philadelphia visitors expressing faith and union
with Believers. In September, Richard Bushnell and Proctor Sampson were sent out. Two of Abel's children, Jane
and Sarah, with their father, were eager inquirers and

Sarah decided to return home with the two brethren. As a plot was suspected to detain her by force, it was planned that in company with her father she should go secretly at midnight; the morning found her far on her way toward her new home, while Jane had to endure full measure of persecution.

Early in 1828, Abel Knight, John Dodgson and Samuel Carr arrived at Mount Lebanon, determined to settle in Shaker land, and Abel bought a farm about a mile distant from the Shakers. Thomas Rider arrived in April with a company of twelve, and the next day came John Shaw and Ann Busby from Westchester. They at once went through with all necessary preliminaries and launched out as Shakers.

As the Philadelphia people were evidently disposed to gather to the Shakers, Elder Calvin Green and Abram Hendricksen were appointed to visit them. In June, 1828, the Knights removed to their new home in New Lebanon, but the mother eventually returned to Philadelphia with her other children, leaving the father and two daughters. Sarah Knight passed away while young, but Jane, till old age, was a mighty pillar of the faith in the Gathering Order.

Among those who came with Abel Knight was George Wickersham, whose parents had been among the communists at ill-starred Valley Forge, and who, a youth of sixteen, could not be satisfied to resign his dream of a happier and better life. He, by his marked ability, faithful labor and pure and noble spirit added much to the temporal and spiritual inheritance now enjoyed by the Mount Lebanon Shakers. About fifty were gathered at one time from Valley Forge besides those who came at other times. Among them were many children, who in nearly all cases became steadfast Shakers.

The "Pennsylvania Pilgrims."

On the Philadelphia journey, Elder Calvin visited the descendants of a small band of German people, known as Pilgrims, who, about one hundred years before, had emigrated to America for the sake of freedom to live according to their faith, which seemed to be a forerunner of Shakerism. Having received a special illumination from the Spirit of God, they adopted the virgin life, believing it to be necessary that they might follow Christ. Numbering only about forty, and not trying to propagate their beliefs, the society, who lived true to their tenets, dwindled away by death until the last one disappeared,— the name of the site of their settlement, Germantown, and a small printed book of their beliefs and revelations being the sole relics of the heroic little community. Elder Calvin speaks of this movement as one of many that for a half century before the rise of the Shakers were continually springing up in different countries, whose beliefs and revelations correspond very closely with those of Mother Ann Lee. "These all form a cloud of witnesses," says the Elder, "of the work among Shakers — all testified that the appearance of Christ was drawing nigh."

Temperance.

In 1828, a temperance wave passed over the country. The drinking and smoking habits of the American people, the chewing tobacco and the taking of snuff, were a part of the life of Shaker brethren and sisters, with no thought of evil or impropriety; but with new light, a new advance was made and the societies of Believers discontinued the use of spirits and the custom of placing wine or cider before visitors. The

Anti-Tobacco Testimony

had to be given repeatedly as members entered from the outer world, where the use of Sir Walter Raleigh's "Virginia weed" was almost universal. Among the spirit messages, given about 1840, to Believers, was a prohibition of tobacco, from the departed founders of the faith. At this time, those who were over sixty years of age were exempt from the edict. Contrary to this teaching, however, the custom grew up again in later years. On the pages of the "Shaker Manifesto," in the year 1873, appears an "Obituary," which reads as follows:

"On Tuesday, Feb. 20th, 1873, Died, by the power of truth and for the cause of human Redemption, at the Young Believers' Order, Mount Lebanon, *in* much beloved Brethren, the Tobacco Habit."

"No funeral ceremonies, no monument, no graveyard; but an honorable Record thereof in the Court above. Ed."

At one time, the custom of smoking a pipe was considered, for women of one generation, as unobjectionable as that of drinking tea for those of another, and many an old Shaker saint rested and consoled herself with her pipe. One of these smoking sisters, a humorous, steadfast soul, was Nancy Lockwood, whose spirit was so quaintly wise and full of sunshine that, were her story fully written, Mrs. Wiggs in the "Cabbage Patch" must evermore stand in the shadow. She thoroughly believed that the cross was the source of real happiness, for she had "proved it." The following incident is a sample of the way in which she met life. She had just seated herself in the spinning shop to enjoy an after dinner smoke, when some one casually remarked that the Ministry wished that all the sisters, who could, would give up smoking. Sister Nancy looked at her

11

pipe and said to herself, "What do I smoke for? I never thought of it before. Is it because other people have the habit? Is it only an indulgence that I have practised since I was a child?" Who or what answered her, she never told, but she arose and, extinguishing the tobacco, deposited her old pipe on a beam over her work place, saying, "There! you stay there till I take you down." There she worked for many years, with the token of her conquest before her eyes. With a twinkle in her eye that lighted her whole face, she was wont to end the story with, "After that I used my mouth for glad and heavenly songs instead of smoke." Years after, when the old spinning shop was torn down, there lay Nancy's pipe in its resting place on the beam.

Another aged sister was Lavinia Salisbury, who had served as nurse and deaconess, Eldress for a time at Mount Lebanon, Eldress for many years at Canaan, stately and dignified in presence, pure, noble, intellectual and spiritual, whose motherly, devoted spirit and knowledge of affairs made her a powerful helper, long after her retirement from active service, in years when she was the oldest person as well as the oldest member of the North Family at Mount Lebanon. In childhood she had learned to use the pipe and retained the habit of a quiet smoke after each meal. A young sister, detailed to work with Sister Lavinia, was unaccustomed to the incense of the pipe and used to slip away during the half hours of indulgence. She was noticed and questioned. Eldress Antoinette Doolittle interviewed the aged smoker and told her of the trial of her young fellow worker. The sweet, old saint met her with the calm assurance, "Eldress Antoinette, I am glad of your gift! I have already left it off." She had felt in her own soul the inspirational message from the spirit world and had rendered prompt obedience, dropping at once and forever the habit of over seventy years. Such was the spirit and practise of those who had truly embraced the Gospel of purity and who followed on to do the works as they came to know of the ever advancing teaching of their faith.

Spirit Manifestations.

The period from 1837 to 1844 was remarkable for a series of spirit manifestations throughout the connection, more fully described in another chapter. Their effect was manifold, but especially was the fact established of the connection and interdependence of the Church on earth and the Church in the Heavens. The spiritual life and sensibility of Believers were greatly quickened, their sympathies broadened, and the world-wide nature of the work was so emphasized as never since to have been lost sight of.

Later Leaders.

In this period appeared some whose influence is clearly apparent and strongly felt in the life of the Order. In 1830, came

FREDERICK WILLIAM EVANS,

the young Englishman, — free thinker, radical, materialist, — who, with his brother, George H. Evans, precursor of the more famous Henry George, had come to America and, in company with Robert Dale Owen and other reformers, had planned a community. Frederick was on the way to find a suitable location, when, hearing of the Shakers as practical communists, he turned aside to see them and appeared at the Office at Mount Lebanon on a day in June. Kindly received at the North House, he was "surprised that the expression of his infidel sentiments did not seem to disturb these religionists, who were not touchy, but eminently sensible, candid and open." He remained, was met by spirit manifestations on his own person so convincing that his materialism changed its basis, he found his inner senses opened, his spiritual nature awakened, and he returned to New York only to announce his determination to remain among the Shakers.

His faith was not learned from priest or book, but, like other prophets, from direct spirit illumination. To the end of his life he was the bulwark of Shakerism; the voice which would not be stilled and to which all men listened; the convincing, cogent reasoner, whose arguments could not be met nor refuted; the iconoclastic reformer, whose ax was ever in his hand to demolish the old and useless, while ever building up the new; the seer, whose vision was bounded by horizons far out-reaching earth and present day revelations. He stood always upon a mountain top, calling aloud to his people — Come up Higher! He was in the Elder's Order from 1836 to his translation in 1892.

Contemporary with him was a sister, a Mother, who, in her more quiet way, was as truly seer, prophet, voice and bulwark of the faith as her coadjutor.

MARY ANTOINETTE DOOLITTLE,

born in New Lebanon, N. Y. in 1810, united with the Shakers, of her own choice and determination, at the age of fourteen. A little pamphlet, fascinatingly written by her own hand, tells the story of her childhood and early faith, her coming among the people chosen of God and her own heart.

The story of her after life, of her half century as Eldress, are written in lives mighty now within the Kingdom of God in the Heavens, recorded also in the superstructure,

NO. 13.   ELDER HERVEY L. EADS.

heared so largely by her wise brain, warm heart and tireless hands, upon foundations laid by earlier fathers and mothers — the life, spiritual and temporal, of the family and society at Mount Lebanon.

The labors and influence of these two leaders cannot be bounded by any one family or society. The whole connection, north, south, east and west, felt and feel still the impress of the wise counsels, magnetic inspiration, strong personality and devoted consecration of Elder Frederick W. Evans and Eldress Mary Antoinette Doolittle.

Perhaps no other two among the mighty souls of the period from 1830 to the century's end have left so strong an impress on their people and the world at large.

A life parallel with that of Elder Evans in time as in force of character, power of leadership and influence on the thought of his people, is

HERVEY L. EADS,

bishop, theologian, man of affairs. Born near South Union, Kentucky, April 28th, 1807, he joined the Shaker society, in his mother's arms, at its first gathering, in the following November. Before he was one year old, he was placed in the Children's Order. He lived in a log cabin until he was fifteen, attending school three months of each year after he was four. After reaching the mature age of six, he worked steadily at manual labor, learning seven or eight different trades. He entered the Ministry in 1836, as associate with Elder Benjamin S. Youngs. In 1844, without warning or explanation, he was removed from the Bishopric and transferred as a private member to Union Village. He experienced many changes from Elder to private member and again to the Bishopric, at the opening of the Civil War being returned to the position so suddenly vacated. Elder Hervey loved music to such a degree that when a vacancy occurred, although over seventy, he stepped in, learned to play organ and piano and led a class in music. He passed away in 1892, at the age of eighty-four years. Differing in many points of polity and theology from his equally original and forceful brother of the east, the battles of wit and wisdom in argument between the two were many and fierce, but their Gospel love and union were never interrupted. Another son of South Union was

DANIEL BOLER,

for thirty years Senior in the Central Ministry, who was born in 1804. His father's family were swept into Shakerism by the revival wave of the following years. To avoid the persecutions of his mother's people, the father took his son at ten years of age, and the two came on foot to Mount Lebanon, N. Y. Elder Daniel was wont to tell, in after years, how he wore his shoes backward and walked "toeing in" through the sand, that the tracks might lead his pursuers in an opposite direction. He absorbed the spirit of the faith and in an eminent degree stood as an exponent of its principles. Less widely known outside the Order than some of his contemporaries, few so completely filled the sacred office of Father and Minister of the Divine Unction to the people. He passed to the Spirit Land from Mount Lebanon, in 1892, at the age of eighty-eight.

In 1834, came a young Scotchman,

DANIEL FRASER,

son of a silk weaver of Paisley. Endowed with a vigorous, inquiring mind, a deeply spiritual nature, and of a prompt, practical, mechanical bent, in his connection with manufacturing interests in England, he had received an impetus toward reform of social conditions, and started for America, hoping to found a community. Landing at Baltimore, he heard incidentally of the Shakers and lost no time in seeking them out.

His life and thought are indicative of much that is best in the later development of Shakerism. Dietetics and hygiene were his especial interest, and, as he was a practical chemist, he was of great service to the North Family in the days when the vegetarian philosophy, of which he was an ardent adherent, was being worked out to practical issues.

His biographer says: "Deeply impressed with the importance of a work which demonstrated the possibility of living a divine, angelic life while yet in time, and with the extended range of reforms included within its compass, a new purpose took shape in his soul and he abandoned every other project that he might first eliminate from his own being the elements and forces of the lower selfhood.

"Although he had proved his capacity to lead others, he now sought not position nor distinction in any respect, but, accepting the teachings of Jesus, he entered the Kingdom of Heaven as a little child. In this humble attitude, he was able to comprehend the principles not only in their theological aspect, nor merely as a system of ethics, but with that deeper, stronger grasp given to those who, by doing the works, know of the doctrine; and, perceiving how limited were the capabilities of human beings, how futile all their efforts, save where self is crucified and the divine intelligence works through them to will and to do, he nobly resolved to bring an offering unto death of the 'old man and his deeds,' that he might be re-created in the image of Christ. In one of the meetings, he bore his testimony in these words: 'Brethren and sisters, I find that I have a great big Scotchman in me and it is my intention to crucify him!' When he had been in the family but a few weeks, a sister, noticing that his hands were burned by the sun and blistered by use of the hoe, warned him about overdoing in his new occupation; he laughingly answered, 'O, these things are good for spoiling the worldly gentleman!'

"In early manhood he lived far ahead of his time and the evening of his life found him still in the van of every living theme. He did all that lay in his power that in Zion might be fulfilled those beautiful prophecies which should make of her a centre of redemptive forces."

When his failing strength released him from active service, his feelings were expressed in these lines:

> "Come, O Death! thou great uplifter,
>   Touch me with thy genial rod;
> Sever earthly ties asunder,
>   Lay my form beneath the sod;
> Then in spirit I can triumph
>   In the City of my God."

DAVID PARKER

was a prominent Believer in New Hampshire at this period. A native of Boston, he became a Shaker at the age of ten years. Of unusual ability, he made such advancement and showed such maturity of judgment that at the age of nineteen he was appointed trustee. He was widely known as a shrewd and honorable business man — "one of the best business men of the State." In 1837, at the age of thirty, he was placed in the Ministry. In 1848, he ably defended the Shakers before the New Hampshire Legislature against the calumnies of apostates and, at his earnest request, a searching legislative investigation was made of the life and practises of the Shakers, which resulted in their honorable acquittal of all charges against them.

ABRAHAM PERKINS

was well known to the people of New Hampshire as a leader of remarkable spiritual power. When a young man, well educated, a teacher, a lawyer of great promise, for the sake of spiritual growth and obedience to religious truth as he saw it exemplified among the Shakers, he had united with the Order of Believers. At the age of ninety-two, with form still erect, step quick and face radiant with the innate goodness that had marked his life, he passed to the Home Land. He had lived largely in the realm of inspiration, and as Elder and Bishop, he was unsurpassed in faithfulness, self-sacrifice and devotion.

Millerism to Shakerism.

The decade of the 40's is known in American religious circles as the "time of the Millerite excitement." William Miller, a Massachusetts farmer, a soldier in the War of 1812, a man of limited education, but of earnest spirit and conscientious principles, an honest reasoner and devoted Christian and by some regarded as of more than ordinary intellectual power, set himself to the study of the prophetic books of the Bible. By comparison and literal interpretation, he traced to a focus lines of prophecy that seemed to point to a second appearing of Jesus Christ on earth and boldly preached that the end of the world was at hand. The day and the hour were foretold when Gabriel's trumpet should sound, the dead in Christ be raised and the living, who were prepared, should be caught up to meet him in the air. The fiery eloquence of the preachers of these doctrines was well calculated to stir the imagination, quicken the conscience, enkindle the zeal and inflame the fanaticism of the simple-hearted, sincere and scientifically limited minds of the common people. Many disposed of houses and lands, prepared ascension robes and went out on hill-tops and mountains at the fated hour to await the trans-forming moment. It did not come. An error was dis-covered in the calculations, a new day was set, and thus it went on. In this remarkable movement among the plain farmer folk of the United States, scholars have seen the com-plementary uplift to a spiritual tidal movement in Persia, from the Mohammedan faith, resulting in one of the most singular religious cults of the present day.

In the early part of 1846, Enoch Jacobs, editor of a leading Millerite paper in Cincinnati, Ohio, visited the Shakers of Union Village. Here he found a belief that accorded with prophetic writings, and his literalism changed to a satisfactory spiritual interpretation of prophecy that should harmonize with hard facts of experience. He be-came a Shaker, changed the name of his paper, "The Midnight Cry" to "The Day Star," and began to teach Shakerism. In July, the Millerite society of Philadelphia sent a letter to Mount Lebanon, asking for teachers of the faith. This was answered in person by Elders Richard Bushnell and Frederick Evans. Other visits were made, meetings were held and sixteen of the Philadelphia society visited Mount Lebanon. In October, a community was organized, although a number united with the Mount Leb-anon society.

A company of colored people, led by a noted colored woman, Rebecca Jackson, gathered to the Philadelphia so-ciety. A natural leader, a woman of remarkable psychic powers and spiritual experience, Rebecca Jackson was widely known as a missionary and preacher among her people. After a short time the colored contingent, with "Mother Rebecca," went to Watervliet and the original Philadelphia society became nearly extinct. About 1860, the colored members felt a call to return and open the testimony again in Philadelphia, where the little community, mostly of colored people, continued to flourish.

The Millerite movement sent many into Shakerism, the societies of Canterbury and Enfield, New Hampshire, and Harvard, Massachusetts, receiving large additions from this source. Some of the western societies, notably Whitewater, Ohio, were also greatly increased by followers of William Miller.

From Quaker Stock.

Robert White, of New York, a wealthy Quaker of English ancestry, a man of strong convictions, benevolent, cultured and intellectual, became interested in the Shaker faith through business intercourse with representatives of the Order, and, after much opposition and persecution from friends and family, including his own children, he united with the society at Hancock in 1846, three years later removing to Mount Lebanon. He continued to support his family, dividing his time between their residence in New York and the home of his soul at Mount Lebanon. He was the friend and correspondent of Theodore Parker, and from Robert White, the famous Boston preacher received his conception of the Mother in Deity, so familiar in his public invocations. Members of the White family are names of note in American literary and scientific circles. Richard Grant White, author and critic, was a nephew of Robert White, while one brother, Chandler White, was one of the circle, connected with the N. Y. Chamber of Commerce, whose personal and financial support made possible the enterprise of the Atlantic Cable. Robert White was a great lover of the beautiful in nature and he imported into the region of the Shaker villages the locust tree, which imparts so tender a touch of beauty to the landscape. The Lebanon and Hancock homes of this brother abound in trees of his planting. He is remembered with great affection by the Shakers of Hancock as he did much to advance the interests of that society; the three noble women to-day at the head of the three families of Hancock, Eldress Caroline and Sophia Helfrich and Catherine Pepper, were brought to the society when little girls through his influence.

He had one child, Anna, who did not join in the persecution of her father. On the contrary, she early began to feel the drawings of the same faith. When an infant, her parents were on the way to Quaker Quarterly Meeting at Hudson, N. Y., and passing through Hancock, stopped at the Shakers. An aged sister, Mother Lucy Miller, entered the room and taking the baby girl in her arms, said impressively, "This child is an Israelite indeed!" The father never forgot the remark. Having received a liberal education, Anna White, at the age of eighteen, after much opposition and disinheritance by her uncle, who had promised to make her heir to his large property, united with the Shakers, entering the North Family at Mount Lebanon, in October, 1849. It was the time when the aged saints of the first generation, who had seen the wondrous days of Mother Ann, were still lingering on the shores of time, imparting spiritual gifts of love and faith, devotion and self-sacrifice. Ruth Landon, successor to Mother Lucy, was here. She met the young girl and, scanning her closely, eager to read her very soul, if it were worthy of her high calling, she said to her: "Well, Anna, if you are faithful, I can promise you all the tribulation you can endure; but you will always find strength to endure it." After more than a half century of toil in the vineyard, the cheery, vigorous Head of the North Family says, "I have proved her words true!"

Led by the Spirit.

Among many remarkable instances of individual experience, one more lends itself to this story. To Whitewater, Ohio, about the year 1848, came an English lady by the name of Betsey Gass. She had with her a little daughter, Mary, two years old. An older daughter had been left with friends in England. Like Mother Ann Lee, from early childhood she had felt intense longings for holy living. Her people were possessed of wealth and station and she had been liberally educated. She married and had two children, but her early intuitions returned as irresistible convictions, and, unhappy in her married life, her soul was continually crying out for a life of purity.

At last, when her younger child was six months old, she resolved to leave home and seek relief in travel. Without revealing her full plans, lest her departure should be forcibly prevented, she set out for America. On the way across the ocean her heart failed her. Had she made a mistake? Was she doing wrong in thus flying in the face of all precedent, taking her life and the life and future of her child into her own rash hands? Was there any possible life of purity and peace, aside from the path marked out through all time — the submissive subject of man as father, brother, husband, within the sacred precincts of the home circle? A breath from above touched her; a word of comfort, of assurance, fell upon her ear, and as if in vision was revealed to her the fact that in America was a people who lived as she longed to live, who had the light her eyes were aching to behold.

Reaching New York, she went to friends in the west, and for a number of months traveled about visiting different cities in the United States. She started one morning from

Cincinnati, accompanied by her child, now two years old, and the child's nurse, intending to visit Niagara, but missed the train. In the uncertainty that followed, the nurse proposed: "Come and visit the Shakers!" "The Shakers, who are they?" The nurse maid had known them and could tell enough of their beliefs and peculiarities to catch the heart of the woman who had not forgotten the message on shipboard in her hour of doubt and homesick foreboding, — the promise of a people and a kindred yet to be revealed. She accordingly visited the society at Whitewater, was kindly received and hospitably entertained by the motherly Eldress, who, however, thought it extremely improbable that this refined, cultured English lady would be able to accommodate herself to the homely, primitive ways and works of the Shakers. But the guest asked the privilege of opening her mind, requested, in a few days, that she might give up her child to the society and sent to England for her daughter and her property. These, however, were retained by her relatives, although the income of her property was regularly sent to her. The elder daughter was educated in England and at the age of nineteen joined her mother and sister in Whitewater.

Betsey Gass was for many years teacher of the Shaker School at Whitewater, and her sound English education fitted her for thorough work along higher lines than was accorded to the American woman teacher of the period. The Whitewater School took high rank under her direction. She was the first woman to receive a teacher's certificate at the Regents' Examination in the State of New York.

The three have been strong pillars in the society at Whitewater, and the one who, at the age of two years, was by her mother given up to the Shakers, after serving the North Family of this society as Eldress for many years, is now in the Central Ministry of the West. Eldress Mary

Gass is widely known, esteemed and beloved throughout the Communities.

Pension versus Principle.

In the year 1840, the societies of Harvard and Shirley were the apparent target of some secret persecutor, who, under cover of a Petition to the Legislature, aimed to overthrow by legal compulsion their consistent refusal to uphold war. The Petition called for legislative action requiring all citizens to pay an equal proportion of military tax, either in service or money.

Elder Grove Blanchard accompanied by a Shaker brother went to Boston to present their case. They arrived just in time; the Petition had come before the legislature and had been referred to a committee. They had an article drawn up, and Elder Blanchard, going with it before the committee, had an opportunity to see its effect. The article ran as follows:

"Agreeably to the Act of Congress of March 18th, 1818, relating to Revolutionary Pensions, the following persons who are members of the United Society (called Shakers) were entitled to Pensions of the following amount with interest inclusive, viz.: —

Amos Buttrick	$4,143 30
Jon. Kenney	669 63
David Melvin	2,219 67
John Warner	2,219 67
Levi Warner	669 63
Samuel Barrett	2,691 79
Gideon Hammond	2,691 69
Samuel Whitney	4,143 30
Abijah Worcester	4,143 30
Nath. Turner	541 16
Total	$24,131 24

"Agreeably to Act of Congress of June 7th, 1832, relating to Revolutionary Pensioners, the following persons who are members of said Society were entitled to Pensions of the following amount, interest inclusive, viz.: —

Benj. Winchester	$479 37
Sam'l Blood	940 15
Joseph Wythe	275 20
Jon. Crouch	497 37
Total	$2,191 09

"Agreeably to Act of Court, Amos Buttrick was entitled to a Pension during life of $40 per year, which would now amount, with interest inclusive, to the sum of

	$15,251 66
	2,191 09
	24,131 89
The several sums total.......	$41,574 89

"The above persons are of the societies of Harvard and Shirley. The two societies comprising about three hundred members are about three-sevenths of all belonging to the State, and in the same ratio as the amounts are for the two societies, would now be entitled to $97,005.74.

"Of the said sum nothing has been sought, in consequence of the conscientious scruples of the above-mentioned persons — being agreeable to the established principles of said United Society of which they are members."

In the words of Elder William Leonard of Harvard, who has related this episode, "It presented the conscientious faith of the Believers in a form so new; it made their detestation of the war spirit appear before them in all its bearings so clear; and their determination to maintain the principles of peace, whatever might be the sacrifice, so deeply laid, that they were not only amazed, but nearly all were completely disarmed, surprised and taken. Out of seventeen members of the committee, twelve immediately raised one voice in favor of the remonstrance, and it was all settled without further difficulty."

In a letter, written in 1846, Elder William says: "May we not justly reverence and bless those venerable saints who were willing amidst their numerous acts of self-denial to sacrifice the price of blood, and at this age enable Believers of the latter day to show to the world, to a fighting, degenerate world, that neither the honor, fame, gold nor silver that is to be gained by shedding human blood has ever stained Christ's holy banner of peace on earth, good will to men; which pure standard is waving from the walls of Zion as an ensign of righteousness to the nations!"

The Story of Amos Buttrick,

who lived in the Church Family at Shirley and passed away in 1844, is a remarkable one. A valiant and heroic soldier of the War of the Revolution, he referred the matter of accepting a pension to Mother Ann, whose answer was that it was the price of blood and would bring him into bondage if he received it.

In 1792, not fully comprehending her reply, he applied for and received the pension to which wounds and service entitled him. As the Church was being gathered and true foundation principles were being established, Father Joseph took up this matter for serious consideration. "He was directed," says the account, "by the unerring spirit of truth to shut out all such pension money, together with pension lands and all kinds of remuneration for war services." Amos, therefore, in obedience to his faith, "although Believers were then poor, suffering from the iron hand of persecution on the one side and poverty and great privation on the other, took the silver and gold which had been pronounced the price of blood and returned it to the Government."

When the pension agents received the petition of Amos to take back the pension, it was so unheard of a proceeding that they did not know what to do. A special resolve had to be passed by the Legislature to provide for the reception of the rejected grant, and perhaps the following is the only receipt of the kind recorded in Bay State annals:

"COMMONWEALTH OF MASSACHUSETTS.

(No. 10496)

Mar. 12, 1792.

TREASURY OFFICE.

Received of Amos Buttrick, a State Pensioner, by the hand of Joseph Hosmer, Esq., Eighty-two pound, seven shillings and eight pence, as a deposit in the Treasury, agreeably to Resolve of Court of the 8th inst., having signed duplicate receipt.

ALEXANDER HODGDON,
Treasurer."

"Before the War."

In 1818, Eldress Molly Goodrich wrote thus from South Union, Ky., to Elder Calvin Green, of the difference between a slave and a free country: "It seems sometimes as though the very air is impregnated with that idle, careless, indifferent spirit imbibed by creatures through that sense of slavery. It feels a heap harder for the people to be really industrious, neat and clean, to be really subject and obedient to what they are taught."

In the years that immediately preceded the Civil War, the pro and anti-slavery excitement made it extremely dangerous for non-slaveholding residents of the Southern States to express their sentiments. Shakers, who were opposed to chattel as to all kinds of slavery, loving the souls of both the slave and his master, but detesting slavery, were obliged to exercise great care and circumspection in all they said and did. It speaks well for their discretion and brotherly kindness that so little friction occurred between the Shaker Communities in the border states and the sensitive slave owners who were their nearest neighbors.

"The Lord's Side."

A laughable story is told of the days when it was unsafe for anti-slavery principles to be fully expressed. In one of the Kentucky societies lived a good deacon and trustee, who had said what he thought a little too freely, and one of the slave-holders very decidedly said to him, "Mr. Shaker, I am your enemy, and if I should meet you away from your home and alone, I would kill you!"

Nearly two years had passed before the anticipated time came. The deacon had been away from home on business. Entering a piece of woods on his return home, he saw his avowed enemy coming toward him. When within a short distance of each other, the deacon sprang from his horse and threw the lines over a small tree. Off went his coat, and rolling up his shirt sleeves, this non-resistant hailed his enemy: "My friend, this is the place the Lord has appointed for you and me to meet. Now we will see who is on the Lord's side!" Not a word was spoken by the other, but by the use of the spurs the horse and rider were suddenly out of sight, and the good deacon, remounting his horse, rode pleasantly to his home and never again was troubled by his enemy.

X

IN WAR TIME

PUT up thy sword,— thinkest thou not that I cannot
now pray to my Father and He shall presently give
me more than twelve legions of angels?" "They
that take the sword shall perish by the sword."
"The servant of the Lord must not strive, but be gentle,
peaceable, easy to be entreated." "The fruits of the Spirit
are love, joy, peace, longsuffering, gentleness." While
thinkers in the outer world are slowly coming to insist
that all war is criminal, that never was there a justifiable
war; while Peace, Arbitration, Disarmament, are becoming
the watch cries of an increasingly great array of men and
women in all countries of the earth; — the Shaker Communities, small, unnoticed and unknown among the nations,
have steadily and consistently kept their stand on the peace
platform of Jesus and Ann; have refused to fight, have
persisted, through wars and rumors of wars, in treating as
brothers all classes and conditions of men. White haired
veterans of the wars of the Revolution and 1812, who
afterward became good Shakers, abhorred as the "price of
blood" the bounties and pensions legally their due; the
dark days of the 50's passed in political strife and contest, the black rising tide of slavery engulfing, one after
another, the land-marks of freedom and human rights; the
quiet Shakers pursued their way, showing justice and
mercy alike to slave and slave-holder.

NO. 14. SHIRLEY VILLAGE, MASS.

The Civil War broke out. Defeat and disaster humbled and sobered the too exultant North. Drafts were ordered. Shakers were enrolled and some were drafted.

This tale is told of one young man, summoned from the society at Shirley, who was examined and accepted.

"He returned home, determined to remain there and to place his whole trust in God. He prayed fervently, was sorrowful at his prospect, and continued thus till an officer took him from the village. When forced away, almost heart-broken, he more than ever determined to stand on the power of non-resistance.

"The first night he was placed in prison with deserters and in irons. Their curses on the Government, their ruffianlike conduct and their horrid oaths so shocked him, and contrasted so fearfully with his own God-fearing people at his quiet home, that it seemed to him like dropping from heaven into the very hells of perdition.

"On the Island, he could not be persuaded nor threatened into a course to make him take his first degrees in the drill of a soldier, and was of course kept in confinement. Finally, one of the officers, designing to arouse his fears, threatened to have him shot, if he did not comply. He entirely mistook his man. He had lived a life which had wholly disarmed death of its terrors; he meekly replied, 'I would consider it a great favor if you would shoot me, for I would far rather be shot than to be kept in my present condition.'

"In all this, they could feel no wilfulness nor rebellion. They saw so clearly that it was the effect of acting from principle, that they liberated him and assigned him the duty of waiter. He enlisted the sympathies of every one who knew his case. They admitted his friends to see him, and although he had passed one surgical examination, they favored him with another. Last of all, they released him on furlough, sent him home and never recalled him."

An appeal was made to President Lincoln and Secretary Stanton, expressed in the following Memorial, which was presented in person by the signers. A pleasant interview was had with the President and the Secretary of War. Elder Evans used often to relate that after listening to all the representatives of the Shaker Societies had to say, President Lincoln leaned back in his chair and asked, "Well what am I to do?" The Shaker Elder answered, "It is not for me to advise the President of the United States."

Looking at him appreciatively, President Lincoln exclaimed: "You ought to be *made* to fight! We need regiments of just such men as you."

Memorial.

To His Excellency the President of the United States:

The undersigned, in behalf of the United Society of Shakers, composed of eighteen distinct communities and located in seven of the states of the Union, respectfully ask for exemption from service of such of the members of their society as may be drafted under the Act entitled, "An Act for enrolling and calling out the National Forces and for other purposes." This application involves a matter of very small practical importance to the Government, inasmuch as the whole number of members of the Society subject to the conscription does not exceed one hundred and ninety, from which number, after deducting those of foreign birth and physical disability, not more than seventy would remain among whom the draft would take effect. This favor is asked of the Government for the following considerations: — That non-resistance and non-participation in the affairs of earthly governments are primary and fundamental articles of the religious faith of the Shaker Societies, and that by these principles, which for near a century have been by them conscientiously carried out in practise, they are equally debarred from furnishing substitutes (directly or indirectly) as from rendering personal service.

No Shaker has ever trained, voted or been voted for, or held any office of honor, trust or emolument (except Postmaster) under the Civil Government or participated in politics. But they have suffered in person and property and even been imprisoned for their non-military testimony; but were finally in most of the states exempted from military duties and equivalents. As the Shakers hold all their property in common the Societies have large amounts of money now in the National Treasury, which legally belongs to them through parties who served in the wars of the Revolution and of 1812, subsequently uniting with the Shaker Order; but who, by the Society, were not permitted to draw either their Pensions or Bounty Lands.

These sums, principal and interest, amount in the aggregate to $600,000. (See Schedule A.· for facts). The societies in Kentucky, not yet heard from, would materially augment this amount; while the sum the Government would receive for exemption of one-third of all the members of the Shaker Societies liable to the Draft, under the Net (their number being not over seventy) would amount to not over $7,200, and should the whole number liable be drafted, the amount of compensation would not exceed $21,000, only about four per cent of the aggregate of the moneys referred to as being now in the National Treasury.

Your Petitioners, in behalf of the Society, respectfully urge the equity of considering the sum just left in the Public Treasury as at least an equivalent for any money that might be claimed as due from any of the members of the Society under the Act referred to. The property of the Society is devoted to religious and charitable purposes. Shakers support their own poor, aged and infirm; and bear their full proportion of every form of taxation for the support of the poor outside, as well as for all Governmental organizations — National, State and Municipal. And, while we present these facts as an earnest of our conscientious faith and religious principles which render us it imperative upon us to suffer in property or person, rather than violate those principles, either by ourselves or others, we humbly and respectfully solicit the Discharge of such individuals of our Communion, as are or shall be, under the Conscript Act, drafted for Military Service. And your Petitioners will ever pray both for yourself and for the continuance of this free Government, towards which the Shaker Societies ever have been, are, and will continue to be, truly loyal.

F. W. Evans,
Benjamin Gates.

As a result of the petition, the drafted men were given an indefinite furlough, which had not expired when the troops were mustered out at the end of the war. The State of New York alone, in 1863, owed to the Shaker Societies, on the score of unclaimed pensions and bounty lands, the sum of $150,000.

In the Border States

the Shaker Societies suffered much during the Civil War. A story is told of an old Quaker in the days of the Revolution, who, living near Valley Forge, met General Washington and said to him: "Friend George, my religion utterly forbids *me* to use carnal weapons; but it requires me to feed the hungry and clothe the naked as far as I am able. Thee and thy officers, to the extent of my means, may dine at my table; and I will do what I can for thy soldiers."

This was the attitude of the Shakers in war time who lived in the region over-run by the hostile armies. But they went further and impartially fed and cared for the soldiers of both sides and for the swarms of unhappy refugees, both white and colored.

Eldress Nancy Moore, of the South Union Ministry, kept a Diary, from the opening of the conflict in 1861, until the autumn of 1864, and to her vivid pen we are indebted for lifelike pictures of incidents through that long siege of toil, watching and anxiety, dread, danger and loneliness. Situated on the direct road between Bowling Green and Russelville, two important centres, they were in a convenient halting place for troops.

In October, 1861, Generals Johnson and Buckner took wagons and horses to the value of $1250, for which the Shakers received $680 in confederate scrip. Some of their neighbors accompanied the press-gang and kindly pointed out where their property might be found. One of the most forward in this was, in the years that followed, often glad to secure the good offices of the Shakers to protect himself and his property. Robbers, in guise of soldiers, came one day to the Office, seeking cloth, and when it was shown, they seized and made off with it. This taught the sisters a lesson and they at once hid away the best of their goods. Talk of drafts made the younger brethren nervous and some of them decamped, escaping to the northern states and to other societies.

A company of Texas Rangers were one day on the premises. The principles and mode of life seemed beyond their powers of comprehension. One asked, "How many live in the brick house?" "About ninety," was the reply. Astonished, he said, "If so many of us lived in one house, we should fight and kill each other." At last, in despair of comprehending this strange mode of existence, he wanted to know, if they did not swear, nor fight, nor kill, nor drink whiskey, what they *did* do. "This must be a Heaven upon earth, and you are certainly a very good people," was his conclusion.

Events of 1862.

In January, they were called up at midnight to provide food for 1,200 soldiers who had encamped on their premises, and that night they made 600 pounds of bread for them. The force spent two or three days here and the Shakers provided them with food. At first, the officers were stern and aggressive, but finding only gentleness and kindly treatment, they became warm and friendly and were a protection against worse marauders. Upon leaving, one of the officers said to the sister who waited on them, "Madame, I fear you will kill us with good food." "Better that than with a bullet," was the reply. Measles were brought by the soldiers, and for a time they had sickness to add to their burdens. All their hay and provender were taken by the soldiers. Brother Urban Johns then secured from Gen. Hardee an order forbidding the soldiers to take anything more from the Shakers.

One day, as a company of cavalry was passing through the village, during a brief halt one was heard to say, "These

fine buildings belong to all of them. Everything is held in
common, as it was in the church of the old Apostles. Here
everyone works, from the least to the greatest. Do you not
wish everybody was like them?" "Yes!" was the unani-
mous response, and a voice said, "If they were, we would
not be fighting the Yankees!" Another company was given
a dinner, and before the soldiers entered, the Captain spoke
to them in a low voice, "These are religious, orderly people, and you must be very quiet and orderly while here."
They obeyed, and seemed very grateful and appreciative.
Such conduct was the exception rather than the rule, yet
the treatment they received from the regular troops on the
Confederate side seems to have been more courteous than
from the Unionists.

At the storming of Fort Henry, the cannonading was distinctly heard at South Union. After Fort Henry was taken,
Bowling Green was fired by the Confederates. The country
between there and Nashville was full of marauders, stealing,
burning, or threatening to burn every bridge, mill, depot
and storehouse, to prevent them from falling into the hands
of the Federals. One day, a large gang of men swarmed
about their houses, demanding cloth and other supplies,
raging like madmen. The plucky little company of sisters
gathered on the doorsteps of the Office and held the fort,
while with pleasant words they strove to soften the hearts
of the rough soldiery. Bringing out pies, milk and other
dainties, they managed at last to get rid of their rude, suspicious and troublesome guests; but the whole family
watched all that night, lest they return and rob them.

Days grew to months and months to years, in the steady
round of accustomed and unaccustomed toil, — striving to
keep the house decent and in order, caring for the large
family of boys and girls, increased by many war-made orphans, and all the time, cooking, by day and by night, feed-

ing squads of soldiery, who, by twos and tens and twenties, by fifties and by hundreds, called for meals, for lodging, for provender, — and departing, carried with them corn, vegetables, fruit, chickens, horses, everything they could lay their hands on. Brethren, who to save their lives would not use pistol or shot-gun (every gun save one poor one had been seized by army officers), were forced to guard their premises by day and by night, and, while toiling to raise their crops, had them continually carried off by soldiery or thieves. While the Confederate army lay at Bowling Green, constant demand was made for supplies of every kind. Their horses had to be kept tied out in the woods for safety, often through sleet and storm.

On February 14th, 1862, they heard that Bowling Green was in the hands of the Federals and threats were made of burning Shaker Village. For several weeks they had been looking for thirteen hogsheads of sugar, that had been purchased when the blockade was first begun. On that day, it arrived at Russelville, and eight brethren, with two four-horse, and two ox-teams, started to get it. "On the night of the fifteenth all watch through the night, watch and pray!" The morning finds them thankful for safety. The town of Russelville was full of soldiers, horses were being pressed and everything of value being taken. It was only by hiding their horses and exercising the greatest courage, perseverance and despatch, that the brethren, after two days, succeeded in getting out with the sugar.

On the 16th, Union soldiers appeared for the first time at South Union and were met with joy, gratitude and expressions of loyalty. But soon their supposed friends seemed turned to foes, for they were seen setting fire to bridges and culverts. Great consternation prevailed! Their joy was turned to fear and horror, lest they had betrayed themselves to their enemies, and the supposed

Federal uniform was but a cover for rebel soldiery. Strong men trembled, women sank down, prostrated with terror. The thought, that, by their credulity and thoughtless confidence, they had betrayed their lives and the inheritance committed to their charge, was overwhelming.

At this juncture, the eight brethren arrived from Russelville and investigated the matter. The regiment proved to be Ohio Volunteers, acting under orders for the protection of the people. As the campaign in Tennessee was not yet decided, it was thought best to destroy all connections, but at the protests of the brethren, they stayed their hands, and were afterwards glad of having done so. The panic over, the Shakers could rejoice with three-fold joy, but it was several days before the shock ceased to be felt. It taught a salutary lesson, however, and they often had occasion to remember that the "army blue" did not always cover loyal hearts.

From September, 1861, until March, 1862, no United States Mail arrived. They were shut away from their friends in other states, and no small part of their suffering was their utter loneliness. Even from their companions in distress, the society at Pleasant Hill, they did not hear for months at a time.

On March 24th, letters were brought for the first time, from the Ministry at Mount Lebanon, from Canterbury and Enfield and from Ohio. It was a time of great rejoicing. On April 10th, the first U. S. mail reached South Union. Their horses having been stolen, Brother Urban Johns made a trip to Pleasant Hill and secured some more. The sick and wounded soldiers at Bowling Green now absorbed their energies, — sisters cooking and brethren carrying supplies. Strawberries, three and four bushels daily, were picked by the sisters and sold in Bowling Green by the brethren.

May found John Morgan and his band of guerillas in Kentucky. On the twenty-second, four hundred Union cavalry encamped on their premises. They were quiet and orderly and gave the Shakers in each family a serenade from their brass bands. They were treated to a supper for which they returned thanks in music. A free breakfast was served them, "spread under the sugar trees in the door-yard." Most of the family had been up all night cooking. As the band filed past, they played a farewell, then waving their hats and cheering, they passed on their line of march, each company as they passed repeating the salute.

On the first of June, their two new black horses were stolen, but were afterwards recovered. This month they were gladdened by a visit from the Mount Lebanon Ministry — Elders Daniel Boler and Giles B. Avery, Eldresses Betsey Bates and Eliza Ann Taylor. They stayed for two weeks, imparting strength and encouragement, then departing by way of Louisville, they were met and escorted to Pleasant Hill. The Elders and Elder Sisters from South Union accompanied their guests to Louisville, where they had a day's shopping. Starting to return, when twenty miles out, the train was overtaken by a telegraph despatch, a military order to return. Back they went, they knew not why. Two days later, another start was made and this time they reached home in safety.

Throughout the summer of 1862, the country was overrun by small bodies of Union troops hunting down bands of guerillas, among whom were neighbors who knew well the Shaker premises. In August, Bowling Green was in a panic from guerillas, people fleeing for their lives; and a report was brought to them of a plot to drive the Shakers from the country and burn their village. Elder Hervey Eads was transferred, after eighteen years absence, from

Union Village to his old home at South Union and placed at the head of the Ministry. Brother Urban Johns was made trustee and sent to the Office. Now that the railroad was in constant danger, the U. S. mail came only as far as Bowling Green, fourteen and one-half miles distant. The hospital service at Bowling Green demanded all their stores of preserves and canned fruits and had taken their sugar, $1,000 worth, with promises to pay, promises long delayed in the fiulfilment. Alarming rumors were constantly afloat; now it was Morgan, with 12,000 guerillas at Franklin, twelve miles away — next day's report reduced the number to thirty men; now it was Bragg with 30,000, then Buell with 45,000 troops, covering the road for sixteen miles at a stretch, centering at Louisville. Amid these alarms, a sister had a comforting vision of a host of angels encamped over and about them, protecting them. While Buell's army was at Louisville, Confederate soldiers on parole were constantly passing, many of them in sad condition, and these were fed and kindly treated.

Pleasant Hill was in the centre of the rebel forces who were devastating, robbing everyone, high and low. The Shakers witnessed the fighting of battles and cared for the wounded of both sides.

Early in November, five Union regiments — 6,000 men and 7,000 horses — encamped on the grounds of the South Union Shakers. The object of the force was to clear Kentucky of Morgan's guerillas. The soldiers began to arrive about six P. M., and by seven the roads were full. There had been no rain to speak of for three months and the dust hung over like a thick cloud. Through the evening the sisters were alone, the brethren being away attending to the soldiers. The sisters were all night busy baking bread, with cavalry riding back and forth through the streets and soldiers prowling about the premises. Bee hives were robbed, potatoes, fowls, everything they could find was taken. Four thousand camp fires were lighted, — a magnificent sight, whose glory was somewhat dimmed by the knowledge that two thousand five hundred valuable white oak fence rails were going up in smoke and flame. Their barns and storehouses were cleaned out, and the account against the U. S. Government for that night's work was 12 tons of hay, 215 bushels of corn, 4,800 bundles of fodder, 5,000 bundles of oats and 2,500 fence rails. Vouchers were given for $378. A subsequent estimate of fence rails destroyed during the war amounted to 20,000. At this time the sisters sold fourteen dollars worth of gray cloth and $75 were given for damages. The next day, after the soldiers had gone, the brethren had a busy time drawing water to quench the smoldering camp fires and the sisters had a sorry time viewing the waste of corn and good food, with which the grounds were strewn. With true Shaker thrift, they saved a large amount to be used in soap making. Eldress Jency had dreamed about a week before of seeing this very army and of her own grief at the waste of food and provender.

Letters were now received for the first time for months. Those from Pleasant Hill were especially welcome and told that the sister society had come off much better than they could have expected. When the Confederate army invaded the Blue Grass country, 20,000 troops marched through their village and they were obliged to cook, day and night, for nearly a week. A few horses and wagons were taken, but otherwise they were uninjured.

November 10th brought to South Union a force of two thousand cavalry marching to Russelville. As soon as they were gone, two hundred and fifty more came from the west, encamped on the grounds and demanded one hundred pounds of bread and one hundred pounds of meat. In the night, another band came and demanded supper and

forage for the horses. The men were intrusive and unrea-
sonable. During this month of November, 1862, the people at the Office gave two hundred and ten meals to stragglers, while a sick soldier was cared for and his life saved
by careful nursing. In December, Morgan again raided
Kentucky, and Brother Urban Johns, who had been obliged
by business matters to leave home while still suffering from
an attack of fever, was shut up in Louisville and could not
get home, causing great anxiety to the burdened and
harassed family.

During the period since the Union armies had held par-
tial control of Kentucky, aside from stragglers fed at the
Office and the six thousand troops who had devoured their
substance like locusts, there are recorded nearly three thousand meals provided for soldiers, while many companies are
mentioned as fed, with no estimate of numbers. They were
so imposed upon by irresponsible and non-paying parties,
that Gen. Munson provided them with a safeguard which
put a stop to such demands.

In these times of trial their spirit friends did not withdraw their comfort and assistance. Several remarkable instances are on record of communications of importance
from the spirit world. One night, Brother Urban Johns
was aroused from slumber by a voice calling to him that
there were robbers about. Heeding the warning, he went
out and looked about; but though he could find nothing, in
the morning it was discovered that attempts had been made
on the horse barn, without success, but that enough forage
had been taken for several horses. It was afterwards
learned that a plan had been laid to take every horse in
Shakertown that night.

A spirit voice was heard by a mediumistic sister, Maria
Price, to say that Gen. Rosecrans' battle at Murfreesboro
was a decisive one. She asked if this would end the war.

NO. 15. CHURCH FAMILY, SOUTH UNION, KY.

The answer was, — "Not so! They will go on and on, until slavery is wiped out." On July 10th, 1863, Maria Price had her arm suddenly stretched out and raised up. She inquired, "What is it?" The answer came, "Vicksburg is taken!" "How was it taken?" she inquired, and was answered, "By unconditional surrender!" Then the spirit sang a song of victory, which she learned. Again she was informed by the same agency that Port Hudson was taken, and when she asked if it was port or fort, the answer was spelled, "P-o-r-t," and another song was given her.

Events of 1863.

On the night of January twenty-first, horses were heard dashing about through the village. A fire was seen, and the brethren turned out to find the depot in flames and some cars on the track, filled with corn, wheat and other merchandise, also burning. The owners of the goods were at hand, but had been, under peril of their lives, sworn not to touch it and they stood by, not able to raise a finger to save their own property. The Shakers turned in and saved what they could. About $6500 worth of corn, wheat and dry goods were destroyed to keep them from the U. S. Government. The marauders had broken into the Shakers' storehouse, but on being told to whom it belonged, they had said, "We will not trouble them, we do not wish to destroy private property." Elder Hervey and a brother jumped on a hand-car and went up to Bowling Green to inform Gen. Munson, returning the next evening with a guard of thirty soldiers, to protect the Government stores there and at Auburn.

During this winter, the Shakers had many hours of enforced rest, for lack of light. Oil, lamps and fixtures, or-

13

dered in the fall, were delayed and did not reach them until
February, and the early rising Shakers had thereby many
extra hours of sleep, which were doubtless good for their
overwrought nerves. Robbers, guerillas and Union protectors successively swarmed over them, all alike acting the
part of the grasshopper plague.

On a rainy March night, six teamsters were forced upon
them by a rude and brutal officer. They were fed and allowed to sleep by the fire. One of them had chills and fever.
Eldress Nancy, conscience smitten by the poorness of the
accommodations, so much better than they usually found,
moralizes thus: — "I fear we are coming too much under
the influence of the spirits which accompany the armies,
which causes so much hardness of heart toward our fellow-
mortals. For surely the time has been in this society, when
we could not have suffered a well man to lie down on the
bare floor, without bed or covering, much more one who is
sick with ague chills and fever, to come dripping wet and
then have to dry his own clothes and rest the best he could
by the fire."

During the last two summers, they were annoyed by
bands of people from all parts, who came on the trains and
promenaded their grounds, sight-seeing, even invading their
dwellings and shops, expecting to be fed, sometimes paying
and sometimes not, but very much in the way at all times.
In June of 1863, the brethren laid down a stone walk from
the Office to the dwelling-house. A Union captain, who,
with some Confederate women friends, was visiting the
place, told the ladies that the improvements in the village
were a strong argument against slavery. They ought, he
said, to engrave deeply on the stone: "Laid down in the
year of the Rebellion, 1863. While the people of the United
States were fighting and killing each other, the Shakers
remained quietly at home improving their village."

On July 28th, came a report that John Morgan was captured. Brother Urban Johns went to New York in September to make purchases for the family, and before he returned he visited the Mother Church at Mount Lebanon, where he was warmly welcomed and his visit long remembered. Eldress Antoinette Doolittle went with him to the great metropolis and assisted him in his purchases for the lonely society in the war-swept South. Seven members died during this year.

This year also the societies in Ohio had a little taste of what their sister societies of Kentucky experienced almost daily. Morgan's bands made a raid into Ohio and the society of Whitewater was visited. The band was seen by a boy in time to give the alarm. The record reads: —

"The raiders, 6000 to 11,000 in number, injured the Shakers very little, aside from hindering the harvest. They took but two horses from the South Family. They treated our folks very respectfully and did not enter the buildings, only getting something to eat. After the raiders had departed, we supposed our trouble had come to an end. But not so. The next day comes the Union army some five or six hundred strong on horses, — Home guards of Indianapolis, headed by John S. Hobart, claiming to be authorized by the Government to take all the horses he could find; with threats to burn and kill if the horses were not produced. Elder George Rubush was compelled to bring up the drove of horses. Two of the finest were selected."

The supremacy of the Union army in Kentucky opened the vexed

Question of Draft.

In May, 1863, all male citizens who had not taken the oath of allegiance to the United States were required, under penalty of banishment south of the federal lines, or death, to do so before the first of June. Two brethren, represen-

tatives of the society, went to remonstrate against taking the
oath, as rendering them liable to be drafted. Gen. Shackle-
ford, at the headquarters, wrote, "You will not be requested to take the oath." In August, 1863, Elder Eads
drew up a petition to President Lincoln, which is a good
summary of their relations to the Government up to that
time.

PETITION.

*"To the Honorable Abraham Lincoln, President of the United
States:*

KIND FRIEND, Strike, but hear! The armies of the south, like
a great prairie fire, swept over this part of Kentucky in the fall
and winter of 1861, licking up the substance of the land. We were
humbled before its power and for many months remained the quiet
subjects of the Confederate Government, obeying all its behests
save *one which,* nobly and generously, they permitted us to disre-
gard, and that was to take up arms in their behalf. They encamped
for days, as many as a thousand at a time, in our lots and occupied
our buildings. We chopped and hauled wood for their camp fires
and slaughtered our animals for their commissariat, and at all
hours of the night we were compelled to furnish food for thousands
at a time.

They pressed all our wagons and horses of value for army
purposes; but for these they paid a moderate price in confederate
scrip. It was then we prayed earnestly, — O Lord Almighty, if it
be Thy will, deliver us from our enemies! the worst of whom were
our elated and high headed neighbors. This our prayer was partially answered, when your loud ordnance was heard to open on
Bowling Green, fourteen miles northeast of this place. Since that
time we have suffered much from the ebb and flow of the tide of
war, until a good part of what the fire left, the merciless and surging billows have in their turn swept away, so that we have been
left, as it were, writhing sometimes under the heel of one power
and sometimes another.

Your armies have visited us, from a small squad to five or
six thousand at a time. Our barns were cheerfully relieved of their
contents, our fences turned into camp fires, (for these we have
been paid by you) but gratuitously have we furnished food for

thousands of your men. Of this we complain not. To our uniform kindness (if we must say it) all your armies that have passed us, all your hospitals within our reach, all your post surgeons and commanders can bear witness. When your supplies were cut off at Green River, your officers pressed our sugar for hospital purposes, our cellars disgorged themselves of nearly a thousand dollars worth, for which so far, on account of some informality, we have striven in vain to obtain one cent of remuneration.

We state these things now, not by way of complaint, but merely as grounds (coming to your knowledge) on which we may rest a hope that we may be treated on the sensitive point, with as much lenity and as much justice, as we were by the Confederates while we were subjects of their government.

It is impossible that one's friends can be as tolerant, as just and generous as their enemies? Must our prayers be reversed, and we cry to the Lord to be delivered from our friends? After we have uncomplainingly borne until we can scarcely bear any longer, must we receive from our friends the most unkindest cut of all, besides the derision, jeers and mocks of our enemies? Shall the main support of one hundred and fifty women, children and invalids be taken from them? Must this indeed be added to our yet untold sufferings? Heaven grant it may not be! We have yet in our society about twenty-four young men between the ages of eighteen and forty-five years, a majority of whom would be capable of doing some kind of service in the Federal army, but who are the main support of the women, children and invalids above mentioned, a number of whom will not shoulder a musket, nor bear about their persons the weapons of war; who, having been taught from infancy to love, and not to fight, their enemies, would sooner lay down their own lives, than to aid, even remotely, in taking that of another. If this was respected by the Confederate government can it be ignored by the Federal? It is to be hoped not. Were it possible to convince us that we could love a man and shoot him at the same time (!) we could hardly spare either the numbers or the few thousands of dollars demanded in lieu of them. Add to this the serious fact that these young men, through us their leaders, have pledged themselves (we do not swear) not to fight against the Confederate government. Must we be compelled to violate this pledge? Certainly not; still, as long as we are able, we will feed the hungry and clothe the naked, as an act of humanity and Christian duty, but not for the purpose of supporting war, but will cheerfully render unto Cæsar the things that are Cæsar's and unto God the things that are God's.

We are aware that you are oppressed and harassed on all sides, and deeply do we sympathize with you and therefore make our words few. If you cannot exempt all the Shakers in the north, who have scarcely felt the war, never having witnessed your marshaled hosts nor the desolating and deathly tread of an army, — is it selfish in us to claim that our pledges, our losses and our sufferings, and that in the midst of our enemies, demands that our Society in Kentucky should be the object of your commiseration and fostering care? Or can it be God's will, that after having been spared by our enemies, we should be blotted from the earth by our friends? Surely not.

To take the young men of our home to sure demoralization and slaughter, or further wrest from us our means of support, with all that has been done, would seem cruel.

Our principles are above conditions. There is not money enough in the vaults of the nation to buy them nor to induce one truly honest Shaker to engage in any war against his fellowman. We do not expect that absolute equality of burden is attainable in the present condition of things, only an approximation toward it: but where it can be, it should be. We ask for simple justice, nothing more, — hardly that. We look upon you, not only as the friend of humanity and the rights of man, but as the chosen instrument of God, in this time of the nation's peril. But the instrument of God dares to do right. Now that our young men are threatened with enrollment and draft, and are only held (some of them) by their friends, from crossing the Tennessee line, — we ask and feel almost certain you will, from the foregoing consideration, grant exemption from draft to the few young persons of our community, on whom so much depends, seeing especially each one has more to do for the support of others, than the only son of a widow, now by law exempt.

With what ease you can render us the simple justice for which we pray, and enable us to hold within our sacred precincts these of whom we shall shortly be bereft if we "find not favor in thy sight."

Only tell us, at the earliest possible moment, consistent with your other duties, that you will release them. You will then have done for us a favor equal to all the losses we have sustained and will receive the cordial and heartfelt thanks of a grateful. Community. We will not weary you more, but humbly wait and hope and pray.

We are sincerely,
Your friends,
JOHN N. RANKIN,
H. L. EADS,
Leaders of the Society of Shakers at So. Union, Ky.

To the Honorable Abraham Lincoln, President of the United States, Washington, D. C.

In December, several brethren were drafted, but the provost Marshal at Bowling Green informed them that he had received the following despatch from Washington:

"To the Provost Marshal, Bowling Green.

SIR: — If there is any religious Community within your district, whose conscientious scruples abjure war, or the payment of commutation fee, you will parole them indefinitely, still holding them subject to any demand from the authority here.

(Signed)   E. M. STANTON,
Secretary of War.

Washington. D. C., Dec. 30, 1863.

This was "good and glad news indeed" to the Shaker Community.

In 1864.

During this year were two months of severe sickness, something of the nature of cholera, eighteen or twenty being taken down the first week of July. On New Year's Day, the sisters sent to the sick soldiers at Bowling Green roasted turkeys, baked chickens and other good things.

In March, Brother William Ware returned from a four weeks' trip selling garden seeds through Tennessee, in a country where guerillas were robbing and plundering every-

one. Although he had some lively adventures, he came
back unharmed. A few days later, the *Louisville Courier
Journal* reported all the places he had visited as destroyed
by fire. On April 14th, four suspicious looking characters
came prowling about the buildings, demanding to see cloth
of all kinds, evidently scouting for chances to rob. The next
night houses in Auburn were robbed and nearly $2900 taken
in money. "Perhaps the Lord was helping us with outstretched arm for the sake of the righteous of His own
peculiar care," writes Eldress Nancy. A man hired to spin
their wool remarked, — "I know that the hand of Provi-
dence is stretched out over this town to guard and protect
it from harm. Every time there is an intended raid on
this place, something turns up to thwart their intentions."
Even good old "Aunt Jenny," the colored woman who
worked for the sisters, and who had often informed them
of impending danger from their enemies, made use of similar expressions, that God had His arm stretched out to
protect the place. If the cup of cold water given in the
name of a disciple shall not lose its reward, then surely, the
nearly six thousand meals provided for soldiers and stragglers, aside from whole regiments and companies of whom
no account was taken, received a like remembrance.

One Sabbath in July, a company of troops, wearing the
Federal uniform and carrying the Stars and Stripes, rode
through the village. Two of the number dashed down a
lane and turning in where some horses were feeding, one
began to exchange his lame horse for two good ones belonging to the Shakers. Two brethren interfered and ordered them to stop, and one, saying "You are my prisoner!"
took into custody the young man who was helping himself
to a horse. At the same time the sisters began to ring
the big bell.

"What's that bell ringing for?" they asked.

"To call the soldiers from the depot," was the reply.

"What soldiers?" "Federal soldiers!" The mounted one now made off at his best pace, leaving his comrade in the hands of his captors, who were in doubt whether they were dealing with Federals or Confederates. Soon the whole troop came dashing back, swearing and excessively angry. The captured youth was restored. He had asked, a few moments before, if he was to be killed, and the brother had said he believed it was the order to kill robbers at sight. The youth evidently expected to be slain at once.

When the lieutenant in command found his armed soldier a prisoner in the hands of unarmed Shakers and no horses in sight, the little boys having spirited them away, he raved like a madman. Bullets were fired at two of the brethren, who jumped behind trees and were not hit. The two concerned in the affair having made good their escape, the lieutenant fiercely ordered that the men who had arrested his soldier should be produced, but no one seemed to have seen them. Swearing and raging, he accused the Shakers of being traitors, of harboring guerillas, and declared he would hang or shoot some one, or have a horse, before he would leave the place, and threatened to burn the whole village. Explanations failed to calm him, until even his own soldiers seemed ashamed of the raid and told him it would not do to shoot unarmed men. The sisters brought out their usual panacea of pies, milk and fruit, which the men ate and grew good-natured, but the lieutenant was "too mad to eat," and went into the Office, where good Eldress Jency patted him on the shoulder, saying she hoped to see him in a better humor before he left.

The neighbors, who had come to attend meeting, were grinning and tittering about to see the Union soldiers so vindictive and the Shakers mistaking them for "rebels." One of the troop was heard to say that he "wished the

women would go into the house and they would make the
bullets fly like hail." After an hour or so, they started off,
and Eldress Nancy writes: — "My prayer is that we as a
people may learn wisdom and exercise more of it in future,
live more strictly to what we profess, which is to take no
part in the conflict and live in peace with all men; at least,
that we do nothing to stir up the lion in either party."

When the army of Gen. Bragg lay in the neighborhood
of Pleasant Hill, the Union army under Gen. Buell approached and a battle was expected. The Shakers were
removed from their large dwelling, which was made ready
for the reception of those who should be wounded. Buell's
force, however, passed on their way, and although only one
field separated the hostile armies, the peace was not broken.
Amid all the plundering and raiding, in the Border States,
the Shakers of Pleasant Hill found an unlooked for protector, no less a personage than the notorious guerilla leader,
John Morgan. Brought up in the vicinity of the Shaker
Village, he had great respect and affection for the quiet
people, and, hearing of a plot to loot their village, he
promptly came to the rescue and issued immediate orders
forbidding any such proceeding. He informed his troops
that he had long known the Shakers, that they were a harm-
less, inoffensive people, that they took no part with either
side, injured no man and had no desire so to do, and none
under his command should injure them in any way. The
Shakers viewed him as one raised up to help them in the
day of trouble and he has ever been held, by all Shakers,
in grateful remembrance.

As the war drew to an end, the communities were still
under great trials. There was, if possible, less order and
control of lawless spirits than during martial rule. The
country was over-run by reckless bands of ruffians, and to
break open houses at midnight and demand money, goods,

NO. 16. CENTER FAMILY DWELLING, PLEASANT HILL, KY., ERECTED 1824.

food and drink, was a common thing. Yet these people were mercifully watched over and protected by higher powers. The Government, as its hand began to be felt, gave them protection and the societies came out of the terrible conflict, where they had seemed at the mercy of every fierce and cruel element, and are still in existence.

Elder Evans, a pronounced land-reformer, in a terse

Summing Up

of principles, says: "There would have been no Civil War if no chattel slavery. And no chattel slavery if no wage slavery. No wage slavery if no land monopoly. If no land monopoly, no poor landless people. If no poor landless people, no soldiers and nothing to fight about. With an inalienable homestead, men can feed and shelter their families, if they will cease to kill. And if they cease to kill there will be no war. 'Thou shalt not kill.' "

Visit of Secretary Stanton.

In October, 1867, Secretary Stanton visited the Mount Lebanon Shakers, and, in a meeting of the North Family, after some very interesting reminiscences of Abraham Lincoln, made the following remarks: "Brethren and Sisters, in behalf of myself, wife and child, I return thanks for the love I have felt from you. This opportunity I count as being among the happiest moments of my life. I have had a busy life, but always tried to do the right in whatever office I have been called to fill. From my earliest recollections, you Shakers have been talked of in my father's house, and I always felt a desire to visit you. To Benjamin Gates, who will always be a brother of my heart, and to his Elder Brother, Frederick W. Evans, I am indebted for this privilege.; they came to me in time of your distress and laid before me your condition. I understood the case, and after consulting the President, we acted according to your desire, and I have always been thankful that I could in any way befriend you. I hope your society will always prosper, that God's blessing may rest upon it and that you who have joined hands today may be reunited in the spirit land." As the party left the room, Eldress Antoinette Doolittle said to him, "We are thankful to you for remembering us in our affliction, and we also pray for your prosperity." He stopped a moment, looked earnestly at her, then with great emotion and eyes filled with tears, said: "Sister, when my head was weary and my heart was heavy, the thought that the prayers of the righteous were ascending to heaven in my behalf was my only solace. God bless you!"

XI

YESTERDAY AND TODAY 1865-1904

Time of Transformation.

THE rapid increase in wealth among the people of the United States after the Civil War, the development of material comforts, the opportunities for commercial enterprise as invention and discovery joined hands with science, introducing an era of social, intellectual and business expansion, the impulse of activity, the sense of physical power — all combined to change the current of thought. Man, in America, felt himself a young giant just come to a knowledge of his might. Of the earth, earthy, he paid less attention to religious thought. The spiritual struggles of a former day were unknown to him. He turned to external interests and when the religious instincts moved it was in the direction of physical activities.

A race freed from bondage was to be civilized and educated or remanded to a worse than chattel slavery, and the contest waged with tremendous force in political and social centres; a continent hitherto almost unknown was to be explored, settled and controlled; political parties, aristocracies of money, brains and enterprise were to be born, or strangled in the birth; benevolences, charities, improvement of conditions in houses and schools, streets and sewers, races and incipient nations, opening of railroads, mines and cities, absorbing and assimilating huge masses of crude and undeveloped humanity from all the nations of the world,— these were the tasks which he — the man of America — found awaiting him. The question of his soul's salvation or the gaining of Heaven became absurdly irrelevant.

This outward activity to the neglect of the inner nature had its effect in the decadence of spirituality. The conception of sacrificing personal freedom or ambition, for the service of Christ or the Kingdom of Heaven, became almost as remote from the minds of men as the self-immolation of the Hindoo fakir. All religious bodies were affected by the change of attitude. Churches of the old order suffered; Shakers of the new order diminished in numbmers. To these changes in the outer world, the religious communities adapted themselves as well as possible, never losing hope, because of the faith so long accepted, that to their Order had been entrusted the living Testimony of Eternal Truth.

Public Meetings.

During the period covered by the sixties and seventies, several missionary tours were entered upon, led by Elder Evans and united in by leading Shakers from different societies. These were not, like former movements, in response to revival outbreaks that opened the way for the Shaker faith. The effort was rather of an educational nature, — to promulgate, explain and illustrate Shaker beliefs, customs and character. A series of meetings was held in each of the cities of Troy, New York, Brooklyn and Boston. While only a few converts were made to Shakerism, the meetings were large, respectful and attentive and a wider and clearer knowledge of Shakers and their faith was extended. Similar meetings had been held some years before in a circle of towns in western Massachusetts and eastern New York.

In a report of the meetings at Boston, signed by Elder Albert G. Lomas, of Watervliet, it is related that the party of over fifty Shakers stopped at the Marlboro House, where they had a large parlor at their disposal. Their first public recognition was through the Anti-slavery Association. Elder Frederick was the leading spirit. From their number were appointed Deacons, Deaconesses and Care-takers, so that the company settled at once into regular order of a Shaker family in Boston.

The first meetings were held in Meionian Hall, then in Morgan Chapel, where the spiritual atmosphere was found to be disagreeable, and finally their audiences filled Music Hall. Marching through the streets in Shaker fashion, in their simple, though striking dress, frequent remarks were overheard, — "Who can these people be?" Entering the hall, the rich voices of the Canterbury singers and the thrilling Shaker songs soon drew listeners to them. In the private union meetings held in the ante-room before the public services, such were the spiritual manifestations that all were equipped with power, and it was said that none would have been surprised to have seen Elder Frederick mounting on wings as do eagles. Intense interest was manifested by the audience, who are described as leaning forward like hungry children for their food.

Questions for oral answer were handled at the desk by Elder Frederick in his inimitable way. "If all should live as you do what would be the consequences?" was promptly met with, "If all should live as we do, the consequences to an evil nature would be terrible."

"Do you believe Christ's being represented in the Eucharist?" Provokingly instructive was his answer in these terms:— "Eucharist! Eucharist! what can that be? I shall have to ask for information." Sometimes his most telling reply was his peculiar fashion of straightening his tall form and simply looking, with the dryest of smiles, till the audience burst into a roar of laughter. One time on Music Hall platform, the Elder, who had not the fear of man, woman or conventionality before his eyes, warming up with his subject, found his cravat uncomfortable and proceeded to throw it off. Encountering difficulty in the unfastening, he tugged away while the audience laughed at his amazing gyrations, till, giving it a toss, he exclaimed: "There! that would be a curious operation for your priest, wouldn't it? I claim the Christian right of making myself comfortable," and proceeded with his discourse. Eldress Hester Adams, of Maine, affirmed that she had some of the most beautiful spirit impressions of her life, in these meetings.

Across the Water.

In 1871 and again in 1887, Elder Evans visited England and held meetings in several cities and towns. On the second trip he visited Scotland; on both occasions he went in company with his friend, the noted spiritualist, James M. Peebles, M. D.

Thirty-two years afterward, in a letter to the "Banner of Light," Dr. Peebles says: —

"This was one of the richest experiences of my life. The Elder, being an Englishman, went to his own as a missionary. At the great meeting he held in St. George's Hall, London, when W. Hepworth Dixon, author of 'New America,' took the chair, an immense crowd flocked to hear him. There were present members of Parliament, distinguished journalists, noted clergymen, secularists and spiritualists. The Elder was up to the occasion. The 'Spirit of the Lord was upon him.' If ever a man was inspired, he certainly was. His eyes flashed like fire at times. His voice rang out clear, strong and resonant. Three-fourths of his audience were seemingly hypnotized. Occasionally there was a dissent, as when he begged of the English to dispense with their bishops and priests and noblemen, constituting the House of Lords, and put women in their places. He further shocked them when declaring that the repenting, fighting, warring Jehovah of Israel was nothing but a tutelary divinity, needing conversion to Shakerism. As a whole, the audience was delighted with the simplicity, sincerity, solid logic, and I may add, the Elder's daring denunciations of England's sins and shortcomings."

The next day they were invited to a fashionable London breakfast with an ex-member of Parliament. The reminiscences continue:—

"On the morning that we were to breakfast with the Hon. Mr. H——, the Elder took his plain breakfast at the usual hour. Much of this he had brought with him in a large trunk from Mount Lebanon. When about to start, the Elder deliberately walked to his trunk, took out a good sized chunk of cold, coarse-ground Shaker unleavened bread, which, putting into his satchel, we started off for our appointed breakfast. Ten or twelve guests met in the elegantly appointed breakfast room. The Elder had stepped to his grip, taken out his bread, half as large as a quart bowl, and sitting down at the table, laid it by his plate. As the Elder was the honored guest, tall and reverential looking, the host asked him to 'say grace.' Crossing his hands and sitting as erect as a towering pine, he said, 'In my accustomed way,' and this way was as silent as the depths of silence itself. Not a word from his lips! Soon there was passed him a cup of coffee. He did not take coffee. 'Do you prefer tea, or cocoa?' 'Nay, I take neither.' There was passed to him a nice plate of fish. 'Nay, I do not take fish.' 'Perhaps you would prefer steak?' 'Nay, I do not take steak, or any animal flesh.'

" 'Well, really Elder, what do you eat and drink?'

" 'I drink water when thirsty, and I brought my bread with me, for I did not expect to find any London bakers' bread that was fit to eat.'

"This opened the way for a free, outspoken series of remarks upon bread, animal flesh-eating and its effects upon both mind and body. The breakfast 'hour' lasted nearly two hours, and I have often wished that it might have been reported verbatim."

Fires.

The Shaker communities have suffered much from fires, often of incendiary origin. At Watervliet, in the fall of

14

1871, two fires, within one week, destroyed the barns and sheds with all the winter stores for stock. The vicinity was said to be infested by a gang of desperadoes whose efforts were directed to plunder and conflagration. Attempts were made at robbery of the Shakers as well as fire. The state of mind of the people was thus expressed in a private letter: "We can courageously endure privation and labor hard, but when night comes it brings with it such a feeling of horror that we long for an eternal day. If we sleep, we are only frightened that we have been to sleep. When the bell strikes it is the knell of fear. We know no other way than to be faithful in duty and fervent in prayer, looking to the higher powers for protection." The Second Family at Mount Lebanon lost the Office and a drying kiln by the flames, and at the burning of the former, a sister, Ann Eliza Coburn, was so badly burned that her death soon followed.

The Church Family at Mount Lebanon, in February, 1875, in the most destructive fire ever known among Believers, lost eight buildings including the dwelling-house. The Fire Brigade of Pittsfield, eight miles away, came over the mountain in fifty-five minutes. Neighbors turned out; the Tilden Family, neighboring proprietors and manufacturers, did effective service, and by heroic efforts they, with their employees and tenants, saved the ancient and historic meeting-house. Elder Daniel Boler, of the Central Ministry, and the Family Elder, Daniel Crossman, were injured, while Eldress Harriet Goodwin, in the effort to save important and valuable papers, barely escaped with her life, being removed from an upper window. There was no insurance and the loss was $150,000. Sister societies took hold in earnest to aid their afflicted brethren and sisters, large sums being donated by those who were able. A handsome and commodious dwelling of brick was erected, containing a spacious meeting-room. The family were presented by the manufacturers in Troy, N. Y., with a large bell for use in this building. After the rebuilding, a residence, including workshops, was erected for the use of the Central Ministry. Previous to this time, the Ministry, according to ancient custom, had occupied apartments in the meeting-house. The change was adopted in all the other societies. In November, 1890, the Church Family lost their drying kiln by fire, loss about $4,000. On the eighteenth of September, 1894, a midnight blaze destroyed a number of buildings belonging to the same family, with two, the property of the North Family. One contained a year's store of roots, alone valued at $1,500. These buildings were at the East Farm. The family once dwelling there had several years before been incorporated with others. This loss was estimated at $5,000. Liks the previous fires at Mount Lebanon, it was the work of an incendiary.

Two days later, at about the noon hour, the society at Harvard was visited by the fire fiend and the great Shaker barn, with all its valuable contents, besides a smaller barn, ice house, lumber house and several sheds were destroyed. In January, 1897, Enfield, Conn., lost by the flames a large barn with several other buildings, hay, grain and valuable implements. Twenty thousand dollars would not have made good the loss. This was the third barn on the same site that had been destroyed by fire. In nearly every case these fires were the work of incendiaries.

Alfred, Maine, was visited in 1901 by a conflagration that destroyed several buildings, including the dwelling-house and the residence of the Ministry. The society, although small and composed mostly of sisters, set bravely to work to replace the old time dwellings with a smaller, more convenient one, better adapted to present day needs. Canterbury, N. H., in the same year lost several buildings. Other societies, east and west, have suffered in like manner. Ohio and Kentucky Shakers have suffered like their eastern kindred, often at the hands of avowed enemies. One fire at Pleasant Hill destroyed a silk factory, with a costly plant of valuable modern machinery.

Western Visit of the Central Ministry.

In 1889, a state of things had come about in the western societies that called for the personal attention of the Central Ministry, and Elder Giles B. Avery and Eldress Harriet Bullard with Eldress Anna White, by appointment, visited these societies. After several weeks, thoughtful study of conditions resulted in the closing up of the society at North Union, the merging of this society with others, the abandonment of the South Union Bishopric and the appointment of one Ministry, central at Union Village, Ohio, over all the societies west of New York State.

Self Improvement Society.

In 1891, among the young sisters at Mount Lebanon, was started a society, whose aim was "harmonious development of being, physical, intellectual and spiritual, unity of sentiment and individuality of expression." It was also proposed to "establish a radical improvement in habits and manner, address and conversation and the cultivation of the mind in substantial, beautiful and interesting things." The rules forbade the use of "all unkind or sarcastic remarks to or about one another, all manner of slang, by-words, extravagant expressions, false statements and white lies; and encouraged the use of grammatical language and correct pronunciation."

Literary, scientific and philosophical study took their attention, and original work of a superior stamp resulted from this earnest effort at self-education. The efforts of this society have been very apparent in the manner, thought, address and writing of the class engaged in it.

Society Changes.

The society at Tyringham, Massachusetts, had been many years before united with Hancock and Enfield, Connecticut, and the estate sold. Groveland was merged with Watervliet, New York, and the property was sold to the State. It is now the site of the State Asylum for Epileptics. Canaan, N. Y., was merged in the societies of Mount Lebanon and Enfield, Conn. The Lower Family estate has become the seat of a private benevolence of great value to society — the Berkshire Industrial Farm for Boys.

Colonies in the South.

Through investments, resulting in property exchanges in different states, the society at Mount Lebanon became possessed of extensive lands in Florida, and, in 1894, a little company was sent to establish a society in that state. They located at Narcossee, and, by dint of hard work and great frugality, have succeeded in establishing themselves and are engaged in raising and marketing pine apples and other southern products.

The Union Village society in 1898 bought forty thousand acres of land in Camden County, Georgia, and started a small colony there. This and a previous attempt in the same state have proved failures. Much doubt was felt in many minds of the advisability of these moves. It was felt by many, that concentration rather than scattering of force was demanded by the condition of the societies; that empty buildings and untilled fields in the north hardly called for new territories and the erection of new dwellings and store-houses in distant states. Others saw in the opening south, opportunities for obtaining a livelihood with less outlay of strength, less waste of energy, than in the cold climate and on the rocky soil of the north. The experiments were tried without loss of union among those who differed in opinion. Perhaps it is too soon to say whether or not true wisdom prompted the last attempt.

In 1902, Elder Andrew Barrett, of Narcossee, Fla., Eldress Mary Gass, of Whitewater, Ohio, and Eldress Clymena Miner, of Union Village, Ohio, were constituted the Ministry of the West, the centre of the Bishopric being Union Village.

Changes of Polity.

Among the reforms brought about through the influence of Eldress Antoinette Doolittle, during her administration, was one which proved of much import to the domestic economy, as well as the stability and success of the North Family, Mount Lebanon. Financial and business interests were placed under separate management of brethren and sisters, and for a number of years the sisters had full control of their own business affairs. The measure proved highly satisfactory and the same policy obtained in other societies. But at length it was felt that the era of separation in business polity had served its purpose as the preparatory stage to a stronger and more real union, and in a return, in some ways, to the early customs of the Order was seen an onward step. Following the plan already in successful operation in the Canterbury society, in January, 1903, the business interests of the North Family were united; a treasurer was appointed from the sisters, a finance committee of brethren and sisters was chosen to meet monthly and de-

cide all questions of business policy and one set of books was
to be kept.

Thus, without renouncing, in any degree, adherence to
the Shaker principle of following an authorized leadership,
the faithful, covenant-keeping members are more fully recognized, brought in closer touch with business operations
and their influence and judgment accorded a larger place
in the family polity. This change is one that must necessarily develop both individuals and the united body, while it
is a broader expression, in harmony with the spirit of the
times, of a principle inherent in communism and observed
in practise by the early organizers of the Shaker Communities.

With the World's Work.

One of many pictures of Shakerism and its mission given
by that associate Shaker, James M. Peebles, M. D., is that
in an issue of the "Shaker Manifesto:" "Though absent
from you in body, I am often with you — and the Zion of
our God — in spirit, with you in moral travel and with you
in your earnest efforts to rightly educate and build up a
divine humanity, golden with moral beauty, purity and
love. Shakerism, seen in connection with the incoming
cycle, is all rainbowed with promise and aflame with the
light and love of God. Power does not consist in numbers. The gulf stream, in comparison with the ocean, is
small; it sometimes seems as if the ocean would swallow
it up; yet there it remains in the ocean, but not of the
ocean; there it remains an everlasting river, flowing
steadily, bearing the choice treasures of the tropics to colder
climes, changing temperatures, modifying the swift-footed
winds, spreading the greater blessings of summer warmth
— and all as a potency and promise of golden fruitage

and a waving harvest. So with Believers, in the world but not of the world, so with truth victorious in the end." Among the reforms with which many Shakers are in touch is

Vegetarianism.

Through the constant efforts of Elder Frederick W. Evans, assisted by the calmer, more persuasive spirit of his coadjutor, Eldress Antoinette Doolittle, supported by a few earnest, progressive spirits among official and private members, the North Family at Mount Lebanon early took the position of adherents to a bloodless diet. From the earliest years of vegetarian agitation, Elder Frederick, with a few others, had abjured all meat. For many years the vegetarians had a special table, but in time the whole family united and they have found, as years have passed, that the abundant, varied and nutritious diet of grains, vegetables and fruits has answered every physiological need; while the lessening of labor on the one hand and the satisfaction of mind and conscience on the other amply repay any slight sense of deprivation that may at first have been felt. Following their lead, other societies have, in a measure, adopted the non-meat diet, and there are many individual vegetarians throughout the connection.

Cooperation with Peace Movements.

Shakers have from the first been associated with the movements for Peace Reform in this country, attending the Peace Conventions and actively engaged in the cause. Elder Evans was for many years one of the Vice Presidents of the "Universal Peace Union." When the branch society at Salt Point was organized, the Shakers for six years attended the meetings and helped bring that association into being. The last attendance of Mount Lebanon Shakers was at Mystic, Conn., in 1899, when a party of brethren and sisters from the North Family accompanied Eldress Anna White. A paper, "Voices from Mount Lebanon," was read by the leader of the party and the Shakers added much by their singing to the pleasure of the meetings.

Eldress Anna was also associated with the late Princess Wiszniewska, daughter of Victor Hugo, leader of the "Alliance of Women for Peace," whose centre is at Paris, France, and, having obtained five hundred signatures to the Petition for International Disarmament, more than any one else in the State, she was appointed Vice President of the Alliance for the State of New York. The active work is constantly carried on at Mount Lebanon, and few women visitors are allowed to leave the North Family residence, without the Petition being offered for their signatures. Hundreds of names are thus secured.

Work with Humane Societies.

Every important philanthropic movement receives the sympathy and, if possible, the cooperation of the Shakers. Especially does the work of the various Humane Societies receive attention at the North Family in Mount Lebanon. At the present time, one of the sisters acts as Local Secretary for several different societies, improving every opportunity to win advocates to anti-vivisection and animal protection. Branch societies have been organized by her in the neighborhood; children in the Shaker families and among guests and neighbors are won to these causes, and signatures and funds are daily secured to carry on the work of establishing their principles and securing legislation in their favor.

As sociological and humanitarian problems have increasingly absorbed the attention of men and women of thought and unselfish purpose, the moral and economic status of the Shaker Communities has attracted notice and invited visitors and correspondents from all over the world. Many of the leading Shakers have come from the ranks of the great reform movements and they have attracted their comrades and associates to the sphere of the higher spiritual influences so manifest in Shaker homes. Anti-slavery and Land Reformers of an earlier day, apostles of Temperance, Peace, Labor, Equal Rights and Social Reforms of the present, all find sympathy and cooperation at this centre of good influences.

NO. 17.   LEBANON VALLEY AND MT. LEBANON, N. Y.   TACONIC MOUNTAINS IN THE DISTANCE.

XII

SPIRITUALISM

"IN some degree," writes Elder Giles B. Avery, "and operating in some manner, spirit manifestations have ever been the inheritance of the Christian Church; to this, the Shaker branch has not been an exception."

"If a man die, shall he live again?" It is the question of all humanity;—of savage and civilized, old and young, happy and sorrowful, saint and sinner, ancient and modern. From years before the flood, the question echoed on the ears of Job. From psalmist, prophet, seer and sage, from Chaldean plain and Persian hilltop and Galilean lake; from Egypt and Babylon, from Tyre and Alexandria, from Rome and Athens, from London and Paris, from Pekin and Boston, it arises. Egyptian mummies wait thousands of years for an answer; seers of old hope for it; Socrates expects it; Jesus implies it; but, down the long centuries, Humanity's love racked, sorrow wrung heart yearns, begs, demands an "I know it!"

To one, the Bible glows with its truth as gleams an illuminated cathedral window; to another, the Bible is opaque as that same window gazed at from without. To one, the confession of Apostles' Creed — which apostle neither wrote nor saw—"On the third day He arose from the dead" is the end of all discussion: "He lives. I shall live also!" To another, the stone has not yet been rolled away from life's great mystery.

Far on in the centuries, there came to a childish ear, in a humble home in a small city of a New World commonwealth, — a tiny rap! Quick, low, abrupt, — unaccounted for! A series of raps, showers of them. The raps were found to mean something, to respond sensibly to questions, to reveal, when applied to, facts and occurrences of the past known only to the secret thought of the inquirer. The mysterious visitants claimed to be present personalities, people who had left earth life; who, buried in graveyards near or far, living in times recent or remote, now claimed to be alive, conscious, intelligent, able and anxious to speak to inquiring friends.

Time brought greater developments. The circles spread over society, like ripples on a lake when pebbles are dropped in. The light of higher encircling spheres shone into the dense shadows of earthly vision. Men's minds were wondrously quickened. Wizard intellects arose, and from the secrets of spirit spheres came discovery, invention, thought, which once would have burned or crucified the earthly agent as an emissary of the Devil. Water and air became responsive to man's will; compression forced free air to delve and toil for him and to light the darkness of his world.

Electricity, banishing darkness, moving earth's mountains, chaining earth's cataracts, speaking across mighty distances, linking ocean to ocean and land to land, not only gave to man a glorious new sense of freedom, might and power, but, like spirit arms reaching across immensity, drew man's head to a Parental breast, and Wisdom supernal, Love divine and Care angèlic gave to humanity a new sense of childhood, a new knowledge of Fatherhood and Motherhood.

Man's spiritual being seemed brought en rapport with the world for which it was created, for whose use and occupancy it was designed. Diseases healed, beneficent actions performed, national crimes averted or atoned for, enslaved races freed, great discoveries and useful inventions revealed, — these are among the mighty works claimed to have been accomplished through this last inflow of light and power from the world of spirit. Fewer to-day than a decade ago doubt the existence of life beyond the grave; yet, alas! too many see naught in life but corporeal matter, nervo-cerebric pulse and ganglionic thrill, that will, in due time, cease, and life, with all its sublime possibilities, become the empty cell wall and the impassive dust.

Shakers the First Modern Spiritualists.

Shakers first received this great spiritual visitation of the nineteenth century. Ten years before the first suggestive rap fell on the wondering ear at Rochester, the light of spirit illumination had shone into every Shaker Community.

Shakerism was founded in Spiritualism. Its very essence and life principle is that of conscious, continuous action and reaction between the worlds of spirit and of sense. Ann Lee's child life was full of vision and spirit teaching. Her maturity won, through soul agonies almost unthinkable, access into the light of open revelation. All of the first great leaders and teachers were spirit led, instructed in the minutiæ of faith and practise by open vision, by direct divine revelation. Voices and visions and spirit hands led and guided all along the way, nor was a stone laid nor a tower erected of the spiritual temple of this faith, that was not "after the pattern shown in the Mount."

From the first ingathering in the early part of the century, the rapid increase in numbers, great hopes were raised. Old prophecies were indeed being fulfilled; people were "flocking like doves to the windows." The world was to be redeemed, and naturally, the faithful looked for a mighty inflowing of convicted and rescued humanity to the communistic homes, where the pure and undefiled religion of Jesus and Ann was lived. The cry was — Room for the thousands! The inheritance for the heirs of the Kingdom! Building to building, hilltop to hilltop, fertile valley to valley were added, in their anxiety that home and place and opportunity might not be lacking for those who were to come. Was the toil hard, the burden heavy? Cheerfully they bore it, eating scanty bread and drinking cold water, denying themselves all luxuries, wearing clothing coarse and poor and plain, that so the Kingdom might be made ready for the children of the Kingdom who were to come to their inheritance.

There came a check to the incoming, a period of heaviness and sluggishness in the life and fervor. The old time rejoicing before the Lord was checked. Down into the valley of humiliation went the people, as their quickstep grew slower in march and dance. "Be not discouraged, the Heavens are closed, but they shall yet open for you," the Spirit had said.

Suddenly, the opening came. Came, as come all divine visitations, at a time and in a manner least thought of, farthest removed from expectation; so strange and foolish in its first manifestations, that the watchers might well be pardoned had they failed to see the signs of the Son or Daughter of Man in the cloud of witnesses newly arisen.

The Children's Hour.

On the 16th of August in the year 1837, at Watervliet, N. Y., the work began, among the children. Some little girls, of ten or twelve years of age, were seized in the house of worship with shaking, turning and similar exercises. They soon became entranced, and in this unconscious state began to sing songs entirely new to the observers, to ask and answer questions and carry on conversation with beings invisible to those about them.

At their early bedtime, they were put to bed by their care-takers, but, unconscious of their surroundings, with arms in motion as if flying, they were wandering in beautiful fields and groves, in delightful gardens were gathering delicious fruits, plucking beautiful flowers, laughing, singing and chattering, as children would with dear and trusted friends. These phenomena went on day after day and night after night. Their care-takers have left on record what they saw and experienced with them. No matter where they were placed nor in what position, no change was affected in their occupations and conversation.

A class of boys of the same age was affected. Some of these were thrown violently on the floor and all the efforts of strong men were unavailing to raise their stiffened bodies. Then they too began to talk of being in heavenly places conversing with angel guides and singing the songs taught by angel friends. It was not all of heaven and happiness. Sometimes they were with those in suffering and torment; they seemed suffocated, as by sulphur fumes; their bodies were distorted and bore every mark of intense agony, while their screeches and cries were terrible to hear.

In one of the western societies, some young girls were walking in a grove and heard beautiful singing in the air just above their heads. While learning the melody, they became entranced. At North Union, one Sabbath afternoon, the children were holding a service of their own, when the Elders were hastily summoned to the Children's Order, as something strange was going on. They found the children in a state of trance, walking rapidly to and fro, singing, laughing, talking with those invisible to Elders and care-takers, nor could they be stopped even by forcibly holding them. Before the end of 1838 these manifestations were in full tide in all the Shaker Communities.

Always among the children! Those affected were not unusual children, nor had they been subjected to any special training or effort. No one had tried to "make little angels of them." Shaker child culture has always been simple, plain and practical. Children are taught to be honest, truthful and obedient; they are trained to industry, neatness and cleanliness of person as of lips and heart. The lessons of the simple faith are inculcated, but for the rest, the Shaker child is a free, happy, rollicking, little human being, loved and cared for tenderly, the law of kindness on the lips of every one who has to do with him. These were natural, unaffected children in 1837, when this strange visitation seized them.

To say that their Shaker friends were startled, perplexed and anxious is to express the general feeling very mildly. There was no trickery; the circumstances, the character and ability of the children, the fullness of detail in the phenomena, the naturalness of the children when freed from trance conditions, all made that hypothesis untenable. It was real, evidently.

No harm seemed to come to them from any bodily exercise, however violent; nor, from their worst impersonations of souls tormented in flame, did not return any the worse, or with the smell of fire upon their garments; nor was the exhaustion more than such extreme muscular tension would naturally produce. A nap would suffice to set the little impersonator of torture upon his feet again. The trance condition lasted a few hours, or for one or two days; one case of a six-days' trance is recorded. Sometimes the subject was lying perfectly still, apparently dead; sometimes relating audibly, or, in movement and action revealing the scenes through which the soul was passing.

The practical, spiritually-minded Shakers accepted the visitation as in the order of Divine appointment, watched over and protected the children and waited for the gifts and blessings, instructions or warnings, intended by the unexpected outbreak.

Soon the children began to talk to their audience, to exhort, to urge to faithfulness, to warn and to encourage, — using language far beyond their years or ability. Sometimes they made personal appeals to individuals, speaking of events or experiences about which, of themselves, they had no knowledge whatever. It is interesting to read the accounts of these experiences, as recorded in after years by the children themselves.

They tell of being taken to see Mother Ann and the beautiful spirits who surrounded her; of her talking to them, asking them if they would always obey her.

One speaks of Mother Ann asking if she would always bear the cross, were it great or small, and of her childish heart going out in love and gratitude, as she earnestly promised that she truly would be a faithful cross bearer; of Mother Ann putting into her hands the gift of a little cross, telling her that she would understand its meaning better by and by.

These children had evidently been carefully guarded by their spiritual friends, within and without the body, from any undue elation or self-conceit that might naturally spring from such wonder filled lives. They were duly impressed with the sacredness of the trust, the necessity of being true to their pledges of faith and constancy. In many instances, their after lives bore fruit of earnest truth and devotion to the cause whose heavenly side had been so strangely revealed to them. It must have been a wondrous morning-land of light, "trailing clouds of glory" into later years, such as no poet's dream has ever known.

15

Work with Adults.

An older class became affected by these experiences, then the adult members of the society were seized by them. In the religious meetings or about their work, on the highway or in the fields, the body would be acted upon as if by subtler elements, beyond physical cognizance, — whirling, jerking, leaping, dancing, head and arms thrown about as if to be pulled out. The acute mortification caused by such involuntary antics was accepted as a good dose of spiritual tonic. Often the subject was visited by bands of friendly spirits, with whom ecstatic hours were spent in sunny fields and beautiful groves. Sometimes, cities and towns, libraries and workshops were their field of observation. The visiting spirit often revealed himself in gestures, tones and mannerisms, so perfectly that he was at once recognized and called by name, — while the instrument acted upon might be in complete ignorance of the personality affecting him. All this was years before a medium had been heard of in the outside world.

Often the spirit visitant brought gifts, which the agent affected was to distribute. Love and blessing were freely showered about. Flowers and fruit were often given and other articles, which to the prim, demure Shaker, with his hatred of show, vain glory and worldliness, must have seemed uncanny enough. For instance, from a departed friend, — the plainest, simplest, most self-denying Shaker of Shakers, would come gifts of gems, jewelry, gold chains and rings, fine robes of white or beautiful fabrics in rainbow hues. Bells, musical instruments, pens and paper, singing birds, doves and lambs were added to the collection of treasures, imparted by spirit hands. Whatever the gift or ministration, the Believer, childlike and submissive, accepted with grateful simplicity and improved, growing in spiritual understanding and comprehension of the nearness, reality, and homelikeness of the spiritual world. It brought the minds that had wrestled with hard tasks and mighty problems down to the simplicity and heavenly-mindedness of the child, — the typical child nature, innocent, pure and true, beloved by Jesus and by Ann.

In 1838, the media began to speak in unknown languages, sometimes the loss of speech altogether is recorded. In some instances this infliction lasted for one or two weeks, the victim being in great straits to make himself understood by his friends. Some could be sent into a trance at a moment's notice. The visionist would be sent on an errand to Mother Ann saying that the Elders wanted advice or counsel, perhaps, though without specifying for what. Immediately, the answer would come through the lips of the entranced, always to the point and what was needed. In one society, forty members were at one time thus ready for service at a moment's warning, in this strange foreshadowing of later developments of psychic powers and capabilities of the human being, powers and capabilities which the beginning of the twentieth century sees but in the infancy of their unfolding.

Many new and beautiful forms of exercise were learned while on these pleasure trips with the angels, which were learned and practised in the worship. "The manifestations soon took the form of solemn messages. The guardian angels of the people seemed to speak in the name of the Father and Mother in Heaven. Zion was to be searched as with candles, Believers were shown how there had been departure from ancient ways and right paths. It was a time of heart-searching, repentance and sorrow. Special blessings were conferred on the aged and hope given to the young. Every manifestation seemed designed to inspire a deeper love for sacred and divine things and to establish a deeper confidence in the beautiful gifts. Some, who had indulged a lukewarm or infidel spirit, were arrested in astonishment and began to reconsider their position. Near the close of 1838, Father Joseph Meacham and others visited the society and endeavored to renew Gospel Order and a better understanding of the life of a follower of Christ."

This has been known among Believers as "Mother Ann's Second Coming" and "Mother's Work." It was the result, she affirmed through media, of the prayers of aged members of the Order, her own first born children of the faith, who had for years been praying that something might come to convict and establish in the foundation principles of the Gospel, the young people who had grown up under the protection of the communities, but who had not experienced the deep work of faith. They exerted a constant pressure on Elders and leaders, for more liberty and indulgence in their worldly tastes and selfish desires; they did not believe in so much self-denial and restraint as was enjoined by the laws of the community and the example of the older members. There had been a gradual yielding to them by Ministry and Elders, in the hope that they might receive the conviction that would establish them in the faith and that then, the discipline might be restored. The results as well as the teaching of Mother Ann in her vigorous work among the people showed the futility of such a course.

Educational Epoch.

About the year 1840, a fresh tide of spirit power flooded the life of the societies. The simpler childlike revelations passed and to minds rendered obedient by the lessons of the two past years, more earnest work was given. Written as well as oral messages were imparted, in some instances, books of several hundred pages were indited, which have been of value in the work of faith and the instruction of Believers; some were of a prophetic cast.

The instruments employed were often persons, who, in natural ability and education, were by no means fitted for such tasks. These inspired writers were released from all secular duties, and, in order to be prepared for the complete absorption of the bodily powers in the work of the spirit, they lived on a simple diet, largely bread and water, abstained from unnecessary conversation, and, withdrawn into a room alone, in silence received the messages imparted. This continued for more than a year. In February, 1843, the Sacred Roll was imparted, and the Book of Holy Wisdom, written at Watervliet, was published at Canterbury, N. H., in the year 1849.

Some of the media were inspired as public speakers, some as singers, twenty new songs a day being sometimes given through the same medium. It was declared that every person has one or two guardian spirits, whose character is determined somewhat by the character and will of the individual. Sometimes these guardians minister directly sometimes through others nearer in nature and influence to the person in their charge. Kindred natures attract each other, and will and purpose can draw or can repel the good as well as the evil among the spirit bands.

Father James Whittaker and Father William Lee with other well known leaders were recognized by their characteristic ministrations. One historian of this epoch says: "The close of the year 1841 was remarkable for seasons of worship, in which were manifested deep humiliation and prayer. Hours and hours were spent in meditation, preparatory to the reception of the beautiful gifts to be poured out upon faithful souls. The year was one of astonishment as well as of great joy." Many messages were of a reformatory nature, the people being called to advance toward purer, more spiritual living. Swine's flesh, tobacco and ardent spirits were forbidden and from the year 1841 were discontinued throughout the societies.

Elder Andrew Houston wrote a lengthy description of a strange scene at Union Village, which seems a remarkable prefiguring of the developing principle of telepathy. In a meeting of great spiritual fervor, living members of the society at Mount Lebanon were present and together with many well known spirits out of the body were plainly visible to those of clairvoyant powers, expressing themselves through media, each in characteristic tone, speech and manner.

At Watervliet, the public crowded to the assemblies, and at one service scholars were present who affirmed that four different languages were spoken by the media, — Hebrew, Greek, Latin and Spanish. They could hardly be made to believe but what the inspired ones had learned these languages. Some were inspired to read from invisible scrolls long accounts of the transactions of former times. One Elder writes: "It all has to be in Order. Mother Ann herself does nothing but by reference to the Elders, the very spirits do not interfere but by permission. The inspired and the visionist are under control and cannot speak nor act but by liberty."

Holy Mount.

At Mount Lebanon, by special revelation, instruction was received to establish on the highest peak of the mountain east of the village, a spot called Holy Mount, as a place for worship. Hither, twice each year, one day in spring and one in autumn, went all the people. Starting in the fresh morning hours, they walked in solemn, yet glad procession, family by family, climbed the long, steep hight, and here spent the day in worship, in song and dance before the Lord, mingling with hosts of the immortals, whose presence was sensibly, oftimes visibly apparent. It was a holy, a joyful day,— lifted above earth and earthly tasks and burdens; the long climb, its rocks and cliffs, its stumbling places and its dark, forest depths, all typical of the hard, burdened, shadowed path through earth life, up the spiritual steeps of redemption. Hand might clasp hand, love's keen foresight remove some obstacles from the path, pleasant resting places be made by kind hands going over the way before, where a sweet rest, wide views of the glorious country of God be enjoyed and inspiring songs be sung; — songs and hosannahs and the beautiful watch-cry of the faith be shouted, "More Love!" Yet, each step of the way must be trodden by each one for himself. His own, her own, work of climbing must be done alone. But at the top, — the long, glad day of spiritual feasting and joy! What lessons were not taught the Believer, in its bright exercises, of spiritual requital for past toil? Here, on the summit, rose in spiritual sight, the spiritual temple of Mother Ann; its walls of purest marble, its adornments, gold and gems of celestial polishing; its windows open to celestial airs, its arches ringing to strains of celestial melody and echoing to words of celestial wisdom. Little children, free and happy, were led by their angel guardians, and were seen feasting on fruits, which, invisible to the eyes of others, were real and tangible to them. A similar spot was chosen in each society. From that of Mount Lebanon could be seen the society of Hancock on their summit, and the two societies would shout and wave their greetings to each other, — Mount calling and answering to Mount the joy of the Lord!

Was it all fancy play, a wild extravaganza of fantastic brains? Nay! remember ye not who said, "I thank Thee,

O Father, Lord of Heaven and earth, who hast hid these things .from the wise and prudent and hast revealed them unto babes?" To the babe in Christ, the child spirit of the true Believer, these sacred mysteries are revealed. Earthly, natural forms are to him as the shadows of the actual, spiritual facts. Fruit and flower, landscapes, works of art and literature, whatever brightens, gladdens or uplifts humanity are to him ten-fold more real when seen and felt through the sense of the interior, spiritual being. To him is the right to the life and glory of the spirit land, for, in a sense true of no other, is he the child of the Divine Father and Mother. This opening of the spiritual world into the earthly life of Believers was so actual and practical that it lifted the communistic toiler into the life of spirit spheres, and no longer was there a question of the possibility of angel communication. It was a natural, every day fact.

Pleasant Grove.

In October, 1842, at Canterbury, a spot was selected in a beautiful grove, which was named "Pleasant Grove." The ground was smoothed, boulders removed, trees uprooted, a fence built with two gates, one at the north-east, the other at the south-east, through which brethren and sisters could enter two by two, wide enough also for the admission of carriages conveying the aged and infirm. A house, twenty by sixty feet was erected, one story in height. Near the fence beautiful firs were planted which grew into tall trees. In the centre of Pleasant Grove was placed a large slab of beautiful Italian marble, six feet high, three feet wide and three inches thick, resting on a heavy stone foundation carefully mortised and cemented. A message was engraven on one side and on the other the name of the place and the object of its erection. Around the centre stone was another

NO. 18. OLD MEETING HOUSE, EAST CANTERBURY, N. H.

enclosure, ten feet by five, called "The Fountain" and protected by a pretty white fence six feet high. To this spot the people came to worship. Similar places were arranged in all the societies, each called by some spiritual name as directed by the controlling power.

At Union Village, "Jehovah's Chosen Square" was described as ten rods on a side, set with forest trees, ash, oak and hickory. The centre fountain was eighteen feet square and over the gate was the inscription: "Purity, Holiness and Eternal Truth I do require of all who enter here to worship Me saith the Lord." Each society had a spiritual name by which it was known among Believers. Mount Lebanon was known as "Holy Mount," Watervliet as "Wisdom's Valley," Hancock as "City of Peace," Enfield, Conn., as "City of Love," Canterbury as "Pleasant Grove" and Union Village as "Wisdom's Paradise."

The procession to Holy Mount was continued till 1854, when, by spirit direction it was given up. For nineteen years Pleasant Grove was kept in good preservation, then all was removed and no use has since been made of the place. The same was done in the other societies, and little or nothing is ever said of the sacred spots which once meant so much in the spiritual education of the people.

Peculiar Gifts.

For three years, from 1842 to 1845, the Sabbath service was closed to the public and a notice to that effect was posted on the door of the meeting-house. The message came from the leaders of the heavenly host to the leaders on earth that Believers should retire within themselves. A common exercise at this time was for a company of brethren and sisters to march, singing, over the fields sowing seeds of blessing. At one time, under spirit direction, a general inspection was made of every room and articles of furniture, books, pictures and ornaments were accepted or rejected in accordance with spirit direction. Gifts of healing were common and one Elder is mentioned at death's door with consumption who was restored to health and lived for sixteen years, dying at last at the age of eighty-three. In 1842, a singular manifestation was known as

"Mother Ann's Sweeping Gift."

Four brethren and four sisters accompanied by the same number of singers went through all the rooms, speaking and singing in every room. This work of spiritual cleansing had a most salutary effect on the life of the people. Eight days were thus occupied and the sixteen persons selected were released from all other duties and, during the time, fasted and spent in meditation and prayer the hours not employed in this special ministration.

"The Midnight Cry"

was the name given to a startling performance enacted, like the preceding, for eight years. A company of twelve media, six of each sex, was organized. Two leaders carried lamps in their right hands. Each wore on the right wrist a strip of scarlet flannel, bearing the words: "War hath been declared by the God of Heaven against all sin and with the help of the saints on earth it shall be slain!" Under the direction of the medium, this company marched through every room in every building, occupying about two weeks in the work. At midnight of the third day, a company of four sisters passed through all the halls and the sisters' apartments in the dwelling-house, singing. This "Midnight Cry" awakened all from slumber and everyone arose and joined the ranks. The next night, at two o'clock, a company of brothers and sisters again aroused the family, who at three A. M. gathered in their chapel and engaged in an hour of active worship. This strange alarm had a wonderful effect on the minds of those thus suddenly aroused.

Meaning of the Gifts.

These various actions, inspired by spirits, sometimes recognized and sometimes not, but all claiming to be prompted by Mother Ann and the first Elders, and in some cases by inspiration given directly to the media by Mother Ann herself, seem to have had an educative force and to be, on a spiritual plane, of the nature of kindergarten work in modern educational methods, — preparing minds and hearts for the reception of higher spiritual truths; training the powers of the soul through pictorial and simple object lessons for dealing with spiritual facts. Simple deductive reasoning first, abstract thought and broader, advanced deductions later, with simplicity, receptivity, obedience, humility and teachableness as the necessary foundation for true spiritual education, seems to have been the plan of development of these unseen teachers.

Incoming of the Nations.

Among the visions given to the little children in 1837 were visits to so-called cities in the spirit realms, where they were instructed, in conversation with their angel guides, about the residents. In one case, they visited a city inhabited by those who had been negro slaves; but, slaves no longer, they were waited upon and served by their former masters, who had thus to square up accounts and earn their own right to freedom. Some, recalcitrant and rebellious, sulking in a corner, had to wait until suffering brought them to the point of willingness to redress the wrongs inflicted on their unhappy slaves, in earth life.

In 1842, there came at Mount Lebanon, and then through the other societies, a strange epoch of visitation by representatives of all nationalities. Indians, Arabs, Ancient Jews, Chaldeans, Persians, Hindoos, — people of remote lands and ancient times, thronged to the City of Zion. The revelation of Christ through Mother Ann had come to them, and, as in vision many times repeated while she was on earth, with open mouths and eager hearts, they pressed forward to secure the treasures of the Gospel. Sometimes they came to the Elders begging the privilege of confessing their sins, asking forgiveness of the people assembled in worship and pleading to be admitted to the ranks of Believers. For months and years these visitations continued. Certain spirits became well known and dearly loved by the people whom they visited. The Indians often came in tribes, headed by their chief, sometimes led by a squaw. Applying to the Elder or Eldress, permission would be given them to come in. The family would be called together and then, through the sensitives or media, the native Indian would be revealed in all the savage glory of war-whoop, dance and song; talking in their native tongue or in broken English, gesticulating, shouting, or sitting in dignified silence as fancy or disposition prompted. Sometimes they would sing a song never heard before, and the whole band of affected media would sing, as one person, the new, strange melody perhaps in English, perhaps in Indian, perhaps a mixture of both. But these tribes came to be instructed. They were bound by a pledge to be obedient to the Elders, and to keep the order of the family by whose courtesy they were received, and, to their credit, they generally did so. They came in work hours, went into the shops and were instructed in the various industries and trades followed by brethren and sisters; into the kitchens, laundries, bake-rooms and sewing-rooms, learning the arts of the housekeeper.

These principles of industrial education thus applied in the early forties, by direction of spiritual. teachers, under Mother Ann, to these savage tribes, antedated by a half century, modern improved methods of educating savage races.

Departure of the Spirits.

After about ten years of these experiences, the spirit visitors announced to the people that they were about to leave them and go out into the world. They would visit every city and hamlet, every palace and cottage in the land, and then they would return again to the people who had first received them. Mother Ann herself spoke to her people in the different societies and said she should go out from them for a season, into the world at large, working for the uplifting and enlightenment of humanity. "The knowledge must be spread throughout the whole earth as the waters cover the sea, that every tongue and nation may learn of the goodness of God and the glories prepared for the upright and honest worker when done with the things of time," were her words.

The people wept at the leave taking, sorrow was felt as for the loss of beloved friends by death, and a sad blank was left in lives that had for so long been spent half on earth, half in the spirit world. The promise remained that in fulness of time, a greater and more wonderful re-opening of the heavenly·world would be given to the people who had first received the endowment of spirit communication. Thus the Shaker Church may justly claim to be the

Parent of Modern Spiritualism.

The spirits took their departure in 1847. An exercise prompted by them, of frequent occurrence, had been kneeling and rapping on the floor; and when, in 1848, in the city of Rochester, N. Y., the famous rappings began at the home of the Fox sisters, the Shakers recognized the familiar sounds, and knew that their visitors for ten years past had, according to promise, gone out "to visit every city and hamlet, every palace and cottage in the land."

Close and interested observers of all that has transpired under the head of Modern Spiritualism, Shakers find no more wonderful phenomena than those that were daily household tales among themselves; while, seeing the disorderly and repellant nature of much that occurs among media in the world outside, they realize how safe and secure was their own dealing with the tenants of the spirit world, — subject as they were and are still, to the control of the central authority, the divinely appointed Visible Order.

Many who have entered the Shaker Church in recent years recognize this power of control, and rejoice that here is a safe centre where even the spirits of the disembodied are subject, in the line of the Anointed Order, and where, under their recognition and control, intercourse is safe, mediumship natural, controlled and protected.

XIII

REMARKABLE MANIFESTATIONS

Lafayette and the Shakers.

APECULIAR and interesting story is on record, told by eye-witnesses of the scene, of a visit made by Marquis de La Fayette to Mother Ann Lee, during the year 1780 or 1781, while holding meetings at Watervliet.

The young French nobleman and patriot, whom Americans have justly regarded with so much gratitude and veneration, was at that time serving General Washington as aide. Young, enthusiastic and sensitive, he has been in later times regarded as an especially finely organized medium for spiritual manifestation and influence. In General Washington he is thought to have found just the strong, serene and beneficent spirit whom his more delicately organized nature needed as a controlling and directing centre.

On some mission for General Washington, he passed with several other officers through Albany, and, hearing of the strange people in the vicinity, he turned aside to Niskeyuna and found the house occupied by Mother Ann and the Elders. Many were coming and going, and the upper room where they were teaching was filled with people, some of whom were violently affected by the physical operations which brought so much notoriety and which, it was claimed, were caused by the Spirit of God acting upon the mind and body of the subject. Abijah Wooster was in particular under strong operations of the Spirit. Lafayette and the

other officers quietly entered the room and stood in the rear,.
looking on with interest at the strange proceedings.

Lafayette was attracted to Abijah and soon passed
quietly through the crowd and, seating himself close to the
affected man, watched him closely, sometimes putting his
hand upon him. Abijah made some remark to the effect
that he seemed to desire this power. Lafayette simply replied, "It is desirable!" and continued his close observation.
Growing restive under the scrutiny, the Shaker brother arose
and left the room, but the young Marquis also arose and followed. Going down a flight of stairs, still followed by his
persevering observer, Abijah made for the barn, where,
seizing a broom, he began to sweep the floor as if that were
his one business. Lafayette quietly watched and waited.
Several other moves were made by the nervous Abijah, in
all of which he was closely followed by the relentless though
silent investigator. At last, in desperation, from a cellar to
which he had vainly fled for rescue, Abijah dashed up a
flight of stairs that led directly to the room from which this
strange chase had started, and re-entered in the presence of
Mother Ann and the Elders.

In all this strange scene, there was no trace of ridicule
or laughter, simply an attitude of absorbed attention, close
observation and thoughtful inquiry. Mother Ann and the
Elders now addressed the young Marquis, whose strikingly
noble, handsome face and figure had of course attracted
attention. His eager questions met full and clear answers.
The nature of the work which was now opening in the new
world, the spiritual meaning of the peculiar movements
which had so absorbed his attention and the requirements
of the new and spiritual life thus unexpectedly presented to
his notice, were all explained to the young nobleman. He
then inquired if he too might not come into the work and
be allowed to share in it. Instead of joyfully accepting this

new proselyte, young, noble, wealthy and influential, as a merely human leader might have done, Mother Ann Lee refused him and told Lafayette that this work was not for him now ; that he was called to a very different life, that hard struggles, fierce battles and much suffering lay before him, but that the time would come when he too might enter into the path from which he must now turn aside to other work, and the interview ended.

It is an interesting fact that when Lafayette died, fifteen days before the news reached America, Shakers at Watervliet were informed by spirit agency of the departure from earth of Lafayette. The story is told by the brother to whom the spirit of Lafayette appeared, telling him the date of his death and asserting that he had seen Mother Ann Lee. The date was verified when the next vessel arrived with news from Europe.

In the manifestations of 1837-44, Lafayette and Washington both were among the spirits who claimed to give expression to their faith and union with the Elders and Spiritual Parents of Believers.

Phenomenal.

A remarkable verification of spiritual communications was a series of questions and answers, of the nature of telegraphic messages, that came through the mediumship of different people, many miles apart, at an interval of several months, the answers preceding the questions. Both questions and answers purported to come from the same spirit — Seth Y. Wells — to whom frequent reference has been made in the previous pages.

The answers came at Mount Lebanon, N. Y., to a sister in the Church Family. She tells her story thus : —

16

"On the evening of March 25th, 1850, soon after I had retired, I heard my name called distinctly. I arose, went to the door but found no person there. Soon after, Seth Y. Wells came to me and invited me to go with him. I reluctantly complied. We went to a telegraph office, where were many spirits whom I knew and more whom I did not know. I was requested to copy all that came over the wires. I did so, though the substance was quite unintelligible to me; for, as nearly as I could understand, it was answers to questions some person had put to some other person; who, or what the questions were I could not tell."

The communications were received and preserved, but were the source of much bewilderment to the Elders who listened to them. Elder Richard Bushnell in particular felt much interest in the dark sayings that were all unexplained.

Five months and eighteen days later, September 7th, in the house of Dr. D. Phelps, in Stratford, Conn., Eldress Antoinette Doolittle and other Shakers were visiting and witnessing the wonderful mediumistic powers of a boy, twelve years of age, son of the gentleman in whose house they were. The medium had never before seen a Shaker, knew nothing whatever of the spirit who came through his organization to Eldress Antoinette, nor had he ever heard of the mysterious answers that had been received at Mount Lebanon, the previous March and almost forgotten.

The spirit of Seth Y. Wells came and addressed the Shaker Eldress. The sentences were rapped out letter by letter. The questions were given and numbered and the answers were referred to by the "control."

In 1838, was prefigured the modern movement for kindly

TREATMENT OF ANIMALS,

IN

A MESSAGE FROM MOTHER ANN LEE.

Nathan Williams, a member of the Mount Lebanon society, in the year 1838, experienced the following vision which he describes in these words: —

"I had been employed for many years taking care of horses; my feelings had been much exercised concerning the abuse of the animal creation; it grieved me very much to see them cruelly treated. I felt that some spiritual communication on this subject might be brought forward that would prevent unnecessary suffering to the poor dumb beasts, created for our use. I felt a burden about this for many years, until in 1838, I received the following, which to my understanding clearly set forth the will of our Heavenly Parents.

"At the usual hour of bedtime I lay down to rest without any particular impressions on my mind. In my sleep, I seemed to find myself in a very large company of Believers in front of our meeting-house. There I saw Jesus and Mother. Their countenances appeared very bright and glorious and their eyes remarkably clear and penetrating. Mother began to speak and said: 'I have come to teach you how to deal with poor, dumb creatures. We will begin at the North Family.' Accordingly, we all went on there together. She then called for Elders, Deacons and Herdsmen. She spoke to them and said she had come to teach them how to deal with poor, dumb creatures, that were made for the use of man and put into his care and mercy. 'Mankind,' said Mother Ann, 'by the fall, have lost the true spirit of mercy and have fallen into a spirit of cruelty and abuse. But God has opened a way for us to obtain the spirit of mercy, and all may gain and keep it if they will.' She then requested them to bring forward all the creatures they owned, which they immediately did. She then stretched out her arm toward the animals, and said: — 'All the creatures that are gathered here in union and bought honestly, belong to the New Creation. They do not belong to the children of this world; they are under my care, and my eye is upon them and I know when they are abused and suffer cruelty. Poor dumb creatures were made for the use of man, and were put under his care and dependent upon his mercy and kindness. They have to go out at all times wherever he directs. They cannot speak for themselves to tell when they are sick or in pain, but they must go at the command of man. Perhaps you may think it a trifling matter to abuse and drive them

beyond their strength; but you will find that it is not. In consequence of such abuses, souls suffer loss, judgment and darkness,
and know not the cause. Believers are called to use creatures and
all things in a righteous manner, and if they do so, they will be
under the blessing of God. How cruel it is to abuse dumb creatures,
in a passion, or through ambition, or in any manner! They who
do it shall be called to account and will have to suffer for it. The
dumb creatures were more upright and more subject, according to
their natures and the order of their creation, than the human.'
This she said with keen severity. Mother Ann then went on to say
that Believers had suffered a great deal of loss for their abuse of
dumb animals. Speaking to Frederick Evans, Mother then asked
him to get some salt, and salt the cattle and sheep, and to be kind
to them and keep them in their order and place — 'Be their master,
and do not have them master you,' she added, 'then you will find
a blessing.'

"Mother then left them and proceeded south to the Church,
where she made the same communication and had the same gift.
She was particular to enjoin upon us 'mercy and kindness to all
things.' She gave the brethren who took care of the beasts express
directions, saying: 'You must have comfortable places for all the
creatures you keep and see that they do not suffer in any way
by cold, hunger or abuse. This gift,' Mother Ann concluded, 'must
go through every family of Believers.' She then proceeded south.
During these communications, I awoke four times. I felt myself
transferred, as it were, out of my own state, in the presence of
Jesus and Mother during the whole night. While awake, my mind
was steadily upon the exhortations of Mother, and when I went
to sleep again, I found myself in the vision just where I was before
I awoke. When I awoke the last time, just at the ringing of the
morning bell, I left the work still going on. Jesus was with Mother
through the whole vision, and although He did not seem to say
much, he was equally engaged in the gift and appeared to support
Mother through the whole."

Prophetic Utterances.

Many prophetic revelations were imparted during these
years of open vision, in the societies of Believers. Among
many utterances by those professing to speak in the name

of ancient prophets, was a series of predictions respecting the lands and races of Asia, Europe, Africa and America, particularly of the United States.

These prophecies have been most remarkably fulfilled in many particulars, and in the march of human events, their continued fulfilment can be plainly traced.

Prophecy of the Telegraph.

A peculiar message was received at the lips of two of the young girl media at Watervliet, when in a trance state. It was in 1837, the year that Morse discovered the magnetic telegraph and before the discovery had been made known. The room where the girls were lying was packed with interested observers, among them the Shaker brother who related the incident. The subjects of spirit influence were apparently traveling in some far distant city of the spirit world and were conversing with Mother Ann. The brother wondered, silently, how they made their bodies talk when they were so far away. Answering his thought, the girls told him, from Mother Ann, that their guardian spirits, who were left in charge of their bodies to keep up the vital action, spoke through them. Then, he wanted to know how the guardian spirit received their message. A brief pause ensued, and then the answer came from Mother Ann through the media, and he was told that she could not explain it to him so that it could be understood very well, but it was by means of a telegraph, which people on earth did not then have, but which they would soon possess.

The apostolic injunction to

"Try the Spirits"

is well heeded by the leaders and protectors of the people in the Shaker homes. At one time an individual appeared at Mount Lebanon burdened with an important message which he declared had been delivered to him by Mother Ann Lee herself. Through his mediumship she desired to speak to all her people and impart to them new light and revelation. Elder Frederick Evans informed the messenger that it was necessary that the revelation be first imparted to the Elders before the flock should receive it. Thereupon, the stranger declared that Mother Ann Lee wished her people to know that the time for the necessity of the virgin life had expired, and she now wished her followers to marry and give in marriage, for this was the law of the higher state to which they had now arrived. He had been entrusted with the mission of delivering this message to all her followers. He was quite taken aback, when the keen-eyed Elder quietly replied that Shakers were not followers of Ann Lee. "What, not followers of Ann Lee? The Shakers? Can I have been misinformed?" "Nay, Shakers do not follow Ann Lee. We are followers of the principles of Ann Lee, but if she has fallen from her light, that is no reason why we should do the same. We follow the truth!" "Well, but Elder, what if Mother Ann should appear to you in person and tell you what she told me?" "We would take her down to the visitors' room," replied the imperturbable Elder, "and try to convert her, and if we could not, we should send her where she belonged." Rock-like fidelity to basic principles with ever broadening knowledge and a spirit of true progress has been the secret of Shaker growth and stability.

Many well authenticated instances might be given of the appearance of the departed in the homes of Believers. One of recent occurrence, as told by the one who received the spirit visitant, is cited. In the spring of 1902,

NO. 19.   CHURCH FAMILY, ENFIELD, N. H.   MARCOMA LAKE.

Sister Caroline Whitcher,

an aged sister, for many years an Eldress and recently a Trustee, passed away at Enfield, N. H. One who was much attached to her had desired a promise that if possible she would make herself manifest. This Sister Caroline promised to do if it were possible. She departed in March. For months the sister watched and waited, but no sign appeared, and she began to give up all hope of ever having any sign of the presence and knowledge of the one who had always kept her word. One night in June she had been taking care of a sister who was sick. Late in the evening, she heard loud talking in a lower hall and, surprised at the unaccustomed sound, went out to see if anything was the matter. Surely, she thought, that is Sister Caroline's voice The voice was saying, "I have just been to see Brother Hiram and try to make him more comfortable in his mind. Poor Brother Hiram! In his best days, he was such a good, faithful brother." The brother referred to was quite aged and feeble.

As the watcher looked down into the hall, she distinctly saw Sister Caroline Whitcher in the hall below, with some one else, who, was not plain. Soon, Sister Caroline was at the top of the stairs although she did not see her ascend. She saw Sister Caroline pass into the room where she herself had been taking care of the sick one, go to the bed and, without speaking, pass her hands over the form of the sick one, as if spreading something over her to make her comfortable.

She then went into another room, looked at a sister there in bed, returned to the room where the watcher stood, went across and looked at a girl asleep and then came back and stood in front of the watcher, who now sat down on the edge of her bed. Sister Caroline came and stood facing her, with hands folded in front, perfectly distinct and as in life. She was in appearance about fifty years, in full tide of vigor and maturity. "Well, I am so glad to see you, Sister Caroline," said the one who had so looked and longed for this visit. "I began to think you had forgotten your promise." "I had not forgotten," was the reply; "I have been with you a great many times and tried to make you feel me, but you never realized my presence."

"I have missed you so, Sister Caroline, and I have looked down the road so many times and said that I wished I could see you coming down the road with your broom." This was an allusion to a habit Sister Caroline had of walking with a broom instead of a cane. The sisters had always laughed a great deal about this habit.

The spirit visitor put up her hand to her mouth in a familiar way and laughed. No sound was heard, but the motion of laughing was very plain.

"Why was it I never saw or felt you?" was asked. "Because you were always too preoccupied." was the answer, "and now, I had to come in the night."

"Now, Sister Caroline, tell me how it is over there!" The visitor laughed again, then in an earnest manner, said: — "Marinda, if I could tell you how it is, so that you could realize what it is like," putting out her hand in a straight, forcible gesture, natural to her, "*why, Massy to me!* you would fly right out of your skin!"

"Well, tell me and let me fly!" was the rejoinder. Instead of gratifying the questioner, the visitor said: "And here I am, keeping you up at night, when you ought to be abed, getting rested for tomorrow's campaign! I go in and out, and go all around among you, trying to make things comfortable and easy," suiting the words to gestures with her hands.

"How is it that we cannot see you, but you can see us? Tell me why that is."

"It is because the veil of the flesh is a covering that hides us from you, but we can see you just the same."

The visitor now appeared about to depart and held out her hand. "I took her hand," said the narrator, "and it was as solid to the touch as ever. I felt it just the same."

She then went out of the house and out of doors, opening and closing the doors in passing, like one in the body. She went down through the garden. "I saw her go by the flower-bed and lean over it as if looking to see if the plants were coming up. Then she passed between the bed and a path and looked at a rosebush which she had always called her rose." She then went toward the Infirmary, and, entering the building, disappeared from sight.

While Shakers have little sympathy or affiliation with those coarser phenomena characterized as spiritism, seldom visit seances and have held themselves aloof from the spiritistic developments of the times, they have watched with full sympathy the unfolding of a purer, higher type of manifestation and recognize with hope and pleasure the gradual evolution of a portion of mankind to whom the world of spirit is a living reality. Mediumistic organizations are numerous among Believers. It may be safe to say that very few have really entered into the faith, but have the gift of mediumship to a greater or less degree.

While rejoicing in the presence and helpful ministrations of ministering spirits, it is recognized that they are busy on their side of life with the work of the Order; work for which, on the earth side, Believers are preparing and in their degree assisting. Seers and sensitives feel today the moving of spirit forces, the concentrating and focussing of spirit power. In the wonderful revealings, the mighty deeds and discoveries of later years, is read preparation on the human side for a new era, a higher, deeper, broader life for humanity, and in the minds and hearts of men and women is read a work of preparation. From the spirit side, it is believed, will come when all things are ready, a new revealing of force and power, a new development of human capabilities. Believing that when man shall have attained his true condition, his long forfeited birthright, — the inheritance of the sons of God, then the life-work of humanity will go on with the manifest cooperation of those beyond the veil, many Shakers look for the time when a consciously recognized influence shall come to man's intellect, spirit and physical being, from the higher spirit spheres. Believing themselves, in their Order, to be in the right connection, on the true spiritual plane, according to their faithful harmonious travel in the spiritual life, they expect that to them will come, when the time is ripe and they are prepared, a new, a broader, higher, deeper life and revelation, a leading into a new development, another cycle of spiritual progress. Not under old conditions or forms suited to a simpler age, but under modes and forms suited to the time, the tone of man's thought, the measure of his experience, knowledge and capabilities.

We cannot better close this special study of spiritualism as experienced by Shakers, than in the words kindly contributed from a book, not in press at the time of the giving, — the inspired and inspiring thought of that world traveler and teacher of the Higher Christian Spiritualism, James M. Peebles, M. D. He says:

"Spiritualism, in its broadest sense, is a knowledge of everything pertaining to the spiritual nature of human beings. It is cosmopolitan, eclectic, uplifting and heaven-inspiring. Spiritualists, being believers in Christ, have the spiritual gifts — the gift of converse with the so-called dead, the gifts of healing, the gift of tongues, the gift of clairvoyantly discerning the spirits and other gifts spoken of in the ancient Scriptures. Spiritualists, believing in the great law of evolution, teach that there is great reward for well-doing and certain punishment for every wrong action; that all the good and divine that is attained here will be retained when entering the spiritual world; that we are building now, by our conduct and characters, our homes in the future state of existence.

"When genuine Spiritualism is generally recognized, and becomes, as it will, the universal religion, — when it becomes actualized and out-wrought through the personal lives of earth's millions, it will no longer be selfishly said, mine, thine, but ours, yours, all who appropriate it for holy uses. This is the resurrection — a spiritually exalted resurrection state in this present life. It is Christ — the living Christ within.

"When Spiritualism in its divinest aspects is practised, our country will be the universe, our home the world, our rest wherever a human heart beats in sympathy with our own, and the highest happiness of each will be altruism. Then, when this Christly Spiritualism abounds, will the soil be as free for all to cultivate as the air to breathe; gardens will blossom and bear fruit for the most humble; and orphans will find homes of tenderest sympathy in all houses. This is Spiritualism, pure, simple and practical. It is the handmaid of Shakerism.

"Christianity as taught by the Christ-Heavens-baptized Jesus and the Shakerism of Mother Ann and the Spiritualism of and from the angel spheres constitute the trinity of the resurrection state. These are saving principles; they must conquer.

"Standing now upon the mount of vision and looking down the long vista of time, I see doubt giving place to faith, and faith giving place to knowledge. I see tyranny dying upon the grassy plains of freedom. I see superstition receding before a rational religion. I see error giving place to the inviting brilliancy of truth, vice to sturdy virtue, bigotry to toleration, sectarian hate to charity, policy to principle, monopoly to cooperation, individualism to communism and grating discords to divinest harmonies. I see before us a new heaven and a new earth. I see again in our midst the living Christ. I see the burning of tares, the gathering in of the golden sheaves and a very Eden of peace, and love and good-will crowning our world and baptizing its every heart with the pentecostal fires of a purified life and a divine beneficence as altruistic as universal. Can you not say with me then, —

I have fed upon manna from heaven above;
Have tasted the fruit of a wonderful love;
I have looked on a land where the sun ever beams,
And talked with the angels in mystical dreams;
And though some visions may die in their birth,
They still leave the trail of their glory on earth?"

XIV

NEW IDEAS

EVERY new era of Divine Manifestation, elevating and spiritualizing the nature of man, has been marked by thought changes as man has been lifted nearer the Deific plane. Into an age of creed and ritual came this baptism of power and love from Deity. Ann Lee and those who accept her teachings follow literally the words of Jesus: — "If any man would come after me, let him deny himself, take up his cross daily and follow me." No other demand or requirement has ever been laid down as a condition of admission to the Gospel work. Pure Christianity, named in the eighteenth century, — Shakerism, calls for a

Baptism, Not a Creed

Among Shakers, creeds and theological dogmas are regarded as of no value save as they have a bearing upon daily life. The search-light of God's Spirit reveals to the individual heart its own condition, the Mediatorial Gift of the Parental Spirit, resting in and upon the Anointed Leader, presents the opportunity to find the Way, whereby each comes to God, finds the Truth, and, in obedience and loving service enters into the Life, among those who have trodden the path of faith, and each in turn, by "doing the Will comes to know of the doctrine."

· In meeting the multitudes whose religious aspirations and confessions of faith were expressed in theological dogma

(253)

and creedal controversy, rather than in the manner pointed out by Jesus in his Sermon on the Mount, the early dispensers of this faith were forced to formulate to some extent their spiritual revelations.   But, while exact and clear in exegesis, earnest and logical in their expounding of what they felt to be an endowment of the Divine Maternal Spirit resting upon Ann Lee, yet, they were careful never to limit that endowment, never to preclude the possibility that a greater than Mother Ann in divine endowments might arise, a more complete incarnation of the Divine Father and Mother than has yet appeared.   No grander declaration of religious freedom has ever been uttered than that penned by Fathers in the Shaker Church, in prefacing two early publications.   Remembering the days in which these words were written, they sound as if echoed from centuries yet to come.   In the Preface of the first published book of songs, we read: "Words are but signs of ideas, and of course must vary as the ideas increase with the increasing work of God.   Therefore these compositions, though they may evince to future Believers the work and worship of God at this day, can be no rule to direct them in that work of God which may be hereafter required of His people. As regeneration is an increasing work, and as there can be no end of the increase of Christ's work and kingdom, so that all His people have to do is to keep in the increasing work of God and unite in whatever changes that increase may lead to, which, to the truly faithful, will be a continual travel from grace to grace and from glory to glory; so that the Spiritual Songs of Believers, as well as every other part of their worship must be according to that degree of grace and glory in which they are given, — no gift or order of God can be binding on Believers for a longer term of time than it can be profitable to their travel in the Gospel."

The revisers of the "Millennial Church" assert that as "the light of Divine Truth is progressive in the Church, and as the preparatory work of salvation and redemption increases on earth, — so the solemn and important truths of the Gospel will continue from time to time to be more clearly manifested to mankind."

Among the revelations to Ann Lee and imparted through her life and teachings, were ideas new to the Christian world. Contrasting these ideas with the formulas of belief cherished and insisted upon by Christians of her day and for one hundred years later, the claim of a special gift of spiritual enlightenment is not extravagant; comparing them with the thought of the Churches of today, it will be apparent that the masses of Christian thinkers are slowly climbing up to the standard set more than a century ago by Ann Lee. Among these great truths are:

God is Dual.

Shakers believe in One God — not three male beings in one, but Father and Mother. And here the Bible reader turns at once to Genesis 1 : 26. "And God said" — in the beginning of creative work, whether by fiat or evolution matters not — "let us make man in our image, after our likeness." Did three masculine beings appear, in contradistinction to every form of life heretofore known? Nay! Verse 27 says: "So God created man in His own image, in the image of God created He him, male and female created He them."

The ancient language of Scripture distinguishes God when power or truth are emphasized as masculine; when love or wisdom is the important attribute, the masculine name has the feminine complement. O Theos agapa estin,

God is Love (feminine). The term Adam is well known
to mean humanity, male and female. How can it "image"
a Being utterly unlike itself? Simple and beautiful becomes
the relation between God and man when the true meaning
is accepted. Hence comes

Equality of Sex.

Woman appears in her rightful place, at once the equal
of man in creation and office at the hand of God. Ann Lee's
followers, 1900 years after Jesus uttered the words, "Neither
do I condemn thee, go and sin no more;" and sent Mary
to tell the Good News of a risen Lord and living Savior,
alone of all humanity, have taught the doctrines that have
placed woman side by side with man, his equal in power,
in office, in influence and in judgment. To Ann Lee may
woman look for the first touch that struck off her chains
and gave her absolute right to her own person. To Ann
Lee may all reformers among women look as the one who
taught and through her followers teaches still perfect freedom, equality and opportunity to woman. The daughters
of Ann Lee, alone among women, rejoice in true freedom,
not alone from the bondage of man's domination, but freedom also from the curse of that desire "to her husband"
by which, through the ages, he has ruled over her.

God the Father-Mother.

Fatherhood and motherhood exist in the complete human
being. One is correlative of the other. The apostle said:
"The invisible things of Him are clearly seen, being understood by the things that He has made, even His eternal
power and Godhead." And as all life in the "things that

He has made" originates, as scientists tell us after most careful experiments, not from spontaneous generation, but always from seed or germinal principle, from a father and mother, so in the highest form of earth life, humanity, in the spiritual realm are souls born of God, the Absolute, Self-existent, infinite Perfection of Being, Father and Mother. The very name God, Almighty, in its original Hebrew form, El Shaddai, reveals the infinite quality. El, God, its first meaning, Strength: Shaddi, the plural whose singular, Shad, signifies a Breast and is feminine.

In the beautiful and lofty strains of that magnificent psalm found in the eighth chapter of Proverbs, "Doth not Wisdom Cry," etc., Wisdom is feminine, and all through the wondrous passage the Mother in Deity utters her voice. In the forty-fifth Psalm, the Queen is pictured standing at the right hand of the King. The King's daughter is described in the beautiful vision that follows. "She is all glorious within, her clothing is of wrought gold. She shall be brought unto the King in raiment of needle work," wrought piece by piece, thread by thread, by her own patient efforts. "The virgins, her companions that follow her, shall be brought unto thee. With gladness and rejoicing shall they be brought. They shall enter into the King's palace. Instead of thy fathers shall be thy children whom thou mayest make princes in all the earth." The spiritual children of Ann Lee, who forsook all fathers of church and creed and covenant, of old relationships of blood, old ties and bonds of idea, custom and conformity, and through supreme toil and anguish came to the heritage of spiritual motherhood, render easy of fulfilment the promise, — "I will make thy name to be remembered in all generations; therefore shall thy people praise thee for ever and ever." We may look up through Nature to God. Our

17

natural father and mother, with their united strength and wisdom, truth and love are types of that Perfect Parentage, our Father and Mother which are in Heaven.

Resurrection.

Mother Ann taught that there is no resurrection of the body. "I am the resurrection and the life," said Jesus Christ. The life of Christ is in itself, by its very nature, a resurrection out of, above, the natural, carnal life. "The time cometh, and now is, when the dead shall hear the voice of the Son of God and they that hear shall live!" The Christian resurrection is a resurrection of the soul from death in sin to a life of righteousness, as judged by the Christian standard, not the revivification of the dead physical body. "Resurrection is unearthing." Whoever hears the voice that calls to the life of the Gospel and obeys does rise from the death of sin and from the natural, carnal plane of existence into the life of regeneration.

Regeneration.

"By following in the footsteps of Jesus and in obedience to his precepts, man may be fully saved from sin in this life and ultimately redeemed from sin and all temptations to evil. The true Christian salvation is from the commission of sin, not merely from the consequences of committed sin. The blood (life) that Jesus gave for man's salvation was his life of consecration and obedience to God's will, an example and winning incentive to follow him. The death Jesus died to aid humanity in the work of salvation was his death to a sinful nature, by which he overcame the world within, thus becoming the great Mediator for our race. 'In that he (Jesus) died, he died unto sin once.' No vicarious atonement. As well have vicarious nutrition and respiration as vicarious obedience. The true cross is not of wood but a life of self-denial, a crucifixion of the lower nature. Every soul must work out its own salvation by practising the self-denials of Jesus, aided by baptisms of the Holy Spirit of Christ, an influx of the saving power of the Divine Creator; salvation is not otherwise found."

Atonement.

As a new, practical and living sense is found in the terms resurrection, regeneration, so do the followers of Mother Ann Lee learn from her a new rendering of this old theologic term, which is at-one-ment. By the life of the resurrection, by following in the steps of Jesus, living out his principles, man works out his salvation and comes to be at one with God.

The Judgment.

"The day of judgment for any soul commences when brought to the Christ tribunal, whether in this or the spirit world. This judgment is initiated by the voluntary confession of all the confessant's sins to God, in the presence of a Christ witness, who likewise has confessed all sin." The end of the world shall come to every soul who is born of the Spirit into the Kingdom of Heaven and by growth and patient effort will eventually attain unto the Kingdom of God.

The Soul's Eternal Progression.

Against the favorite doctrines of her time — Election, Reprobation, Hell Torment for the persons of those decreed by the fiat of Eternal Justice to a lake of fire and brimstone, Ann Lee taught the mercy and love of the Eternal Father-Mother. The souls of all men have endless existence. Every soul is a subject for the spiritual resurrection to eternal life, by obedience to Christian principles; thus, and thus only, may it inherit eternal soul life.

The soul's probation is not limited to this world, but extends to the world of spirits, the future state. Thus only can the justice and mercy of God be manifest to souls who are not privileged to hear the testimony of Christ in this life. Jesus Christ went and preached to the spirits in prison (1 Peter iii, 19, 20). Heaven and hell are conditions and states of the soul. Heaven is opened and entered by repentance of sin and a life of righteousness. Hell is formed by disobedience to God's laws and persistence in sin. Mother Ann taught that whenever and wherever a soul felt true repentance, that moment it turned toward God; that mercy was everlasting; that pure, ministering spirits watched over, led and taught repentant souls, both in this world and in the world beyond, and that the soul's advance was continuous in knowledge and goodness, in spiritual power and glory, toward the perfection of the Divine character.

Christ of the Ages.

To Ann Lee came by revelation of the Spirit and through her was imparted to her followers the teaching that Christ (not Jesus) is the manifestation of Deity,—"Immanuel, God with us." Many times and in different races has the Christ Spirit rested upon, entered into and manifested itself through human beings,—special witnesses. The most complete and all-embracing endowment of the manifesting Spirit of God rested upon Jesus of Nazareth. Jesus was a Jew, born of human parents. Struggling with a nature like our own, "tempted in all points like as we are," he conquered by self-control and daily cross-bearing, as we must conquer our natures, "learning obe-

NO. 20.   ELDER ABRAHAM PERKINS.

dience by the things that he suffered." When the multitudes came to John in the wilderness, confessing their sins, and were baptized of him in Jordan unto repentance, Jesus came with the rest. John recognized the superior sanctity of his character and refused to baptize him, as himself unworthy of so sacred a privilege. The short dialogue between them was ended by the word of Jesus: "Suffer it to be so now, for thus it becometh us to fulfill all righteousness." After receiving at the hands of John, the appointed witness, the sign of spiritual cleansing in the baptism with water, immediately followed the descent upon him of the Christ Spirit, which, in the form of a dove, was apparent to John. Then came the consecrating voice: "This is my beloved son, in whom I am well pleased, hear ye him." Jesus the man had become Jesus Christ the Anointed, and through the rest of his life his works were those of the loving, pitying, Heavenly Father. Jesus Christ expresses to man the nature and character of God the Father. Jesus lived a pure life, uncontaminated by sensuality, by any lust of flesh or pride of life. His followers gave up all, shared all things in common, lived in peace, without wars or fightings, and were known by their great love for one another.

The Coming of Anti-Christ.

Jesus Christ and his immediate followers foretold a time when there would be a great falling away, when heresies and divisions would creep in among the disciples. That time soon came. Constantine, the first Christian emperor, made the church a channel for war and conquest. Simplicity and purity were lost and all traces of the early faith as taught by Jesus disappeared. One dogma after another was propounded and adopted by councils of priests, as opposed to the simple truth and pure love of the early church as light is opposed to darkness; until Jesus would not have known those who claimed his name, had he come to earth, nor would he have been recognized by them. Christ has not been recognized when He has come, wherever some strong voice has taken up the word of truth, bravely and simply, uttering it out of a loyal heart untrammeled by priest or book.

Christ Revealed in Woman.

Jesus Christ not only foretold the falling away, the coming of antichrist, he also foretold a reappearing, a coming again to gather and save. In his last interviews with his disciples he uttered some mysterious words, over which theological quibbling has spent itself in vain. At the end of the last opening of the heavens of inspiration, before the darkness of antichristian night settled down upon a world that had once trembled to the angel chorus, there comes a beautiful vision — a vision of a Lamb slain from the foundation of the world, of a Being wondrous in brightness and glory, resplendent as the sun. There is a Bridegroom and a Bride, and the two utter a heavenly harmony, whose opening chord was the song on Bethlehem's hills. "The Spirit and the Bride say Come!" Come! to all humanity! Come to the rest, the feast, the home, the harmony! Come to purity, truth and love! Come to fruition, redemption, perfection!

Not to the wise nor prudent of this world came the word of revelation, but to the child in simple trust with heart of faith. The apocalypse of mystery that descended from cloud to sea at Patmos opened its meanings, when to the child spirit of Ann Lee came the call of God. We have watched her follow that call. We have seen her wrestlings and conflicts as flesh strove with spirit, as the

cross, heavy and death bringing, was taken bravely up.
We have watched her as she subdued and slew the weakness and sin of her lower nature. We have heard her
cries and moans of agony as the weight of a world's woe
pressed upon her heart. We have watched her in prison,
every nerve throbbing with the torture of that forsaken,
narow cell, where for fourteen days she was nourished by
God's gift, sustained by His power. We have seen her in
the prison cell in Manchester, baptized with the Christ
Spirit. From that time she never faltered in her calm assurance of knowledge that to her had been given the revelation of the Maternal Spirit of God.

Ann Lee always acknowledged Jesus Christ as her Lord
and Savior, the Head of the Church; but, when the two
anointed leaders, before whom she had confessed her sins
and whom she had obeyed as her spiritual guides, recognized in her a superior endowment of Divine Maternity,
and with the rest of the little circle acknowledged her as
now their Spiritual Mother, she did not refuse the recognition.

Once, in 1781, a large assembly of Believers were
gathered at Watervliet, among them Joseph Meacham, Calvin Harlow and three of the Goodriches. Mother Ann reproved the people sharply for their unbelief. Especially
the men and brethren, "I upbraid you," she said. She
spoke of the unbelieving Jews in the time of Jesus, and
continued: "Even his own disciples after he arose from
the dead, though he had often told them that he should
rise on the third day, believed it not. They would not
believe that he had risen because he had appeared first to
a woman. So great was their unbelief that the words of
Mary seemed to them like idle tales! His appearing first
to a woman showed that his second appearing would be
in a woman." So great was the power of the Spirit of

God in which she spoke that many could not stay in her presence. After this she sang with great joy and love, gathering the people about her. "Her countenance was beautiful and glorious," says one who was of the company.

Prophecy and Parable.

When long buried cities in Assyrian plains are unearthed by pick and shovel, crumbling brick answers to brick. When parts fit and the inscription reads connectedly, the explorer knows that the parts belong together. When letter fits and answers to its type, we read the thought inscribed. When type and antitype answer to each other, we read God's thought.

The advent and work of Jesus is accepted as divine, because foretold by ancient prophets, typified by many symbols, recognized by men and women under inspiration in his own day; because tested by works accomplished and witnessed to by persecutions suffered; and because the innate force and meaning, the logical coherence, the spirit and tenor of that life and mission find response, conviction and correlation in the mind that thoughtfully studies them, and an ever approximating harmony of imitation in heart and life by those that faithfully and lovingly adopt and follow them.

The Mother Spirit making its advent in Ann Lee receives the same tests. This appearance, long foretold, was necessary and logical. The typical representations were numerous and apt. She was recognized and accepted by many truth seekers of her time, and those who accepted her advanced in the life of the spirit to a higher plane than they had before attained. All who received her received power to conquer self and sin, and to stand erect in a regenerate nature. These have witnessed to her truth.

Her works are attesting witnesses to her divine endowment and her measure of suffering and persecution was filled. The life and mission of Ann Lee bear their own innate stamp of genuineness, and the correspondence to it of the lives touched and molded by it is as complete as in the case of her predecessor, Jesus.

One has well said: "If the perfected order demands the union of man and woman in earthly relations, it must equally demand the union of the two in spiritual relations." In Jeremiah 23:6 is a vision of a far off time when, "Behold, the days come, saith the Lord, that I will raise up to David a Righteous Branch, and a King shall reign and prosper and shall execute judgment and justice in the earth. In his days Judah shall be saved and Israel shall dwell safely, and this is the name by which he shall be called, the Lord our Righteousness." In 33:15, 16, Jeremiah also says: "Behold, the days come, saith the Lord, that I will perform that good thing which I have promised unto the house of Israel and to the house of Judah.' 'In those days and at that time will I cause the Branch of Righteousness to grow up unto David; and he shall execute judgment and righteousness in the land. In those days Judah shall be saved and Jerusalem shall dwell safely, and this is the name by which she shall be called, The Lord our Righteousness." Closely does one answer to the other, both counterparts of one great truth. In the eleventh verse of the same visional chapter 33, is heard "the voice of joy and the voice of gladness, the voice of the bridegroom and the voice of the bride, the voice of them that shall say, Praise the Lord of Hosts." The whole picture glows with the light of redemption, when both shall have done their work, accomplished their mission. A logical thinker among Ann Lee's followers writes thus: "If a man can become a Son of God, there can be no reason why a woman cannot become a daughter of God; and if the Spirit of God descending from heaven and resting upon a man makes him a Christ, then the Spirit of God descending from heaven and resting upon a woman will make her a Christ. That woman should have been driven from her legitimate position by the dominant spirit of man is not at all strange, for the race to a large extent has considered that might is right in all the affairs of life."

The mission of the daughter of God was seen by the prophet Micah, who exclaimed, "Arise and thresh, O daughter of Zion, for I will make thine horn iron and thy hoofs brass; and thou shalt beat in pieces many people; and I will consecrate their gain unto the Lord, and their substance unto the Lord of the whole earth." In Israel's history, the era of conquest and of progress toward full occupancy of the Promised Land, begun and carried on with success for a time by Joshua, was checked and the work ended in defeat at the hands of their enemies, in disaster and enslavement, — "Until that I, Deborah, arose a Mother in Israel!" Then the captivity was turned, rescue and salvation were attained at the hand of a woman, who judged the people in prosperity for twenty years. There hardly needs an explanation of the type, so clear is the spiritual meaning beneath the course of historic events. Again, Jeremiah says: "Behold the Lord hath created a new thing in the earth, A woman hath compassed a man." In the strength and power of the spiritual baptism of which Ann Lee was the recipient and the agent of communication to others, woman did and does compass man; and Ann Lee was able through the endowment of the Christ Spirit to compass the wise and learned of the men of her time.

Jesus referred to the appearance of the Christ in a woman. The time had not come for explanation and his most profound and vital teachings always wore the dress of the parable. In the parable of the wedding feast and again in the story of the virgins, wise and foolish, always read as the prefiguring of his coming again, bridegroom and guests are easily accounted for, but theologians have failed satisfactorily to explain the bride. Who is she? The symbolism is remarkably apt and beautiful when the natural rendering is accepted.

The disciple who stood nearest of all to the heart of Jesus, in the vision of the last days of his life that rounded out the first Christian century, heard the sound of a great multitude, as the voice of many waters, singing, "Let us be glad and rejoice and give honor to him; for the marriage of the Lamb is come, and his wife hath made herself ready. And to her was granted that she should be arrayed in fine linen clean and white, for the fine linen is the righteousness of saints," not a virtue imputed to them that they had not earned, but a character wrought from within, like the foliage, blossoms and fruit that clothe a tree.

Type and Symbol.

With Nature as an expression of spirit, natural form as a type of spiritual reality, man's thought, from the infancy of intellectual development, has been familiar. When from the recorded history, philosophy, poetry and vision, for 4000 years, of a single race, — a race possessed of a special sense of God and religion, — had crystallized a library, a Biblos or Book, later peoples easily learned to reverence its pages as bearing, through Divine control of human agents, the tracery of God's thought and will. But has inspiration ceased? Why should all flow of light and revelation from heaven and from God cease at the say so of a conclave of priests, some hundreds of years since? Why may not inspiration still thrill the nerve centres and vibrate through the brain tissues of mankind? Ann Lee declared it did, and her followers today rejoice in the knowledge that it does, while the world at large is coming to recognize the same truth. No less, on that account, but rather more vital to mankind is the record of past inspirations; and the pages of the Hebrew scriptures are loved, their truths fed upon, their principles taken by all of Ann Lee's followers as the guiding star, the lamp to the feet, the light upon the path of everyday life.

Down the long course of revealed and recorded truth, gleam at intervals symbolic expressions of a deep, underlying principle, whose import is seldom grasped by Christian thinkers. As the plain, matter of fact statement of duality, imaged in man's two-fold being and found in all the lower orders of animal, vegetable and even mineral creation, escaped all eyes sealed by the church dogma of the trinity, so this duplex, symbolic language has gone unexplained. When, by God's direction, Israel framed its ark and mercy seat, two cherubim, beaten from one piece of gold, faced each other, guarding beneath their outstretched, meeting wings the sacred fire of Deific Presence. This two-fold symbol is very suggestive; lower and higher intelligences, human-angelic forms, part corresponding to part, two yet one, facing each other, thus typifying union, guarding the Holy Presence, the Mystery of Redemption. "There I will meet with thee, and I will commune with thee, from between the two cherubim." The covenant between God and man, preserved within the sacred ark, beneath those guardian forms, was written on two tables, the Mercy Seat prefiguring the earthly throne of judgment as revealed in the Visible Order of the Church established under Ann. Again, the call to worship, the signal for sacrifice, for fast and feast and Sabbath rest, — for every event that summoned man to appear in body or spirit before God, was given on two trumpets fashioned from one piece of silver, that the two clarion voices "may be to you for a memorial before your God." The very cloud that followed or led them on their long wilderness journey had a two-fold aspect, dark or bright as day succeeded night.

Most suggestive of the many symbolisms is that given in vision to the prophet Zechariah, recorded in chapter four. The vision related to the building of the second temple by Joshua and Zerubbabel, the two temples prefiguring two appearances of Christ. "The angel that talked with me said unto me, What seest thou? And I said, I have looked, and behold, a candle-stick all of gold, with a bowl upon the top of it, and his seven lamps which are upon the top thereof. And two olive trees by it, one upon the right side of the bowl and one upon the left side thereof." Naturally, the prophet inquired the meaning of the vision, but received no answer, except more enigmas. "This is the word of the Lord unto Zerubbabel,—Not by might, nor by power, but by my spirit, saith the Lord of Hosts." "The seven lamps are the eyes and spirits of the Lord that run to and fro through the whole earth." But the prophet asks further, "What are these two olive trees upon the right side of the candle-stick and upon the left side thereof?" No answer was given to this, and again came the question, "What are these two olive branches which through the two golden pipes empty the golden oil out of themselves?" The reply was a suggestive one: "These are the two Anointed Ones that stand by the Lord of the whole earth." Who are these Anointed Ones? By the believer in a dual God, they are recognized as the Christ, whose two-fold nature, embodied in the human tabernacles of Jesus and

Ann, is represented in the two olive branches. The two golden pipes are realized in the living, Visible Order, man and woman, conveying today the vital, continuous gift of the Christ Spirit to the bowls — the body of the Church, or Believers — through whom the light is revealed. The Hebrew original preserves even in the lamps and their pipes the dual idea; the expression is seven, seven. Truly it was "not by might nor by power, but by the spirit of the Lord," that the work of redemption, "my work, my strange work," as described by another prophet, was accomplished.

In verses six to ten, we read: "Who art thou, O great mountain before Zerubbabel? Thou shalt become a plain, and he shall bring forth the headstone thereof with shoutings, crying, Grace, Grace, unto it. The hands of Zerubbabel have laid the foundations of this house, his hands shall also finish it, and thou shalt know that the Lord of Hosts hath sent me unto you. For who hath despised the day of small things," signifying Ann Lee as founder of the second temple of the Christ Spirit on earth. Hebrew scholars, among them Professor George Bush, formerly of Columbia College, New York, have translated verse seven thus: "And he shall bring forth the cap stone whose name is Ann,— Ann Lee." Another rendering, by Levi David, a German Jew, who lived and died in the Shaker Order, reads: "She shall bring forth a headstone which shall be called Ann, — Ann Lee." The Greek word rendered Grace, and meaning grace, beauty, kindness, etc., is in form Anna, from which we have our proper names, Anna and Hannah. The Hebrew expression rendered "to it" is Lê. A coincidence startling, to say the least, when the thoughtful mind compares the work of the carpenter's son of Judea with that of the blacksmith's daughter of England, in the building of the spiritual temples first and second.

The following is the rendering of the same by **Prof.**
Bush, of Columbia College, New York City:

נֵיזדכבללנוישר בְּזִיעַ הָה הָהָר הַקָּרוּכ

הָרֵרר לָהָ הרצִיא אכרר אש וישר עַלְךָ

MI ATTAUH HAUR CAUDOL LIPNA ZERUBBABEL
LEMISHOR HOTSIA EBEN ROSH TESHUA
ANN, ANN LEE.

What art thou great Mountain in the presence of Him who was
sown in Babylon? Thou art changed into a plain.
And he shall bring forth the Cap Stone whose name is
Ann Ann Lee.

Grace Grace towards her.

Breaking the Seals.

The Apocalypse of John has stood the mystery of the
church, the riddle of the Christian age. Scholars and com-
mentators are dumb before it, their shrewdest guesses barren of explanation. It has been regarded as almost a forbidden book, many having the feeling that it was worse than
useless to try to understand it and almost wrong to peer
into mysteries so carefully hidden from the prying human
intellect.

But to the Believer in the Christ manifestation in woman,
the mysteries stand revealed. Mystery lies beyond, never behind human experience. Prophecies hard to be understood
until after the occurrence of the events foretold are then
clear and plain. Jewish Rabbins were poring over the sacred
texts that presaged the coming of the Messiah, until, behold!
their Messiah stood in their very midst and they knew him
not, but rubbing their book-blinded eyes, blinking in the rays
of His Divine light, they called him blasphemer and wine-

bibber, and picked up stones to kill him. He said that when he came again it would be as a thief in the night, and so it was. The Revelation of St. John contained the prophecy of that coming in picture language, not to be understood until after the events had occurred. While Christians the world over were studying texts and watching the skies for the coming of the Son of Man, Lo! "One like unto the Son of Man" appeared; not the Son, because the Christ Spirit had come to a woman, a humble factory girl, as once had come the Christ Spirit to a carpenter's son. To Believers, Revelation is a book of joy and comfort, its picture language rich with suggestion and aglow with truth; for Believers are living the life therein portrayed. Its mysteries lie behind, having become the background of experience.

A remarkable and original explanation of the types and figures in this book was given, under inspiration, by Elder Frederick W. Evans, of Mount Lebanon, and may be found in the pages of his Autobiography.

To the Believer, the Sealed Book contains the "Plan of Human Redemption and Resurrection." In Chapter one are seen again the seven golden candle-sticks that Zechariah saw and one like unto the Son of Man, — the Christ Spirit. "He cometh with clouds," not vaporous masses in the atmosphere, but multitudes of witnesses, the redeemed, who come with him, for they belong to him. The seven churches of Asia typified, as complete in all the elements of good and evil, seven great churchal eras of Christian history.

The seven thunders named in chapter ten are seven cycles of travail of the Millenial or Resurrection Church. The other sevens of the Revelator,— seals, vials, plagues and trumpets, are the seven cycles of travail of the great anti-Christian world; — the "history of the church and state governments, of generative, fighting, poverty-creating governments which have the poor always with them to make

NO. 21. SABBATHDAY LAKE, ME. MEETING HOUSE AND DWELLING HOUSE.

soldiers out of, and with the soldiers filling the earth with violence."

Then was seen the angel that stood upon sea and earth and lifting up his hand to heaven swear, by Him that created heaven and earth and sea, that time should be no longer. To the arisen in Christ, time is no more. Already, they stand in the Resurrection and in Eternal Life. Again, "I saw a new heaven and a new earth, for the first heaven and the first earth had passed away, and there was no more sea." Not the globe with its atmosphere is meant, but the earthly, worldly life. Eternal life on earth had begun.

We read of the "holy city," that is, the Pentecostal Church, with its seven foundation pillars, — seven principles of revelation, — overpowered, trodden under foot, for forty-two months or 1260 days, a day counting as a year in this mystical language. Power should be given to "my two witnesses;" again they appear and the answer to Zechariah's question: "These are the two olive trees and the two candlesticks standing before the God of the earth." These witnesses are scattered communities and individual Christians, who should preserve the faith, — always two, man and woman, through the ages of religious darkness.

Again there appears a great wonder in heaven, "a woman, clothed with the sun and with the moon under her feet and upon her head a crown of twelve stars. In this is seen the Christ Order. A true Christian man, Jesus, is born of the Spirit; the Dragon — the animal nature, existing in earthly governments as in individuals — smote the Shepherd and the sheep were scattered. The Pentecostal Church was destroyed. The first Christian, Jesus, was caught up to God in the spirit world, and there, during the 1260 days, preached the faith and founded the Christian Church, the true Shaker Church, in the heavens.

18

Again the story goes on: "To the woman were given two wings of a great eagle, that she might fly into the wilderness, into her place, where she is nourished for a time and times and half a time from the face of the serpent." The woman, that is, the Christ Order as embodied in Ann Lee, was persecuted by the English government of church and state, and she fled in a ship which, as with eagle's wings, wafted her to a wilderness, where, for a time and times and half a time, three and a half years, she was nourished, secure from the Dragon's power. But, "the serpent cast out of his mouth water as a flood after the woman, that he might cause her to be carried away of the flood." Out of the Dragon's mouth came a continuous flood of falsehood, slander and misrepresentation, sufficient, had the work been of humanity alone, to have swept away her reputation, influence and usefulness. But, "the earth helped the woman; the earth opened her mouth and swallowed up the flood;" and, over and over, in the story of that life, did the counsel of the wicked come to naught, and the torrent of man's wrath and the floods of falsehood were swallowed by the earth — vanished from sight.

The court of the temple was to be trodden under foot of the Gentiles for forty-two months. The Pentecostal Church was to be lost beneath the tread of antichristian hordes for forty-two months of years. Also the two witnesses — men and women of the true Christ Order, Shakers, — were to prophesy for 1260 days in sackcloth, in darkness and mourning. These witnesses, men and women, raised up at different times and from different races, have always borne testimony to the purity of the Primitive Church, to the precepts and example of Jesus Christ, testifying against the sins and corruptions of the church of their day; and always have they been persecuted and slain by the Dragon — the ecclesiastical power of their age.

Then comes the vision of the work of God in the spirit world. The Jewish Christian Church, brought up out of great tribulation, have washed their robes and made them white by working out a pure, virgin character. "And lo! a Lamb stood on Mount Zion and with him 144,000, having his Father's name written in their foreheads." "And they sang a new song — for they are virgins." "They follow the Lamb whithersoever he goeth," that is, they live as Jesus lived, redeemed in their life from among men. They form the glorified Jewish Christian Church in the spirit world.

At length appeared the white cloud, a cloud of witnesses, of human souls, and One sat on the cloud, like unto the Son of Man, on her head a crown and in her hand a sickle. She is told, —"Thrust in thy sickle and reap, for the harvest of the earth is ripe;" and the earth — those who were ready to obey the Gospel — were reaped, gathered from their carnal, fallen natures. This work of reaping has been going on for one hundred and thirty-eight years and is still in progress. Not a multitude of human beings caught up by an attraction that overcomes gravity and ascending into the atmosphere, but souls caught by the attraction of truth and gathered by a deep conviction of the need of a salvation that saves from sin. These are reaped by the sickle of truth, in the hands of Her whom the great world knoweth not, and are gathered into the garner of salvation from the sins of nature and the worldly life.

Times and Seasons.

The rise of the Beast — the coming into power of the Papacy — is placed by ecclesiastical history about 457 A. D. From this time the Holy City — the Pentecostal Church — was trodden under foot for forty-two months. The temple of Christianity was defiled, the "abomination of desolation" was set up. The two witnesses, faithful men and women of the Christ Order, were to preach in sackcloth for 1260 days. Adding 1260 to 457 gives 1717; adding 1278, the forty-two months, three and a half years, gives 1735. These dates mark the epoch when ecclesiastical tyranny began to wane. Civil Government no longer claimed the right to put to death for religious principles, nor had the priesthood any legal power to prevent others from the promulgation of their faith.

The prophet Daniel completes the calculation. In the book of Daniel, chapter eight, verses thirteen and fourteen, we are told that the sanctuary was to be trodden under foot for 2300 days and then the sanctuary was to be cleansed. The date of his prophecy was 553 B. C. 2300 added to 553 B. C. gives 1747 A. D. In another vision, recorded in the closing chapter, the man clothed in linen said: "Go thou thy way, Daniel, for the words are closed up and sealed till the time of the end. Many shall be purified and made white and tried, but the wicked shall do wickedly, and none of the wicked shall understand, but the wise shall understand. And from the time that the daily sacrifice shall be taken away and the abomination that maketh desolate shall be set up, there shall be 1290 days." The single expression that closes this vison is, — "Blessed is he that waiteth and cometh to the 1335 days." Adding 1290 to 457 gives 1747, confirming the former vision. This marks the time when the light of divine truth began to increase and the sanctuary to be cleansed by the purifying work of the Spirit, the time when the work of the "Shaking Quakers" began in England. Adding to 457 the number 1335 gives 1792, the exact date when the Shaker Church had become fully established in Gospel Order and Government. The "daily sacrifice," that of the daily cross, had been "taken away," when the professed followers of Jesus ceased to bear that cross in daily following the steps of Jesus in virgin purity. The "abomination of desolation" was then set up in the first Christian temple, nor could the sanctuary be cleansed until the judgment should sit to take away the dominion of the Beast, destroy the control of the animal, carnal nature. This is done in the Order of confessing and forsaking sin. Hereby is the dominion of the Beast taken away from individuals, who are thenceforth temples of the living God. Blessed, in truth, were they who came to the end of the 1335 days.

Thus do the ancient scriptures, their prophecy, their vision, their symbolism and their prophetic dates of times and seasons harmonize with what men and women, her contemporaries, saw and felt of the coming of the Christ in Mother Ann Lee, the setting up of the Kingdom and the descent of the New Jerusalem, under her endowment with the Christ Spirit.

XV

THE KINGDOM OF HEAVEN

A S the Gospel of Christ, revealed in the life and teachings of Mother Ann Lee, is based on the truth of an Eternal Father-Mother, those born of the Spirit are of one family, brothers and sisters, children of Divine Parentage. The words of Jesus are no more strange, but natural, necessary and beautiful, with the beauty and love of the eternal home: "Who is my mother and who are my brethren? Whoso doeth the will of my Father which is in heaven, the same is my brother and sister and mother;" and again, "If any man come to me, and hateth not his father and mother and wife and children, and brethren and sisters, yea, and his own life also, he cannot be my disciple. And whosoever does not bear his cross and come after me cannot be my disciple." The generative life of man and all the works, thoughts, passions and feelings thereof are to be hated, that is, turned from, once and forever. Whatever has grown out of the generative or natural life, its relationships, ties and associations, are to be broken and the new, spiritual life is to be adopted.

Husbands and wives were to cease living under natural marriage conditions. They were henceforth brother and sister in Christ. A complete separation was to be made from the old, natural way of living and thinking. Believers well might use the expressive term, "taking up a full cross against the flesh." Before Believers were gathered into Gospel Order in community homes, and for a long time

after for those who did not enter into communities, Shakers
continued to live in the family relation, but they were required to follow a life of absolute continence, according to
the law of Christ. "You must forsake the marriage of the
flesh," said Mother Ann, "to partake of the marriage of the
Lamb, which is to be united to Christ, or joined to the Lord
in one spirit." After the community life was fully adopted,
children of believing parents became children of the society
and were subject to the control of the appointed leaders.

This renouncing of old relationships and voluntarily
taking up the new and spiritual relationships, formed the
basis of the charge against the Shakers of breaking up families. Yet they never violently did this, often sending believing children back to unbelieving parents, wives to husbands, while the utmost care was taken to win by faithful
humility in loving service the hearts of natural kindred to
the life of faith. Mother Ann and the Elders taught that
the work of salvation was to be accomplished by families,
and if but one out of a family connection were saved by the
Gospel, that one must strive and labor for all his kindred.
Nevertheless, the foundation stone of the structure was the
entering into a spiritual family and forgetting, casting aside
as of the old earth and heavens, the natural ties of kindred.

At Mount Lebanon, over fifty years ago, there entered
the Order a young girl from a Quaker home of wealth,
culture and refinement. Devotedly attached to her parents,
brothers and sisters, she sacrificed home and friends for her
faith. She had in her possession two fine Daguerreotypes
of father and mother. These likenesses, then a new thing
in the world, had the cash value of $100. Their heart value,
to a young girl leaving home forever, may be imagined.
Yet this girl, in her enthusiasm of obedience to a principle,
thrust these pictures into the fire. It was a voluntary sacrifice, no one had thought of such an act. She said nothing

of it, but her Eldress, hearing incidentally of the sacrifice, said to her: "Why, A——, you need not have burned them; I would have kept them for you." "O," was the reply, "I did not wish to burden you with them!" "The crackle of them in the flames was music to me," she said a half century later. What wonder that Shakerism has defied the storms of persecution and the enervating, relaxing influences of modern times, when of such stuff has been made up the leadership and the rank and file, down to the present day?

With the passing of the years and the change of attitude of outside Christians, the absolute crucifixion of all natural ties and affections is no longer deemed necessary. While a spiritual separation to the Gospel work and the union of life and heart to the spiritual family is essential, such complete absolution from all the bonds of natural kinship as was once inculcated is no longer demanded. The duty of a child to an aged or feeble parent is recognized, and the union of Ministry and Elders is freely given to association and communication with relatives and friends, providing that it does not tend to distract the mind and divert the purpose from the spiritual calling upon which one has entered.

The promise of Jesus Christ in the first Christian dispensation was renewed and has been remarkably fulfilled under the second: "There is no man that hath left house, or brethren, or sisters, or father, or mother, or wife, or children, or lands, for my sake and the Gospel's, but he shall receive an hundred fold, now in this time, houses, and brethren, and sisters, and fathers, and mothers, and children, and lands, with persecutions, and in the world to come eternal life." An expounder of the early time was wont to call attention to the fact that Jesus promised an hundred fold of every relation but the wife. No wife was promised under the Gospel. Persecutions, he said, were given instead. Since this latest coming of the Christ Spirit, Christians of the Shaker Order pray no more, "Thy Kingdom come." It has come, and their effort and prayer is that it may increase to its fullness in each individual. As many as are called are made welcome, helped to find the new life and gathered into the warm heart of the family of Christ.

Two Orders. Celibacy.

Shakers have been charged with denouncing marriage, and the trite old question is sometimes raised, "What would become of the world if all were to become Shakers?" In view of the condition of a good part of the people in it, the thought has sometimes suggested itself that it might not be a bad idea to let the world run out. But there is not the least danger of the world's population failing from religious motives, nor is there any fear that all mankind will become Shakers in this life. The greater part could not, for they are not on the plane to hear the call of the Spirit. "Not by might, nor by power, but by my Spirit," is the prepared soul gathered from the world into the garners of the Lord.

Humanity exists under two distinct orders and has so existed from the earliest times. Man broke God's inborn rule of continence and thereby lost God's gift of natural, orderly reproduction, in holiness and purity, under law. The act of generation became a lawless violation of the Holy of Holies in the temple of the human. Lust destroyed pure, heaven-born Love, and the whole creation groaneth and travaileth together in sin, passion and despair. War, brutality and crime resulted. But in darkest times, righteous men and women have made the law of God their guide and children of light have been born to bear witness to righteousness and purity. Such were Enoch and Noah, and many more, unmentioned in the annals of their race.

There has also been an order of virgin souls, celibates, who have sought and lived the life of continence and purity. To quote from a Shaker tract on this theme:

"There is a law in our nature responding to a celibate, a virgin life. It has cropped out in all ages from the earliest historic times.

"The Shakers of America are living respondents to the law that absolute purity of body and spirit is an essential preliminary to their happiness — the manifestation and growth of the life of God in the soul. They believe that all may enter into a heavenly state by cultivating heavenly principles, and that it is their mission to keep an open door for all who live as Jesus did and walk as He did walk. He was the first born of many brethren. Having these abundant evidences in view, we say that Shakerism is not founded upon a lie, but on that law which when operative has in all ages brought forth the manifestation of God in humanity. On this rock and with such materials, will Christ — the Elder Brother — found and build His Church, and the gates of hell will not prevail against it. And that the world may not run itself out by its own doings before the appointed time, we kindly advise all to draw a little nearer to the example of the Shakers, so that their offspring may not die off prematurely, and that a measure of the blessing of God, bodily health, peace and prosperity may be theirs."

Celibacy Taught by Jesus and the Apostles.

Jesus and the apostles taught, both by precept and example, that the virgin life, for those "able to bear it," was the foundation of a purer godliness than could be attained in marriage, "because she that is married careth for the things of this world how she may please her husband, and he that is married careth for the things of the world how he may please his wife, but the unmarried woman careth for the things of the Lord that she may be holy both in body and spirit, and he that is unmarried careth for the things that belong to the Lord how he may please the Lord."

In the shrewd and politic answer of Jesus to the logical snare laid for him by the wily Sadducees, he laid down the principle that was to be fully revealed in the second Christian dispensation: "Do ye not therefore greatly err, because ye know not the Scriptures neither the power of God? For when they shall rise from the dead they neither marry nor are given in marriage, but are as the angels which are in heaven. And as touching the dead that they rise, have ye not read in the book of Moses, how in the bush God spake unto him, saying, I am the God of Abraham, and the God of Isaac, and the God of Jacob? He is not the God of the dead but of the living; ye do therefore greatly err." Always the teaching of the apostles was that if a man or woman were unable to live the life of chastity, to marry and live according to the law given by Moses, in orderly and righteous manner. It was not, however, the highest type of Christian living.

Mother Ann received by revelation the same truths shadowed forth in earlier dispensations. Now, in the fullness of time, the veil has been withdrawn from the face of nature; henceforth, those who would live the pure Christ life, as Jesus lived it, must crucify in the flesh the natural life of generation. That all are not called to this life is admitted; but that any can live and walk as Jesus did, other than by crucifying the lower nature and leading the virgin life, is denied.

When one has come to the end of the world in himself or herself, is ready to abandon all self-seeking, pride, lust and sin of every kind, and will turn to the new life with its foundation principles of purity, peace, non-resistance and separation from the world, then the seeker may graduate from the old to the New Order, and the way of entrance lies through,

"The Open Door."

"Behold I have set before thee an open door and no man can shut it." The followers of Ann Lee, Believers in the coming of the Maternal Spirit of Christ in woman, have one unique, strangely sweet and wonderfully effective custom. It is called the "Yearly Sacrifice;" sometimes it is also the "Christmas Gift." On the Saturday evening before the Sabbath that is to be the "Day of Sacrifice," the spiritual heads of each family, at the hour of worship, in a few solemn, tender words, explain the meaning and importance of the gift, call on all to enter heartily into its humiliations and its blessings, and, charging all to withdraw quietly in a silence that shall leave each soul alone with its God, dismiss the brethren and sisters to rest.

Sabbath morning comes to a strangely quiet house. Cheery good-mornings fall softly, as when a sacred messenger is in the home; footfalls are stilled, movements restrained and hushed; merry chatter is unheard. Brethren and sisters, and even the children come to the morning meal in a strange quiet; not sadness, but a hush, as when, in Israel's camp, the silver trumpets had sounded and the people staid in their tents. Morning duties performed, all retire to their rooms, and each withdraws into his or her own soul, searching the heart, scanning the life of the months past. Quietly, one by one, a summons comes to each. Softly, the one called goes to the door of the One best loved, most revered, most trusted, tried and true of all earth's friends. The latch is lifted and the soul stands before the altar. In the tender, searching look of love, it sees the Mediator between the tempted, struggling human soul and God. Always it is one who has been through and through again the searching, testing fires of Divine wrath and love, — wrath against sin, love for the sinner.

Always it is one chosen, appointed by the Divine Spirit, bearing the gifts of the anointing; always of the same sex as the one who comes.

How many times has the Sabbath light touched softly the silvered head of a Father, of a Mother, through whose gift has come.the life of the Spirit, through whom, by soul travail so intense as to rack the body and drain nerve force, has come to the soul the power to arise from old ways and deeds, from life-long habit chains; power to shake off corruption, lust, greed, appetite, selfishness; through whom has come freedom, forgiveness, love, hope, peace! The sacred altar — the loving look, the clasping hand, the parental heart that draws the burdened soul down to itself, buries it in love and blessing, shelters it in protecting arms, breathes upon it blessing and strength! In the eyes that bend above, the soul sees — Christ. It is Christ just from Gethsemane, and the lines traced in fire by that supreme test are still on those patient features. It is Christ in the Judgment Hall, on whose ears may have just fallen the hot denials of a cowardly, impetuous Peter. Ah! that look of love and pity and reproof has not yet crumbled into dust. It is even the Christ look of love and yearning, following after Judas with the thirty pieces of world's tinsel chinking in his palsied hand. It is Christ upon the cross, suffering in Himself, in Herself, the sins that burden the heart of the child; the Christ whose look of pitying love understood, penetrated the heart of Mary, mother of the human Jesus, of Mary, ransomed from devils, of lepers cleansed, of blind men seeing, of lame men healed, of dead men living, — all of whom stood watching their last hope fade and fall. It is the Christ that saw the last, pleading look of the murderer and robber, and stretched out a spirit grasp that held both thief and Paradise. Not a phase of human need, of human sin, of human woe, but that Elder, that Eldress, with the firm, strong, tender, patient face, the deep, searching, loving, Christlike eyes, has met, and helped and saved.

Who can paint the sacredness of that hour when every secret thing may be revealed, must be revealed, if the heart be true and the faith be pure! Contrition, humiliation, mortification? Yea! but it is One, the Giver of life, who hears. It is the Open Door that leads to God. Always to God is confession made; the human anointed representative in the Visible Order sits as witness and receives the gift. Then, when the burden is lifted and the soul is free, comes the gift of love and blessing. God's forgiveness speaks from the sacred lips; His blessing falls in touch of the sacred hands upon the bended head. Sins are removed, burdens are lifted, and, cleansed and purified, free and glad as a child, or a bird in its morning song, the soul goes forth.

The hours of the sacred day — the Holy Day of Sacrifice — pass on. Is there trouble, hard feeling, misunderstanding, among brethren and sisters? Here, at the altar, all wounds are healed, wandering hearts reclaimed, weak souls strengthened. Sunset glories gild Mount Zion and fall on a household purified, renewed, united in new bonds of brother and sisterhood. Worn and weary in their human forms, these Shepherds lead forth their flock to newer and fresher pastures of spiritual food; these Captains of the Lord's host marshal their bands anew for greater victories over self and sin, the world, the flesh, principalities and powers.

Sacred are the claims, holy the hours of this Day of Sacrifice. None who have sincerely and honestly entered that "secret place of the Most High" would willingly lose the shelter of those protecting wings. None but the true Shaker can know this, the most blessed of life's experiences. This open door is never closed. At any time, the lightest call, the softest whisper of need, of desire, and the faithful

Shepherd leads the humblest lamb of the flock apart, into the sacred stillness. And the lambs that follow nearest to the Shepherd, keeping closest to his feet, are the safest and find choicest pasturage.

Much has been said in these pages of confession of sin. First, last and all the time, the necessity of this was, and is, insisted upon. Today, as always, it has a harsh, uncertain sound. It strikes the ear and heart unpleasantly. Many shrink, appalled, in honest unwillingness, at a demand so apparently absurd and dogmatic. Some, outwardly compliant, bring like Ananias and Sapphira but half an offering, pretending it is all, and receive what they did,— death, spiritual death! For only by the complete surrender to God in an honest confession of sin, is it possible for the divine life to enter the soul.

The Gift in the Visible Order.

Among the ideas taught by Shakers, which reconcile many apparently conflicting characterizations of God found in the Scriptures, is one which declares God to be Spirit, infinitely beyond the immediate reach of the finite. Some have regarded Jehovah as the name of a tutelary, or national deity, a spiritual being of high order, yet a God of war, who led and directed the Jewish nation as other nations and peoples had their deities, spirits of power and might, who presided over them. Certain it is that the God idea grew and developed among the Jews as the nation progressed in civilization and religious capacity. Possibly, higher spirits consecutively led and taught and ruled over them. From the Christ heavens came the Christ Spirit — the Manifestation of God — through man, a special witness, and 1700 years later, through woman, a special witness. The gifts of God, through Christ Jesus and Christ Ann, come down through a line of mediatorial spirits, — beings of purity, love and power.

The natural man and woman, dead in trespasses and sins, born into a sinful nature, and, from almost the first movings of sense and intellect, yielding to natural propensities and falling into sin, can no more attain of himself, of herself, purity and goodness, than can the physically dead live and breathe and speak. A germ of life is implanted; the Spirit touch on the heart arouses a sense of need, of want; the soul awakes; it longs and looks, but longs and looks in vain. It is like the blind, instinctive movements of embryonic life. In this state, it comes to the Anointed One, who has the unction of the Spirit, standing in the Visible Mediatorial Order. Beyond, in the invisible world, is a line of mediatorial spirits reaching up to Christ, to God. The soul comes to the one close at hand. That one has become somewhat familiar by more or less of intercourse. Trust and love have begun to spring up to the human friend with the good, kind face, in whose every line and feature gleams a spiritual life which has strangely touched and warmed the heart. The hour comes when a request is made that the mind shall be opened. Sincere, in earnest to take each step that leads to God, the inquiring soul honestly utters everything that memory recalls of sin or shame or wrong. Then and thereby, a relation is established between Elder and penitent. Relief, peace, joy, a sense of pardon and a realization of Divine Father and Mother Love, as a birthright just revealed, come in to take possession of the heart. The relation that binds the penitent, awakening soul to the Elder is the visible, tangible side of the spiritual uniting, the birth from above. The gifts of spiritual healing, strength and sustenance are imparted as constantly, as tenderly, as physical food and care to a little new-born child. The spiritual relationship once established, the soul grows as the natural child grows, by

NO. 22. CHURCH FAMILY DWELLING, EAST CANTERBURY, N. H.

food, rest and exercise, till, in the course of weeks or months or years, the spiritual being develops from infancy into a child, a youth, a strong man or woman in God. Not meaningless were the words of Isaiah: "Kings shall be thy nursing fathers and queens thy nursing mothers, and thou shalt know that I am the Lord." Through the open door of repentance — confession and forsaking of sin — comes the gift of Life from God, passed down through mediatorial hands, the living, loving human savior, father or mother, on the earth. This is the Visible Order of God's Anointed.

"The wings of the cherubim touch over the Mercy Seat; and Urim and Thummim — light and perfection — shine in the breast-plate of righteousness which is worn by those who minister at the altar. In associative relations where persons are gathered together in a communistic home, it is necessary that the character of each individual should be known; and the true brotherhood and sisterhood, formed on the basis of a religious life, can only be permanent by each member putting away the sins and errors of the old life in nature. The power of protection can only be kept through union with and confidence in a spiritual lead, from whom no secrets can be withheld. 'Now, therefore, there is no condemnation to those who walk with Christ,' for they have put off the deeds of the old man and woman and are clothed in the clean garments of the resurrection."

Confession Required by God.

Very early in the great drama of humanity appeared the first confession of sin. In the story of the Eden Garden, whether we regard that story as history, myth or poetry, the man and woman stand in shame and confusion before the face of the divine Friend who had before walked and talked with them, face to face, in the cool of the evening.

19

Not God, the unapproachable, Infinite Being, upon whom no man may look and live, but the Guardian Spirit, the presiding Mediator, appointed for their education and salvation. Through the ages, always has some true, aspiring soul, prophet or priest, reaching after purity through obedience, faith and cross-bearing, stood among men as mediator, before whom as the chosen Witness, confession has been made.

In the first giving of the Law, a most strenuous command was laid upon every soul: "And it shall be, when he shall be guilty in one of these things, that he shall confess that he hath sinned in that thing. And he shall bring his trespass offering and the priest shall make an atonement for him concerning his sin." (Lev. v:5) Ezra (see chapter 10:11) called on the people to make confession, and that it was no silent opening of the soul to a God hearing in secret was proved by the vigorous handling of the abomination of polygamous idolatry into which the people of God had fallen. When the covetous Achan had disobeyed and looted the captured city of Ai, Joshua, speaking as representative of the Spirit Leader of the host, said: "My son, give, I pray thee, glory to the Lord God of Israel, and make confession unto Him; and *tell me* now what thou hast done; hide it not from me." He stood as the Witness to receive the confession, as the Medium through whose lips came the fiat of unforgiving justice. Achan and all his family were stoned to death, and the valley of humiliation, confession and death was called Achor — trouble. Centuries after, the prophet Hosea, looking upon the judgments of God that were to fall because of sin and pollution, is made to say: "And I will give her the valley of Achor for a door of hope." This valley of Achor, the door of hope, is exemplified in the soul history of every true Shaker, and is indeed a priceless gift. Moses received the confession of Aaron and Miriam, and of the people of Israel in all their follies and rebellions. Samuel stood as Witness, and the King in his pride and power humbled himself as a frightened child and confessed his disobedience.

The coming of John, the man sent from God to prepare the way for the advent of the Christ in Jesus, was the signal for a national uprising unto repentance: "And they went out to him and were baptized of him in Jordan, confessing their sins." John was a very practical teacher of religion and the different classes of men received explicit directions as to their duties and obligations. Jesus came with the rest; not a step trodden by mankind of the road to God was spurned by his feet. Confession preceded baptism and after the baptism with water the descending dove marked the descent upon him of the Holy Spirit that made him Jesus Christ.

"Confess your faults one to another that ye may be healed," was the apostolic command. Confession before a witness was practised in the Pentecostal Church, and the promise was fulfilled then, as now in the Millennial Church, — "If we confess our sins, He is faithful and just to forgive us our sins and to cleanse us from all unrighteousness."

"Confession as a necessary rite has been preserved in the Church of Rome to this day, but masculine dominance, with its powerful impulses toward sensuality, has not been able to entirely withstand the temptations of the confessional, and saving grace has, in a measure, departed from what should be the Holy of Holies. Woman should confide to woman her heart secrets; but she had no voice nor place in ministerial administration, until the light that shone in the Quaker Church, from which arose Ann Lee, the first born among many sisters in the Second Christian Dispensation, who revealed the Motherhood in Deity, the starting point of woman's emancipation from sexual thraldom. She who

came up out of great tribulations, baptized and regenerated
by the Christ influence, has wrought wisely in establishing
equality in spiritual as well as in temporal affairs, in the
organization that bears the name of 'The United Society of
Believers.' Each sex comprehends its own frailties and each
has its own spiritual advisers in the order of Elders; and
where there is harmonious action, 'the counsel of peace is
between them,' and the law of virgin purity is maintained.
'Now has come salvation and strength, the kingdom of our
God and the power of His Christ.' "

Need of Confession.

To the thoughtful mind, with any experience of the
weakness of human nature, the needs of human hearts and
the teaching and practice of the so-called Christian Churches,
is sure to come at some time the sense of need of just such
a Mercy Seat, of a visible human mediator. The church, in
life's bitterest stress and crisis, is an empty void, its forms
are meaningless. Priest, of whatever name, has failed.
Thousands today are turning away in bitter despair,— no
less despair because covered by a mocking mask of indifference or agnosticism. "My people have forsaken the altars!"
Why? Because the life, the light, has fled.

It came a second time, that "Light that shineth in darkness," and again the "darkness comprehended it not." The
darkness of the lower nature cannot comprehend the spiritual light of the Gospel, until it has come, through need
and want and longing, by spirit influence, to that open door
in the Valley of Achor. There shall it find hope and peace,
forgiveness and releasement. Then it may enter upon the
life of regeneration.

The needs of humanity's burdened heart have driven
thousands to Romish confessionals, and there did Goethe

place the mocking devil, Mephistopheles, the tempter, with ear to the penitent's lips, with lips ready to drop subtle poison into the aching heart. But, it is said, we are to "enter into our closet and shut the door and there pray to our Father who heareth in secret." Yea! but have you never read, "The prayer of the wicked is abomination to the Lord?" To thousands the appalling fact grows more hopelessly real as years go by, that silent, secret confession in the closet, to the ear of the Infinite, is no confession at all. Nothing is opened, nothing revealed. Real sin, actual condemnation, does not down at thought of God, or the effort at mental appropriation of what is not its own, however strong the effort for faith in the merits of the atoning blood of a murdered Jesus. Christian and sinner alike, Christendom over, are sighing, "I can only do the best I can!" and the former perhaps adds, "I will plead the mercy and redeeming love of Jesus, I know no other way!" Both, more and more, busy themselves in deeds of kindness and charity to the suffering of earth, seeking in practical issues of brotherly kindness the only cure they know for a sin-tortured soul. That a Christian must live free from sin is almost a forgotten dream. George Eliot, most profound, most hopeless reader of life's mysteries, sends her heart-broken Romola to a Catholic confessional, which gives her no relief nor hope. Then, true type of the sin-wasted heart, of the sincere but hopeless men and women of today, she falls asleep in a little boat, drifts out on a sunset sea, and sleeping, drifts. Awaking, at last, on a lonely island, she finds people poor, sick and suffering. She stays and helps them. Silent as to herself, forgetful of her own needs, she gives herself to them and finds relief; but the problems that have worn and wasted her heart and brain are unanswered. George Eliot never tried to answer them; she could not!

The Valley of Achor.

It is a narrow pass, — so strait the gate, so close the stony walls pressing on either side, no room remains for aught except the human soul o'er-burdened with its want and sin. That load, however large and heavy, finds the way of entrance, but never of egress,— there it is lost. Lifted by Love's hand, it is never seen again! Here is the Door of Hope. One entrance on the earth side,— dark, narrow and forbidding! Proud, sensitive, self-flattering human nature recoils in disgust and fear. But, enter! Beyond, at the further end, is the door of Hope,— the golden door, leading into the light. Angel song and spirit presence with outstretched, helping hands await the visitant. Here is real help. The haunting weight of unforgiven sin settles not back in the night season, to torment and scourge with stings of shame and fear. Here, in the presence of the pure, Christ-filled man or woman—and where, but in the human, can Christ be found?— the soul has met and been touched by the redeeming power of Christ, has received forgiveness and the New Life. Henceforth "Light is sown for the righteous and joy for the upright in heart."

The Order of God.

"Touch not mine Anointed and do my prophets no harm," said the inspired Psalmist. Under each of the four great dispensations of God's love and redemptive power, a direct Order of human agency has been appointed: in the first, Abraham; in the second, Moses; in the third, Jesus; and in the fourth, Ann Lee. Each in turn was the centre of the Christ anointing in that era. Moses provided for the continuance of the Order; apostolic injunction and appointment did the same. While the people in the second dispensation obeyed that Order, God could and did lead and bless His chosen people, recognizing them in their obedience. They were blessed in their basket and their store and no good thing was withheld; disobedience and rebellion against the Anointed Order met with punishment. The nation lost its power when it abandoned its Holy Order.

In apostolic days, the twelve anointed called the multitude and the disciples together and said: "It is not meet that we should leave the Word of God and serve tables. Wherefore, brethren, look ye out among you seven men of honest report, full of the Holy Spirit and wisdom, whom we may appoint over this business." This is the true Shaker method. "We may appoint!" No majority vote! It is done by the gift of God and expresses the will of the faithful and true-hearted, those who abide in the Gift of God. The overthrow of the first Gospel Church — the third dispensation — dates from the time, when, insidiously as the serpent in Eden, crept in the spirit of disobedience and rebellion, working out of sight, under a Christian name but denying Christ in any form of visible lead, confessing not that Christ had come in the flesh. This spirit of Antichrist, by which the disciples learned to look away from God manifest in the Anointed Order, to a false God enshrined in their own hearts, or in a printed book, or uttering by lips of manmade priestly orders, commands and oracles of disobedient spirits, resulted in the overthrow of the first Pentecostal Church.

In the fourth dispensation, in the Second Pentecostal Church, again has been established a Holy Anointed Order, and again the subtle spirit of Antichrist would seek, with first century malignity, its overthrow. That Order, true to its anointing, is the Christ Spirit abiding in the consecrated, appointed Leaders. Let those Leaders, by all that is sacred in humanity, its needs, its weakness and its trust, merge individual will and self in the Divine Spirit which has appointed and anointed them! Let every true Believer preserve, by the blazing, two-edged sword of the Spirit, the gate to this Holy of Holies! Guard, as with life itself, against all approach of self-assertion, independence, pride of thought or lust of power; all rebellion, in deed, thought or purpose against that Anointed Order. Here alone can be found safety, protection, the abiding Presence of God, the Spirit of Christ.

XVI

SHAKER COMMUNISM

"AND all that believed were together and had all things common; and sold their possessions and goods, and parted them to all men as every man had need." Brotherly love, community of interest, community of goods! This picture of first century Christianity, gleaming in the darkness of history, like a glimpse through an open door into a bright home circle, showing afar off on a mountain side, through the night, has ever affected the imaginations of men.

Christians have sighed over its lost delights, sadly supposing it an impossibility under present conditions. Often in the past, but especially during the nineteenth century, have attempts been made to actualize a brotherhood where equality and community of interest might exist. Forty-seven different American socialistic organizations which had proved failures were given in statistics a quarter of a century ago and the list has lengthened since.

The conclusion arrived at by a well-known writer, that communism is successful only among people whose misery is so extreme that any change is for the better, and therefore the hard straits of communistic life are agreeable because they have known so much worse, can hardly be accepted by Shakers, a large proportion of whose members come from homes of comfort or luxury and who, in most cases, are quite equal to holding their own in the competitive ranks of the world's industrial army. In no case have

the temporal comforts of the home long held any coming
from such low conditions, who were not spiritually ripe for
the Order.

But why, since all are brothers, cannot well-disposed
men and women lay aside selfishness, live harmoniously, by
moderate labor gain a sufficiency of physical necessities and
in unison attain a higher spiritual, a richer intellectual development, than is possible on the individual, competitive
plane?

The Shaker says, because there exist in humanity two
orders — one of the earth, individual, self-centered, finding
its highest expression in the family relation. Were the conditions of this order adhered to, in obedience to God's laws
written in the physiological relations of man's being, a race
of worthy, capable and moral men and women might be
produced, serving God in serving mankind. But every such
centre has a narrow basis. The man at the head must win
food, protection, opportunity, for his own against all others;
must hold life's fortress for them against the world. Separation, individual advancement, self-aggrandizement have
come to seem legitimate, righteous. Pressed to an extreme,
war has become to many a seeming right, and the murder
of other men, similarly striving, a holy cause. In man's
present moral status, the logical end of the protection of his
own life and those dependent on him has come to be the
destruction of others.

But, Shakers insist, there is a higher, a spiritual order
and relation, unto which men and women may attain. Jesus,
the Apostles, Paul, the early Christians lived on this spiritual plane. Those who would truly follow Jesus must live
as he lived. Having risen above, as did Jesus, the sensual,
generative life, the old family relation and all ties resting
therein and connected therewith,— a new relation becomes
established. Man and woman become son and daughter of

Christ, brother and sister in a pure relation of spiritual love and union, the fruit of the Gospel, and a new life principle, through the baptism of Divine Love, is received.

The Shaker sees clearly that the virgin life is necessary, even the foundation principle of religious communism, and that communism, on other basis than a common religious faith, is an impossibility, although it is granted that well organized cooperative systems may be successful and of great benefit to society. Communistic attempts admitting family relationship have inevitably proved failures, from the excess of private family feeling — necessarily a part of humanity in its natural state. It is equally true that people outgrow this state and are ready for a higher plane of life. Virgin purity is successful, happy and a blessing to man and woman, where the ripened condition has been reached, and the true brother and sister relation in Christ is found; and that is possible only in a pure and sustained Christian Communism. The virgin life is held as fundamental to the existence of the community, as the private family relationship is fundamental, essential, to the existence of the natural order. One is the seed garden of the race, the other its harvest field; the one is transitory, the other eternal.

The thoughtful writer of "A Century of Communism" says: "It may not be generally known that some of the most earnest communists who failed to reach their ideals under such organizers as Owen, Ripley, Ballou and other grand souls, afterward realized them in these centres of divinely affiliated action generally known as Shaker Communities, but such is the fact."

Shakerism from its earliest organization assumed the form of community, the united interest. Resting on principles, governed by laws, that link the Church Visible with the Church Invisible, the system is a theocracy, where God's will is acknowledged as the impelling force, God's law the

controlling power. When democracy — the vote of the majority — is advanced as a desideratum in government, the
basic principle of that government is endangered. Yet, as
every great truth has two sides, a theocracy holds within
itself the essence of a true democracy. Ever, in a noble
sense, is "the voice of the people the voice of God."
Through the human is the voice of God apprehended. This
is the soul of Shaker revelation and belief. The judgment
of the consecrated, faithful member has always been recognized as conveying an expression of the will and purpose
of God.

It is the ideal of this system of government that such
should be the union between the head and the body of the
people, that the aggregate thought and conscience of the
members could be gathered on any question of polity or
economy. But God speaks, as of old, to the Anointed Leaders, the Consecrated Shepherds, and it often happens that
a call comes to which the ears of the rank and file are deaf.
Then the gift of obedience is the way of safety, and in the
spirit of obedience no call of God has ever been accepted
and followed to the hurt of the individual or the Order.

Officials are nominated by the Ministry, and, in union
with the Covenant-keeping members, are appointed, and
may be removed in the same way, when unfaithfulness, in-
capacity, or the needs of the work demand. One expounder
of the system says: "The Ministry and Elders are not considered infallible oracles, but the most appropriate for the
time, occasion and locality. The Order is an infallible institution, and where Ministry and Elders are governed by the
Christ Spirit, which constitutes that Order, they are the
oracles of God. The administration is not that of man or
woman in their human capacity, but Godliness acting
through man and woman — a unity in Christ character."

Communism has existed with Shakers in organized form since 1792, as a principle of life, since the establishment of the Church in Mother Ann and her little company of eight. An early document referring to the family at Niskeyuna, believed to be the work of Elder Calvin Harlow, shows the beginning of the communistic life in the Shaker Order. It states:

"The Church at Niskeyuna held the property as a joint interest. After we became acquainted with them and believed their testimony, they gave what they gained by their industry, with the use and improvement of their farm, for the benefit of the whole society, to be improved in the following manner, viz.: There should be a free table and other necessaries for the entertainment of those who went to see them, that the poor might have an equal opportunity of the Gospel with the rich. All who were able had liberty to contribute according to their faith, toward supporting table and other expenses and the poor. None were compelled or even desired to contribute, but such as could do it freely, believing it to be their duty; and they were often cautioned, taught to deal justly with all, and were often examined as to whether they were in debt, or whether their families were in need of what they offered to give. The teaching plainly implied that those who went to visit the Church, who were able to support themselves should do so, or give as much as they received. And those who were able to give more ought to give more than sufficient to support themselves. It is well known that many poor people came who were not able to support themselves while there, nor even to bear their own expenses back to their families. Many poor came for alms and none were sent away. None had liberty to work there but those who would freely give their services as a matter of their own faith."

Shakers of an early day saw visions of great multitudes and they prepared for them,— large houses, thousands of broad acres, room and opportunity for hundreds. Present day Shakers carry the burden of property thus amassed, under widely different industrial conditions, holding it as a sacred trust, an inheritance all strive to pass on intact. Frugality, thrift and industry stamp every part with peace and contentment, while most striking to the casual observer is the absence from all faces of the modern demon, worry. Life problems of the world outside find earnest thinkers here. Laws of social biology that the world is waiting for have been found and applied; light, the millions strain their gaze to see arise from afar, is shining in their midst. Principles the world's best thinkers strive to bring men to adopt have with the Shakers been so long a habit of daily living that they are familiar to his ear as household tales. True democracy of feeling exists, real fraternity and as much equality as possible amid the variety of nationalities, dispositions and abilities that drift into communistic life.

Under the peculiar patriarcho-democracy develop some of the sturdiest natures, strong and original minds. The weak are sheltered and cared for; the strong bear the burdens of the weak; all, weak and strong, bear and do to the extent of their ability, and that not of compulsion but from esprit de corps, not for self but for others. The broader the nature, the wider the outlook, the more is toil a joy as a labor that reaches out to bless mankind. Herein the religious enthusiasm of the earlier days finds expression, changing features with the spirit of the times to the broader altruism of the world's best self.

The Shaker sees in the life he lives so contentedly in health of body and mind, much that the world's workers sorely need, and he regards his little Zion as a city set upon a hill to give forth the true light, a power centre to vibrate electric currents wherever there is human need. He neither marries nor gives in marriage, and his body as well as soul and spirit is consecrated to purity, truth and toil, but he regards himself as harvested from the world for a special

NO. 23. IN THE PATH. NORTH FAMILY DOORYARD, MT. LEBANON.

life, and does not grudge that other men, not so called, should live in their order the common life of nature.

"The poor ye have always with you," is a behest the Shaker never forgets, and from the honest laborer who assists in their fields to the shiftless tramp who haunts their doors, all, according to need, are remembered, fed, clothed and treated with kindness and sympathy. In cases of loss among themselves, the societies assist one another, while their deeds of charity, when disasters occur in the world at large, are well known.

For more than a century and a quarter has this communistic system endured the strain of opposition, persecution, loss, hardship, betrayal and treachery, with the usual percentage, among its temporary members, of the indolent, selfish and incapacitated. The system grew naturally out of the baptism of divine love and revelation that welded the people together and the early conditions of poverty and persecution, which increased the strength of spiritual relationship making it stronger than natural ties of kindred. The same bond holds them still, in years when no man speaks ill of them and when respect and kindliness are shown them everywhere.

Distinctive peculiarities of dress have largely disappeared. Principles alone are regarded as a fixity; creeds, patterns, forms must in the nature of things be transitory in order to give correct expression to higher conceptions of truth, and they constantly adapt modes of thought and action to the progressive principle inherent in the system.

The true Shaker, to whom his religious faith is his dearest possession, after the tender ties of spiritual relationship, would certainly count next in love and sacredness his communistic home. Many are the songs that thrill with the joy of union, many the testimonies that reveal devotion to the angelic life, whose common love and labor are an inspiration, sweetening and uplifting, in defiance of human limitations.

Elder Frederick W. Evans, in a letter to Robert Dale Owen, contrasts the basis of his unsuccessful American communities, twenty in number, founded at a great outlay of wealth, talent and sympathy, with that of the successful Shaker societies, and, quoting the words of Jesus, "Take no thought for your life, what ye shall eat, or what ye shall drink, nor wherewithal ye shall be clothed, but seek ye first the Kingdom of God and His righteousness, and all these things shall be added unto you," asks these pointed questions:

"Has it not been the desire, the constant wish of your big, benevolent heart to gather the people into communities, that, as the prime object, they might be fed and clothed? Has not this been the mainspring of your life-long labors, to educate the ignorant, to feed the hungry and clothe the naked — to lower the rich and elevate the poor? And have you not sought as an end that which is but the effect of an end? Have not your people hungered more after the fruits of the Kingdom of Heaven than after the Kingdom itself and its righteousness? Is not here the cause of the universal failure of the mere earthly man to form a community, and the true cause of the success of the mere spiritual man, who, without possessing a tithe of the external, worldly wisdom and advantages, without even thinking or caring about a community or socialism, has been instinctively drawn into it by laws to him as unseen and unknown as were those which organized and fashioned him in his mother's womb?

"The inspiration that made the Shaker led them to be good to each other, to clothe the naked, to feed the hungry, even when they were their own persecutors. They loved each other so genuinely, so practically, that each one felt it a privilege and a duty to let every other brother and sister possess all that he possessed and enjoy all that he himself enjoyed. They had all things common. They learned by experience that the direct tendency of their new spiritual religion was to throw all who would embrace it into the form and relation of community — that was a legitimate, an inevitable effect."

All who enter the Shaker Community give up all, give up themselves. Not at first, not of compulsion. Too hasty surrender, in early enthusiasm, is discouraged. Time, experience, knowledge of conditions without and the heart within are first required. Meanwhile, the acolyte shares the good, joins in the labor and feels that he is helping in the upbuilding, while his probationary covenant brings him into practical union with the society. After the necessary advance has been made in spiritual travel, a final and complete consecration of self, time, possessions and faculties is accepted. But this does not debar one from departure. No black veils nor barred doors shut in the rebellious from the world for which he sighs. He need tread on nothing worse than broken vows and grieving hearts, and, though he can raise no claim to property once voluntarily renounced, enough is always given to smooth his way in the world to which he persists in going and, as far as possible, the principal that he brought is returned.

None, not even Bishops, Elders or Trustees, hold a dollar of the property for their own use. It is a sacred heritage. They are stewards, responsible to God and the people for a strict account of their stewardship. On journeys for the good of the cause or the needs of the people, many will not eat, save of the simplest, cheapest fare; a dollar spent in mere self-indulgence is to them sin, betrayal of trust.

Strength and faculties are devoted. Time is occupied by all in industrious labor for the preservation and increase of the inheritance. "Labor is worship and prayer," they sing. Food and clothing, luxuries and outings, are evened

20

up; special tastes and likings are considered. It is one big family. The Divine Father and Mother are invoked in silent prayer together, before each meal and in each company of room-mates, night and morning.

Labor is apportioned according to strength and ability, those in positions of trust and responsibility bearing the heaviest burdens, toiling the most hours; — "I am among you as one that serveth" is the motto of the leaders.

Respect and veneration are shown to those advanced in years. "The love and solicitude for future generations is beautifully manifested in the energy, industry, and economy of the aged, who, welcome to repose and the free enjoyment of their previous labors, still are anxious to do all in their power to aid in the cause. With whitening heads and waning strength they generously go forth to sow that which they cannot expect to reap in this life. It is not infrequent to see brethren in their eighties setting out fruit and shade trees for the blessing of generations to come and sisters in their labors making equal efforts. The interest for a spiritual increase is even stronger. They are never too old to sow the Gospel seed and to rejoice in its growth in souls. This ever expanding, ever renewing life and love of the spirit, this continual influx of deific influences permeates the whole being, gives endurance to mind and body and keeps the spirit bright and joyous; for with such, death is forever vanquished and eternity is begun, angelic relationships are formed and the Kingdom of Heaven exists within and around them."—(Biography of Daniel Fraser.)

Shakers have no set creed, no limit of revealed truth, beyond which no further divine enlightenment may come. Avenues are open to the spirit world, through that to God. New revelations are always possible, are expected, and are, in their economy, necessary, as man advances, individually and collectively, in light and knowledge of things human and divine. "Ours is a self-mending machine" is the homely expression of a great truth.

Shaker communism has in its fundamental religious obligation a support and bulwark which other communistic organizations lack. The open page each life should present to the Visible Anointed Order has proved a safeguard and protection to the home, such as no form of community arising from mere social or political principles could obtain. All lives lie open to the Elders and through this relation all are protected. Misunderstandings are corrected, subtle influences counteracted, overbalancing forces adjusted, concealed ills of the flesh or spirit healed. The troubled and the troubling life currents flow in and out of the Centre Fountain to find healing and uniting. The divine life impulse may touch all hearts at the centre of the home — its Altar and Mercy-seat.

The qualities demanded by the duties of the Shaker Elder are of the highest, — delicacy, strength, courage, persistence, hope, energy, endurance, patience and a power of penetration little short of the divine. Various classes and conditions of men and women, all degrees of culture and ignorance, all stages of mental and spiritual development come for admission. The sincere and the hypocrite, the deceiver and the self-deceived, the crank and the fool, the humbug and the fanatic, the weary, the lame, the lazy, the hungry, — the deadbeats from life's thousand paths, all come knocking at the doors of the Shaker Community. The purpose of the life is not communism, but the living in practical work of à highly developed spiritual life, requiring strong, devoted natures. In each applicant may be concealed the germ of a true soul. A Shaker, another name for a Christian of the highest type, may be evolved, an angel may lie hidden in the block, a diamond in the pebble. With patience, discernment and forbearance, the Elders and the family watch and wait, bear and forbear, endure misapprehension, mistakes, wilfulness, peculiarities, rejoicing over evidences of sincerity, progressing insight and the beginnings of true faith. A student of social conditions has said:

"The catholicity of thought evinced by the Shaker leaders, the comprehensive grasp of affairs, the judgment of the trend and comparative valuation of various reforms, the interest maintained in scientific discoveries and inventions, the depth and breadth of that love of humanity which dominates every motive, is something as surprising as it is delightful to the dispassionate visitor."

The Shaker philosopher, Elder Frederick W. Evans, says:

"We are organizing peace and showing mankind a city set upon a hill that cannot be hid. Seventeen villages of human beings that have so crucified within themselves the lusts that war in their members, from whence come all wars, private and public, that they live like the Prince of Peace, celibates, with property in common, having no magistrates, police courts nor prisons. Hygiene is part of our theology. Health of soul and body is part of the institution. The Shaker system is God's method of reaping the human race. The Holy City, New Jerusalem in the Spirit World, is settling down like a cloud upon earth. It is becoming incarnated. The Tabernacle of God is with men and is protected by the American Secular Government. If God is to wipe away all tears from all eyes, so that there is no more sorrow, no more sighing, no more pain, physical nor mental, then there must be abolition, not only of slavery, but of land monopoly, poverty, oppression, sickness and disease, — of army, navy, doctors, lawyers, priests, landlords, of debtors and creditors, of rich and poor; in the New Earth, each one sitting under his or her own vine with mutual National Co-operation; and in the New Heavens, all being brothers and sisters, they enjoy all things in common in a Heavenly Community.

"To the confusion of science falsely so-called, to the mortification of male human wisdom, pride and arrogance, let it be borne in mind that the first successful social organization ever established on earth that secured the equal good of all its members, spiritual, intellectual and physical, was founded by a woman, who could neither read nor write, aided solely by spiritual knowledge. "Thousands have gone forth from these communities," writes Dr. J. P. MacLean, of Ohio, "schooled in the purest morals and implicit faith in the Divine Being. Shakerism has been productive of good. As such, it must receive the encomiums of the just."

XVII

INVENTIONS AND INDUSTRIES

ALTHOUGH claiming to live in the New Heavens, to have been harvested from the world and to lead a pure, spiritual and peaceful existence, the Shaker is by no means a dreamer or a mystic. Hardheaded, shrewd, sensible and practical, he neither cheats nor means to let himself be cheated, prefers to give more than the contract demands and glories in keeping the top, middle and bottom layer equally good in every basket or barrel of fruit or vegetables sent to market under his name. He aims to employ his whole being and all his time, consistently and honorably, in the service to which he has devoted himself. He sees no virtue nor economy in hard labor when consecrated brain can work out an easier method. There is no quickener to brain and hand like a heart at peace, a conscience clear and a sense bright with the joy of holy living; and thus the world is richer for many tangible proofs of the Shaker's consecrated ingenuity.

The list of inventions and devices of Shaker wit and wisdom is a long one, and if extended into little labor-saving contrivances about the dwellings, shops and barns would seem almost endless. Nearly all of their many valuable inventions have been unpatented. To the Shaker, patent money savors of monopoly, the opposite of the Golden Rule. Whatever he invents is for the use of the whole world. Many times have those not so conscientious patented as their own, inventions which were taken from the Shakers. From statistics outside the Order, the statement has been made that more useful inventions have originated among the Shakers than any other people of the same number.

Ten years before the screw propeller was put into use as a new system of navigation, it was invented and used by Thomas Wells, of Watervliet, N. Y. "Babbitt Metal" was the invention of Daniel W. Baird, of North Union, Ohio, and his claim was established in a court of law whither he had been subpoenaed as witness in a law suit, between the man Babbitt and the firm Ward & Co., of Detroit, for infringement of patent. The firm, whose case was established by Daniel Baird's testimony and his little box of soft metal, would have handsomely remunerated him, but he would take nothing save the expense of coming to court. Afterward, he accepted a free pass over the railroads and steamboats under control or influence of the firm. The same brother originated the rotary or revolving harrow. The one afterward patented by another man was contrived after watching Baird's. Daniel Baird also invented an automatic spring, for domestic purposes.

South Union, Ky., was the home of Sanford J. Russell, a Shaker, who invented and, strange to say, patented a sash balance, which without cords or pulleys worked perfectly, moved at a touch, locked at any desired point and, as the "Scientific American" said of it, "furnished 'the best ventilator known."

Elder Matthew B. Carter, of Ohio, invented an ingenious governor of an over-shot water wheel. George Wickersham, of Mount Lebanon, is said to have invented the Turbine water wheel. As early as 1815, a Home-made threshing machine was in use. Boards were matched for the first time in this country by machinery in the same year. It was the invention of Henry Bennett and Amos

Bishop, who used vertical rollers to keep the lumber straight and ropes and windlass to propel the same over circular saws, first making a groove, then a tongue. The improved system was brought out in 1828. A planing machine, since which all others have come into use, was invented at Mount Lebanon. A fertilizing machine was added to the list of mechanical contrivances by Charles Greaves of Mount Lebanon. Elders Daniel Boler and Daniel Crossman, of the same society, invented machinery for splint making, basket working and box cutting. Shaker splint-bottomed chairs and poplar wood baskets and boxes are still a favorite product of Shaker ingenuity.

A Harvard sister, Sarah Babbitt, known as "Sister Tabitha," has the honor of inaugurating a new industrial era, by the invention of cut nails and of the circular or buzz saw. She was watching the brethren make wrought nails, when it occurred to her that they might be cut from a sheet of iron rolled to the desired thickness. Her idea was worked out to a success, and the cut nail became universal property.

At another time, she stood watching the brethren saw wood, and, remarking that half the motion was lost, the idea of a circular saw came to her. Avoiding the ridicule a new idea invokes, she went to work quietly by herself. Making a tin disk and notching it around the edge, she slipped it on the spindle of her spinning-wheel, tried it on a shingle and found it was a success. From this rude, tiny saw, fastened to a spinning-wheel by a Harvard Shakeress, came the circular saw of today. Sister Tabitha's first saw was made in sections and fastened to a board. A Mount Lebanon brother improved on this by making the saw out of one piece of metal. The first circular saw is now preserved and is on exhibition in the Geological Building at Albany, N. Y.

NO. 24. HARVARD, MASS. MEETING HOUSE ON THE RIGHT.

The Improved Shaker Washing Machine was invented at Canterbury, N. H. Canterbury also contributed to the world's stock of conveniences an improved windmill. From Enfield, N. H., came a folding stereoscope, the work of Nelson Chase. George W. Wickersham also invented a summer covering for a flat-iron stove, by which the hotter the irons, the cooler the room. Sewell G. Thayer, of North Union, put into use a stove-cover lifter, which possessed the Shaker qualities of always finding and keeping its own place. A very convenient wood stove also ranks among Shaker notions, and in spite of steam radiators, which have been in use in their dwellings for over forty years, many still prefer this heating apparatus in their shops. Machinery for twisting whip handles, a pipe machine, a pea sheller, a butter worker, a self-acting cheese press are among Shaker inventions.

Few of the millions who daily drive for business or pleasure, in the many forms of one-horse vehicles, know or remember that the first one-horse wagon used in this country started out from the dooryard of the Shakers at Enfield, Conn. The horse collar dates from the same place. The common and useful clothes-pin was invented at North Union.

Union Village claims the large loom for weaving palm leaf Shaker bonnets, the invention of Abner Bedell. The two looms of his making are now in the possession of the Ohio Historical Society. The same brother, in 1837, in-invented and made the woodwork of a silk reeling machine that would reel sixty-three skeins of silk thread in a day; Thomas Taylor, of the same society, invented the iron vessel and furnace by which the reeling machine was operated. An appleparer, which quartered and cored the fruit, was the invention of Sanford J. Russell, of South Union. An invention which has greatly lightened the labors of the sisters who do the family baking is in use at Canterbury. It is a revolving oven, the inner body of the oven having four compartments, each presenting its own door. This is the contrivance of Eldress Emeline Hart, now of the Ministry of New Hampshire.

Metal pens were first invented by Isaac Youngs, of Mount Lebanon, N. Y. The first were made of brass and silver, and some of these pioneer pens are still in use. Silver pens were made in 1819, and the next year were sold for twenty-five cents each. Machinery for rolling the brass and silver plate and shears for cutting the pens were home inventions. In 1820, the inventor writes: "I now have my new shears, with which I have cut two hundred and ninety-two pens in fourteen minutes." The metal used was melted silver coins. He says: "I melted up fifty-five or sixty dollars of silver money." The brass pens had handles of wood or tin, and one tubular handle of tin closed like a telescope.

The first machine for cutting and bending machine card teeth and punching the leather for setting was invented and used at Mount Lebanon.

Broom making was an important Shaker industry and is still followed. Shakers at Watervliet first raised and manufactured broom brush into brooms, invented and made the first flat broom, and an improved turning lathe for the handles of brooms was the work of a Mount Lebanon Shaker. A machine for sizing broom-corn brush was invented at Harvard. The flat broom was invented and made by Theodore Bates, the machine for turning handles by Jesse Wells. The Shaker broom industry began in 1798.

Among the many industries devised by Shaker prudence and thrift, that of drying sweet corn ranks as important. The first done in this country was at Mount Lebanon in 1828, where the business is still followed.

Watervliet and Enfield, Conn. are also noted for their dried sweet corn. At first, the corn was boiled on the cob in large, iron kettles, cut off with knives and dried on boards in the open air. In 1840, drying-houses were erected with run-ways extending out for large, wheeled platforms, on which the corn was thinly spread and raked at intervals. The process was slow and the corn subject to loss from bad weather. Nevertheless, contracts were made with the neighboring farmers, who delivered the husked corn. The modern method with improved appliances is a profitable business. The improved modern kiln for drying the corn is also a Shaker invention.

Three societies, Mount Lebanon, N. Y., Enfield, Conn., and Union Village, Ohio, claim the honor of originating the seed business, which was a leading industry throughout Shakerdom for many years and netted many thousands of dollars annually to the different societies. It started in a small way in the year 1800, gradually increasing in dimensions, until in all parts of the country the Shaker Seed wagon and the shrewd, honest, sedate but kindly Shaker Brother, who sold the seeds, were familiar as the springtime. The business, in all its branches, raising, gathering, papering and selling, gave employment to brethren and boys of all ages and grades of ability. In 1816, the Centre Family at Union Village began to make bags to put up their seeds. A machine for filling seed bags and the printing presses for printing seed bags and herb packages were invented at Watervliet, N. Y. This lucrative and agreeable employment, from a number of causes, has passed entirely out of the hands of its originators. Shakers were also the first in this country to introduce botanical medical practice, the first roots, herbs and vegetable extracts for medicinal purposes placed on the market having borne the Shaker stamp. The manufacture and sale of medicines is still followed in some of the societies. From Mount Lebanon, where the manufacture is conducted by Brother Alonzo Hollister, a skilful pharmacist, the shipments of medicine are largely to London.

Canterbury Industries.

Elder Henry C. Blinn writes thus of Canterbury: "Prominent among the earlier industries stands weaving. In 1796, this was all done on hand looms. From a personal diary handed down by one of the sisters, Ruth Stevens, of Canterbury, the following results are credited to the weavers of the society during 1796: Wide cloth, 4170 yards; binding, 2975 yards; tape, 1140 yards. Carding was performed by hand until 1812, spinning-wheels and hand looms were used by the sisters until 1824, when the spinning jenny was introduced and power looms followed in 1842. Other means adopted for a livelihood were the manufacture of superior Shaker flannel from sheep raised in Shaker pastures, wool hose and underwear, hand knit; also brooms, brushes, scythe snaths, rakes, boxes, chairs, tubs, pails, leather, candlesticks, etc.

"Later, butter and cheese were sold, also apple sauce and some medicines. It is recorded that in 1811 there were made in Canterbury 2884 pounds of cheese. Among the medicines, witch hazel extract of more recent date and a good sarsaparilla, prepared from a formula by Dr. Thomas Corbett, the only Shaker physician in New Hampshire, were for some years in demand and are still on the market. The trustees were counseled not to sell any article unless it were free from blemish. This standard has always been maintained."

The work of the Shaker home is done by the sisters. Hired help may be a necessity on the farms, but the sisters will have none of it in the women's department. The work is divided among different sets of sisters, taking their turns in the different departments, each set serving a turn of four to six weeks. Rug and mat making and fancy work, with their famous preserves and other products of the housewife's art, furnish a lucrative employment. The ubiquitous summer boarder from neighboring resorts finds a trip to the Shakers pleasurable, while in some of the societies, for the convenience of such guests, meals are served. This gives opportunity to serve up at the same time good dinners and pure Gospel, and some are quick and apt to improve the opportunity for missionary work along the various lines of reform in which they are interested. The clothing of the sisters is mostly made at home, part of the clothing of the brethren is also of home make, while in some of the families an old style shoemaker still produces the old style "Shaker shoe," with whose ease and comfort the new fashioned "common sense" boot can by no means compete.

The manufacture of "Shaker chairs" is carried on by the South Family at Mount Lebanon. The chairs are of all styles and varieties, and possess the Shaker quality of thorough workmanship. Palm leaf table mats were formerly made in some of the societies and were a favorite article in the market. Macrame mats are still made at Enfield, Conn. The sisters of Mount Lebanon, Hancock and Canterbury, make a handsome, comfortable woman's wrap, known as the "Shaker cloak," at once distinguished in appearance and possessed of excellent wearing qualities. Hand-knit gloves of silk and fur are also a Shaker specialty. A remarkably effective healing lotion for the skin, named "Healolene," is the invention of a sister now living in the North Family at Mount Lebanon, where it is manufactured.

Maple sugar orchards are a source of revenue to some of the societies, between one and two thousand trees rendering up their sweets to the industrious tappers. In recent years, an improved carpet and rug beater of rattan, steel and corrugated steel, which is simple, effective and has a ready sale, is manufactured by the North Family at Mount Lebanon. Although not a Shaker invention, the convenient handle is a Shaker improvement on the original. For many years an important industry was shirt making. The machines were run by water power and large, airy, beautiful shops for the business are found at several of the societies. In former years wool growing was an important industry, and thousands of acres of the mountain slopes were covered with flocks of sheep besides herds of cattle. These resources have proved unprofitable under the changed conditions of today. Most of the industries in which the societies in past years found lucrative employment have been taken from them by the industrial developments and monopolies of recent times; and while their large possessions of real estate have greatly diminished in productiveness, with the farm lands of smaller holdings, taxation has steadily increased.

NO. 25. TRUSTEES' OFFICE, HANCOCK, MASS.

XVIII

LITERATURE — WORSHIP

D URING the first seventy-five years of their communal existence, Shakers were too busy with temporal conditions and spiritual needs to engage in literary or artistic enterprises, and for the last fifty years, their slowly decreasing numbers, the increasing burden of taxation, the industrial changes forced upon them, together with the sense of obligation to preserve intact the united inheritance, have operated to increase the demand for devotion of time and strength to manual labor, beyond what would otherwise be necessary for support of the families.

For such reasons, as well as from the religious sense of separation from the world and worldly interests, Shaker literary genius has not revealed itself in the world's markets. Shakers have sometimes been regarded as averse to literary and artistic efforts. This estimate is hardly a correct one. In seeking the highest possible spiritual development, Shakers have left behind much in art and literature commonly regarded as of value, yet, in this very renunciation, in attaining purity of life and thought, they have developed a pure, refined, spiritual taste, eminently fitting them for the appreciation of the highest in art and literature.

Writing of the future of the Order, a Shaker sister says: "Arts and sciences will flourish with those living the highest life. Heretofore, the work of drawing the line between flesh and spirit was so great, that no time was left for other thought than watching all avenues to keep out the evils

that would destroy the good that had been gained. All that
is pure and elevating in the arts and sciences will be understood and appreciated."

The societies for many years have kept well-stocked
reading rooms and libraries in the families. Light, frivol-
ous literature is discountenanced, but the advanced thought
of the day, especially along lines of reform, is liberally provided.

From 1871 to 1900, a periodical was published, for two
years at Watervliet, under the name, "The Shaker;" from
1873 to 1876, under the able co-editorship of Elder F. W.
Evans and Eldress Antoinette Doolittle, of Mount Lebanon,
with the title, "Shaker and Shakeress," it stands as the first
and only dual paper known, an able exponent of the dual
idea and faith, man and woman co-workers. For two more
years it resumed its masculine name and character, then, as
the "Manifesto," it reappeared at Canterbury, where it was
published from 1878 to 1900. While devoted to Shaker
thought and belief, the magazine took high rank as a literary production and was widely read, forming a link among
the societies whose loss, when it was discontinued, was
severely felt.

Theology.

In theological and philosophical writings, Shakers manifest the same original and forceful intellectual life, that, in
the routine of daily vocations, has expressed itself in practical devices and mechanical inventions. Shakers are not
addicted to theological discussion, yet there are theological
writers among them of spiritual insight and convincing
logic. It is difficult to subvert or get around in argument
an old Shaker, "dyed in the wool."

"Christ's First and Second Appearing." — The work
bearing this title was first issued at Union Village, Warren

County, Ohio, in 1808, in a small volume, bearing the signatures of David Darrow, John Meacham and Benjamin S. Youngs. Several revisions and later editions have followed. Thomas Jefferson said of this work: "I have read it through three times, and I pronounce it the best Church History that ever was written, and if its exegesis of Christian principles is maintained and sustained by a practical life, it is destined eventually to overthrow all other religions."

Among other works of a theological character, stands preeminent the "MILLENNIAL CHURCH," published at Mount Lebanon, in 1823. Elder Calvin Green tells the following of its origin: A Russian Consul from New York visited the North Family and requested of the Elders an exposition of the faith and practice of Believers, that he might translate and publish it in Russia. Elder Calvin, accordingly, composed the work, and when the manuscript was presented to the Consul, he desired Believers to have it printed. The Elder, assisted by Seth Y. Wells, revised and enlarged the work to the dimensions of the present volume, which has passed through several editions. Secretary Stanton, on his visit to Mount Lebanon, read the book and affirmed that there was "more true religion in it than in any other book he had ever read." It is still a source of spiritual quickening and intellectual enlightenment, and several times have recent messages come from different parts of the world, testifying to light received from this book. A chance visitor, member of a well known law firm of Brooklyn, N. Y., recently wrote: "I have finished reading the 'Millennial Church,' which I purchased from you, and I consider it one of the most powerful religious works I have ever read. It seems to me your morals are ideal. The reading of this book has opened my eyes to the life of the Shakers. It is certainly an enviable one."

21

"Dunlavy's Manifesto of Shaker Theology" was written by John Dunlavy, for many years an eminent leader among western Shakers. A smaller book, selections from the "Manifesto," was printed at Pleasant Hill in 1818, and reprinted in 1846, under the title "Plain Evidences." An interesting and valuable book is

"History of the Kentucky Revival," written in 1807, by the apostle of western Shakerism, Richard McNemar.

"Sermons on Shaker Theology," by Elder Hervey L. Eads, for many years Bishop of the societies in Kentucky, contains an exposition of about every phase of Shaker belief and practice.

Two brief and valuable books are "Plain Talks Upon Practical Religion," by Elder G. A. Lomas, and "Sketches of Shakers and Shakerism," by Elder Giles B. Avery. In the second edition of the latter are inserted views of all the societies.

Biography.

One hundred and thirty years of Shaker history abound in material for fascinating, educative and inspiring biographies. The life of a man or woman who has done something is always of interest. About these hidden personalities have centered electric spiritual activities ; within and without, have dramas been enacted that would have made of each life a wonder-book. But the stories have never been told in print and are unrecorded, save in the memories of their associates. Like the unpretentious and even neglected cemeteries, where their earthly forms are laid in communistic rows, unmarked save by initials on a tiny slab at head and feet, these men and women whose every breath was heroism passed and left no sign.

Of biographical works, the earliest was an account of Mother Ann Lee, entitled, "Mother's Sayings," collected in 1812, by Elder Rufus Bishop, from the first Believers, after a long and united effort in all the societies. It was edited by Seth Y. Wells and published at Hancock in 1816.

A small volume entitled "TESTIMONIES CONCERNING THE CHARACTER AND MINISTRY OF MOTHER ANN LEE," printed at Albany, bears the date, 1827. It is a simple, strong story by eye and ear witnesses of her words and deeds, told by her associates and spiritual children.

A concise story of the Order is found in a small book called "A COMPENDIUM OF THE HISTORY, RULES, ETC., OF THE SHAKER SOCIETIES, WITH A LIFE OF ANN LEE." This has passed through several editions.

From early records has been compiled in more recent years a collation, known as "PRECEPTS OF MOTHER ANN AND THE ELDERS, FROM LIVING WITNESSES," consisting of their personal recollections, clothed in the quaint, expressive garb of their homely, common speech.

The latest is a dainty little volume, published by the Shakers of East Canterbury, the work of Elder Henry C. Blinn, of the Canterbury and Enfield Ministry. The book, entitled "THE LIFE AND GOSPEL EXPERIENCE OF MOTHER ANN LEE," reveals the careful, painstaking hand of a true historian, while the chaste, graceful style of the accomplished author holds the interest of even the casual reader. Its full, yet carefully sifted recollections, its vivid pictures, its spiritual insight, its grasp of the meanings and ideals of the people and their times, render the well-indexed pages a mine of wealth to every lover and student of Shakerism.

"THE AUTOBIOGRAPHY OF A SHAKER AND REVELATION OF THE APOCALYPSE," published in both Scotland and New York, is a work of rare interest, as striking a life story as was the personality of its author, Elder Frederick W. Evans, of Mount Lebanon. It is at once the story of Elder Evans, of Shakerism, an exegesis of the Revelation of St. John and a vision of the time to come.

Smaller works of biography are, "AUTOBIOGRAPHY OF MARY ANTOINETTE DOOLITTLE," "BIOGRAPHICAL SKETCH OF DANIEL FRASER," "BRIEF NARRATIVE BY JANE KNIGHT," and others, all bearing the stamp of originality, vigor of thought and the peculiar charm of manner that marks personal intercourse with leading minds of the United Society." Booklets of an elegiac cast are common. One of the best is "TRANSLATED," in memory of the widely known and greatly beloved Elder Giles B. Avery.

"IMMORTALIZED" contains an excellent biographical sketch of Elder Frederick W. Evans, with Tributes and Letters from his friends and "Choice Gleanings" from his writings.

A dainty little brochure is "ONLY ARISEN," a spontaneous outburst of love from many hearts, at the departure, within a few hours of each other, of two who were perhaps more intensely loved than are many even among these strongly attached and affectionate people, Eldress Eliza Ann Taylor and Sister Martha J. Anderson. The former was for many years a "Mother in Israel," Head of the Central Ministry; the latter was widely known as the beautiful writer, the winning speaker and the inspired singer.

Two others, who began and ended earth life together, form the theme of a beautiful volume, called "IN MEMORIAM," containing a short biographical sketch and memorial tributes to Eldress Joanna Kaime and Eldress Dorothy Durgin, who, at the same age, in the same year, passed from the hills of New Hampshire to the Heavenly Hights. Both were exceptionally beautiful characters with rich intellectual and spiritual endowments, both were peculiarly dear to the hearts of all Believers and both were widely known and esteemed in the outside world.

"The Shakers; A Concise History of the United Society of Believers," published at East Canterbury, N. H., in 1893, is the work of an appreciative friend of the Order, Charles Edson Robinson. It contains a valuable account of the history and a series of vivid pictures of the works and the personalities of Shakers. The book is well illustrated.

"Aletheia — Spirit of Truth. Aurelia's Book" was published at Sabbathday Lake, in 1889, by Sister Aurelia G. Mace. It consists of a series of letters to the press and other articles, in a genial, social vein, revealing Shaker homes, lives and principles. One feels while reading as if in the enjoyment of a good talk with the warm-hearted, motherly author, in whose pictured face, genial and humorous, shine stability, common sense, genius and faith.

A valuable series of "Sketches of Western Shakers," by Dr. J. P. MacLean, the well known Ohio scientist and historian, have appeared in the pages of the "Ohio Historical and Archæological Quarterly." This author, the valued friend of Shakers, east as well as west, shows in his writings not only the true historic spirit, but a rare feeling of equity, appreciation and justice toward this people, a sympathetic realization of the value of their thought and belief and an understanding of their lives and purposes with a kind and discriminating criticism of their mistakes. To the writings of this author may be credited much in these pages, concerning the western societies. The historical studies of Dr. MacLean when completed in book form will be of great value in the understanding of Shakerism.

Educational.

Practical, and in earnest to improve the world he lives in, the natural bent of the Shaker, after expressing the faith that is in him, is toward reform; thus, tracts bearing on almost every phase of hygienic and social reform express his mental activity. While the Shaker societies have a fair proportion of the university trained and college bred, the common school has been the university of most of the members; but all prove discriminating readers, careful thinkers and, what is more, the decision of the mind means, soon or late, the action of conscience, will and faculty.

A little book of great value in spirit and principles is "GENTLE MANNERS," a book of instruction to the young and a guide to good morals.

"THE DIVINE AFFLATUS, A FORCE IN HISTORY," and "THE MUSIC OF THE SPHERES," two small but weighty volumes, by Daniel Fraser, the latter written in his eighty-fourth year, "are calculated," says his biographer, "to hold the attention of the thoughtful reader. Both abound in axioms, and though compressed in style, have a vigor of argument and a clearness of illustration so conclusive as to leave little ground for doubt as to the truth of their statements."

In 1872, six young sisters of the North Family at Mount Lebanon wrote "A DIALOGUE FOR THE ANNUAL SOCIAL GATHERING," whose theme, — "The Gospel Work, Its Present and Future Increase," was suggested by the date, the centenary of the opening of the Gospel in England. The dialogue was printed the next year and in compact and pleasing form preserves the spirit and teaching, as well as the outline of Shaker history, in a manner which speaks volumes for the intellectual training and spiritual culture of the authors.

"EVERY DAY BIOGRAPHY," by Amelia J. Calver, is a Biographical Year Book, published in 1889, at Mount Lebanon. The author, now Associate Eldress, in the Church Family, was for many years teacher of the Shaker School, and the volume grew out of her work with classes.

"Every Day Biography, containing a Collection of Brief Biographies arranged for every day in the year, as a book of reference for the Teacher, Student, Chautauquan and Home Circles," is tasteful and attractive in exterior and a treasure book of reference. It has escaped the dry, catalogue style of many compendiums, is bright, witty, racy and readable. Concise and to the point, its flash lights show the salient points of every career and often reveal the man or woman as in life.

Its three hundred and forty-three pages speak of one thousand four hundred and twelve men and women, renowned in different departments of life, adding an interesting and valuable Miscellany, besides an Alphabetical and an Analytical Index. It is a work of much value and deserves a wide circulation.

"MOUNT LEBANON CEDAR BOUGHS," a volume of original poems, by members of the North Family at Mount Lebanon, was published in 1895, receiving highly commendatory notices from the press. One has spoken of it thus: "A book the literature of which is of the highest type, gems of poetic genius. They are boughs from the Cedars of Lebanon. The trees are still there, waving in grandeur and beauty. They are poems sent forth to enlighten and educate and to make manifest the intellectual power that has been attained in the spiritual, communistic life. Thus the Cedars of Lebanon wave in majesty, distilling dew and sending forth Boughs for the healing of the nations."

In 1903, appeared a volume of poems, entitled, "SONG AND STORY," by Grace Ada Brown, one of the more recent converts to the faith and a member of the North Family, Mount Lebanon. Although not published by the Shakers, many of its beautiful poems are illustrative of Shaker life, the outcome of Shaker history, thought and feeling.

"Pearly Gate Bible Lessons," in three series, by Alonzo G. Hollister, of Mount Lebanon, author of many valuable tracts, is a profound, scholarly and spiritual exegesis of Scriptural Shakerism.

The Bible.

Shakers reverence and love the Hebrew Scriptures as well as the New Testament, constantly read and study them and in their precepts and teaching find the rule of life. Their views of the origin, inspiration and infallibility of the Scriptures have in years past widely differed from the standard belief of other Christian sects.

While not, as a people, learned or scholarly; while, with individual exceptions, unversed in ancient languages and in laws of historic and literary criticism, they have, from early times, held nearly the same ground, in general principles, that the world of scholars is slowly attaining through the long upward climb of critical investigation known as the Higher Criticism.

Shakers have always distinguished between the Bible and the Word of God. To them, the Word of God is not a book, but the Christ Spirit, ever uttering, ever revealing God,— the Invisible, the Unknown, and to the finite being the Unknowable, save as the Christ Spirit, Son and Daughter, who is in the bosom of the Father-Mother, has declared and manifested, God.

"The Word of God," says Elder Giles B. Avery, "is revealing a God character infinitely superior to the Jehovah of the Jews, a living Spirit, Christ, illimitably transcending the crucified and worshipped form of Jesus, and an ever evolving testimony of living truth. The Word of God is light, life and the power of salvation. It is a revelation of God's will and purpose concerning the evolving destiny of man

It is a baptism of divine power in such manner and measure as to magnetize and vivify the whole man — body, soul and spirit — with an intense interest in, love for and devotion to the salvation, development and glorification of the human race. It is a ministration of love so endearing and soul thrilling as to cause its recipient to sacrifice life for the salvation of the object of the soul's affection."

Said Elder Evans: — "Bibles are records of the utterances of Divinity — records of God's word. The prophetic books of the Bible are a priceless boon to humanity. Their claims to Christ inspiration are substantiated by numerous intensely momentous fulfilments of prophecies concerning cities, kingdoms and nations, and by still more important actualizations in the religious progress and spiritual history of the race. All Scripture records of Divine inspiration help to reveal the power and wisdom of God to mankind; and they should be preserved, studied and interpreted by the light of a present, living revelation, as that includes the whole focal light of all former revelations. God's word and work never wane nor retrograde, but are eternally progressing toward the final redemption of all races. Hence, none of the Bibles, not even the Christian's are yet finished."

Worship.

The spiritual origin and meaning of the various exercises in worship have been referred to. The most characteristic were shaking and dancing. Although Shakers find abundant scriptural defense of these customs, they did not derive them from the Scriptures, but were so often led into them by the direct operation of the Spirit that they concluded both to be acceptable to the Divine Will as modes of worship, while they found the spiritual effect of both upon themselves very desirable; the one, in throwing off the sense of evil and the desire for indulgence in sin; the other, in quickening spiritual powers and imparting strength, joy and victory to the soul.

Said Elder Calvin Green: — "They found that sincere devotion and energy of spirit in the exercise and unity of worship, according to the leading gift, was the most effectual means of keeping down the life of the flesh, because in this unity the greatest flow of the superior life of the Spirit was diffused. The natural mind was more opposed to simplicity and conformity in this respect than to anything else in the Visible Order of the Gospel. The proud, self-willed spirit of human nature has ever needed the most mortification and subjection, in order to gain a proper gift in the unity of sacred worship, and those who have refused to unite in these simple exercises have never prospered in the spiritual life and travel."

This condition is as true today as it was one hundred years ago. It is as necessary now as then for souls who would advance in the work of redemption to bring into subjection the natural instincts of self-assertion, independence and pride, and the simplicity of the exercise in worship affords the best opportunity for bringing low these elements of human nature. This self-conquest opens the way for the gifts of the Spirit, the endowment with spiritual energy.

Soon after the Church was established, Father Joseph Meacham gave, as the gift of God, instruction "to labor down into mortification deeper than would ever be necessary again." All recreations and literary studies were suspended; children played but little; they were taught the orders or rules and were severely reproved for breaking them. From 1793, the exercise was a heavy shuffle; there were no hymns. Slower and slower grew the exercise, until by command of Father Joseph it was suspended altogether and the meeting consisted of a solemn song without words, followed by instruction and reproof.

"We were constantly urged to labor in mortification, self-abasement, to think we were almost good for nothing and never would be worth but little. This was depressing, especially to children, but necessary to lay the foundations as deep as any souls would ever be required to travel." This is the testimony of Elder Calvin Green, who was a child at the time.

In 1798, the "Square Order" was introduced and from 1800 speaking by the members was encouraged. Soon after Mother Lucy's administration began and Believers entered into an earnest labor for an ingathering of souls, their feelings were quickened, more life was manifested in the meetings, a quick dance and frequent operations of power were given. During the work in the southwest, hymns were composed and sent to the Church at Mount Lebanon. These were circulated and sung, and, by the summer of 1807, the singing of hymns had become a custom. Previous to that time, the singing of songs without words had prevailed. In the early years of the society, a meeting had been held in the early morning. At the close of the day, each family now sang a hymn and exercised in the Square Order. A song entitled "Gospel Trumpet" was composed and formed an important part of the worship.

Wordless songs passed out of use, and about 1810, short songs often of but one verse were employed. Sometimes these were made up from a few words in an exhortation and sung over and over; sometimes they were prepared with more care and formality. This custom led naturally to the production of anthems. A feeling grew that these would be a spiritual benefit and, by a special gift of Mother Lucy,

anthems were introduced into public worship in the year
1813.

Gradually the meetings grew less formal, extra songs
were sung, sometimes by direct inspiration, words and tune
being imparted together, in the midst of the service.

About two years after Mother Lucy's translation, the
Sacred March was introduced.

Few experiences are more thrilling to a visitor than sitting as an on-looker in the religious exercises of these people, in their plain yet exquisitely appropriate dress, watching the harmonious movement of the march, which signifies
the onward travel of the soul to spiritual freedom and full
redemption, the movements of the hands, that mean the
gathering and scattering of blessing, and listening to the
singing, with no instrumental hindrance in the way of an
accompaniment, as the sweet, soul-filled voices utter in
simple melodies the hope and aspiration of their souls. There
is no striving after effect,— it is pure devotion, the artless
expression of sincere life efforts for purity and holiness.
Many, untouched by art's highest efforts, are deeply affected
in witnessing the worship of these pure, true-hearted men
and women, who aim "to be what they appear to be and to
appear to be what they really are."

Advance in Doctrine.

According to the teachings of Mother Ann, the Gospel
would forever increase into higher and purer Orders, not
by reversing any principle, but by rising higher and higher,
until it should spread through all the world. This has been
the historic procedure. The gathering into Order has proved
the most nearly perfect, for its time, of any system ever
known, and the only institution of the kind that has so long
stood the test of time. A great advance in public teaching

of doctrine marked the opening and followed the great western revival.

The existence and revelation of the Mother Spirit, although understood and believed, had never previously been openly taught. At that time it was personally made known to many, even the children receiving the revelation. Father Joseph had prophesied that in the next opening the Mother Spirit would be held in remembrance, and so it proved. In the west, the prophecy was literally fulfilled, and today, the public testimony to the Mother Spirit is common in teaching and song, wherever Shakers are found.

In later years there has been a gradual change in the character of the worship in the hour of public or family devotion. While inflowings of spiritual power are frequent, and the gifts and leadings of the Spirit are heeded and followed, the tendency is toward expression of thought rather than bodily exercise. Shakers are thinkers; the spiritual current runs, perhaps, deeper, with less of noise and outward demonstration. Thought, instinct with strong feeling, personal consecration, backed by a life habit of practical devotion and self-sacrifice, in free expression by each and every member, as the inner movings of the Spirit prompt, is the custom of today.

Nowhere, perhaps, is the difference between the mental habit of the Shaker and the professed Christian of the outside order more apparent than in the funeral service.

A Shaker Funeral

is not a funeral but a triumph, a transfiguration, a fusion of heavenly and earthly spheres. That pagan dreariness, with which professed believers in a heaven of light and glory enshroud their hours of leave-taking of mortality, finds no place among the people who aim to live every day the life of the angel in the human. The name funeral is being exchanged for memorial service, which it really is. When one of the closely knit band passes into the other life, all share in the triumph; the veil of the mortal grows thinner and sometimes almost disappears, while spirit forms, with song, testimony and blessing, palpably and audibly comfort, uplift and encourage those left in the body. Naturally adopting the simple Quaker custom of personal tributes of love and respect to the arisen one, the Shaker service of farewell is, of all periods of worship, the most full of spiritual help, strength and inspiration.

Shaker simplicity also does away with the meaningless trappings of grief, that for thousands make of burial a burden of debt to crush the future of the living. The strong, sensible testimony of Elder Evans may well be repeated:

"He is Risen; He is not here."

"Thus, the 'prophet like unto Moses' in his life and character as a leader, was also like him in that no man knoweth, unto this day, where his dead body was deposited until it became incorporated with the general soil of the earth from whence it was derived. Dust to dust, but the voice of the spirit still saith, the man 'Is not here.'

" 'Let the dead bury their dead.' The dead anti-Christians, who expect their dead bodies to be re-animated, may reverence 'corruption and dead men's bones' and expend labor and capital to erect costly white sepulchres to contain them,— be it the portion of Believers — Shakers — to decently hide, and then spiritually and piously forget where the body is laid, as an individual body.

"He or she is not here, should be our testimony to all inquiring relatives and friends, who come 'with sweet spices,' to embalm the memory of the rotting body, while they forget to look after the living soul. Let us do as the angels did by the Israelites and again by the early Christians, and refuse to identify the particular lump of matter by testifying, the man or woman is not here. Thus, when I die, may my body be buried, and be laid next in order to the body of the brother or sisters who immediately preceded me to that bourne from whence travellers do now so easily return to commune with the living."

Elder Frederick would have a tree planted by every grave, that thus death should lose its sting, the grave its victory over the living, and the fear of death be supplanted by a spirit of rejoicing. Each human being, having been comforted and benefited by the scenery thus furnished while living, would add to earth's fertility and beauty by the deposit of a body for which he no longer had any use.

XIX

THE GIFT OF SONG

"ON establishing the Order of Believers," writes Elder Henry C. Blinn, "all seemed anxious to keep a respectful distance from the order of the world at large, that the new revelation might be respected and strengthened by force of contrast. The members were expected and instructed to rely on the inspiration of God rather than on the knowledge of any science which the mind of man had developed. Hence, the study of musical science with other branches was at first wholly neglected and for a time rather depreciated. Lengthy anthems and hymns, thousands in number, were learned by hearing. Those musically inclined by nature were employed to communicate the music to others; and in the exchange of social visits among the societies attention was particularly given to an interchange of music. This proved very satisfactory, and for a number of years between 1792 and 1821, no change was deemed necessary."

Soon after the passing of the wordless songs, about 1810, this primitive method of musical instruction became prevalent. In 1815, an anthem was written with notes and sent to Ohio, and a year later an exchange was made of several pieces between Mount Lebanon and Union Village. About this time the Harvard Society began to make use of letters for notes; this device was adopted and employed for many years. The author of the system claimed that it was imparted by inspiration from Mother Ann, as an easier

NO. 26.   ELDER HENRY C. BLINN.   HEAD OF THE CANTER-
BURY MINISTRY.

method and one better adapted to Believers than the one in common use. The first seven letters of the alphabet in capitals were employed, the Roman letters to designate quarter notes, Italics, eighth notes, while half notes had the addition of single lines by the side of the letters. Some years later, Isaac N. Youngs, of Mount Lebanon, and Russell Haskell, of Enfield, Conn., developed and perfected the system of letter notation. A little book, the "Musical Expositor," was issued by Russell Haskell, in 1847, for the expounding of this method. Brother Isaac's gamut, from which he copied and printed with his own hand the book of lessons for beginners, still exists in the possession of Brother Alonzo G. Hollister, to whose thoughtful care is due the preservation of many priceless heirlooms of the old time Shakers.

In 1827, a fresh wave of spiritual life passed over the communities. New songs abounded. "It was a baptism of Gospel fire, the good effects of which lasted for years."

In 1835, a thorough reform was made in the system of music, several helpful articles being written and published at Enfield. In 1837 and during the following years of spirit manifestation, hymns and anthems greatly increased. It is estimated that between one and two thousand songs and hymns were produced and learned. When all these songs had to be copied into manuscript books and learned by heart, it made no small task for so busy a people as the Shakers, yet no book was ever taken into meeting, save by the leaders, and to this day, aged members will, at a word, start off in unison, with the spirit and fire of youth, to sing the quaint, sweet old songs of sixty years ago. The manuscript books, where words were copied, with letters signifying musical tones at the foot of the page, are models of neatness and care. That duty, like every other, was part of the service of God. About 1870, letter notation passed out of general

22

use. From the first, a special gift of harmony has seemed to rest upon the Canterbury society and many of the most refined and soul thrilling of the Shaker hymns have emanated from here. Elder Henry C. Blinn has written upon the

Musical Evolution at Canterbury.

"Abram Whitney, a teacher of music, a member for many years of the society at Shirley, Mass., was the first person to urge the study of music. Upon solicitation, he visited Canterbury and Enfield and gave a few rudimental lessons. Educational interest opened in 1823, by a visit to Canterbury of Brother Seth Y. Wells, of Mount Lebanon. Instruction along progressive lines was given to both brethren and sisters, and this was renewed at more advanced stages, ten years later, when he paid another visit. Among other suggestions, he recommended that twenty or thirty minutes be devoted each day to singing; he also proposed that the day school be opened to visitors and strangers, who might wish to inspect the pupils' work.

"The first attempt at singing in harmony was ventured in 1845, but only melodies were permitted in worship. The first harmony was indeed a feeble attempt, as only a few words at the end of a line were furnished with a second row of notes and these were a third, fifth or eighth below the melody. At this date, Prof. B. B. Davis, of Concord, N. H., was engaged to give a course of lessons to the singers. This new departure was more or less subject to criticism, but the round notes soon led to a deprecation of the other styles. From this time to 1864, interest in music steadily increased. In June, 1853, Joshua Hutchinson, of the once famous Hutchinson Family, visited and entertained the community for several days.

"August 18th, 1870, Dr. C. A. Guilmette, of Boston, was introduced to the society by Prof. Davis, as a superior teacher of vocal music, both in theory and practise. He proved to be not only an accomplished vocalist, but an elocutionist and learned physician as well. A series of lectures bearing upon the vocal apparatus and the means for its development and culture opened a new era, as classes were soon formed for daily drills, of which the Doctor proved a wise and earnest teacher. Rehearsals for correct breathing and tone production multiplied, until the seed of interest was firmly planted in the minds of the society.

"During these early visits, both Prof. Davis and Dr. Guilmette broached the need of a musical instrument as imperative to aid the singing. This subject was urged until an agreement was reached by the leaders. A melodeon, or small cabinet organ, was the first musical instrument purchased, in November, 1870. The first piano was brought into the community two years later by one of the members.

"During a visit of the Central Ministry to Canterbury at that time, sanction and approval of the work accomplished in this line gave the only needed impetus to further culture. Attention was now directed to the mastery of the rudiments, and seven of the most progressed pupils took charge of as many classes. A little book, or music reader, 'Merry Chimes,' was purchased in 1874 and was zealously studied. After the mastery of the present musical notation, helps in this line were kindly given to Believers in other societies, and teachers from Canterbury visited South Union, Kentucky, Mount Lebanon and Watervliet, N. Y.

"All opportunities for culture or advice by visiting teachers have been eagerly improved, and lessons have been solicited and received in drawing, painting, the languages and mathematics, as the means were presented. The first music printed in the present style was in 1875.

"Earnest efforts were repeated as home duties would permit, but the latter have ever been in the precedent. Attendance at outside musicales has been very moderate, but helpful in urging to a better rendering of the music as a first-fruit offering to God.

"The collection of hymns now in use by the society was commenced in the year 1875, under the supervision, and including the choice contributions of our ascended Eldress Dorothy A. Durgin. The printing was under the special advice of Elder Henry C. Blinn. In the arrangement of this volume, several of the most progressed singers studied the rudiments of harmony, and, under the criticism of able teachers who entered the transient membership list, soon became competent to arrange harmonies suitable for the press.

"In 1884, Mr. Herbert Johnson, of Boston, first visited the society and at a later date a quartette of sisters, now existing, was formed, and general attention directed to harmonious part singing. The first concert given at the earnest solicitation of outside friends, was held in Pittsfield, N. H., in August, 1894.

"The family includes several prominent members, naturally musical, who have added talent and scholarship to the consecrated whole, and who are today engaged both as students and teachers in this favorite branch, when home burdens permit. At present date (1902), one hundred ten years after the formation of the society, while musical attainment is still in its infancy, it is, however, one of the leading interests; but the thought of the fraternity along this line may be gleaned from a remark volunteered by one of the singers: 'Despite the endeavors of years, we are still at work on the A B C of musical excellence.' "

This modest estimate fails to do justice to the artistic work of the "Canterbury Quartett." The wonderful harmony of these remarkable voices is a surprise and a delight to those, who, accustomed to the great singers of the day, listen for the first time to these Shaker sisters. It is truly "like the singing of the angels."

Music Books.

A volume, entitled "Millennial Praises, A Collection of Gospel Hymns," was published at Hancock in 1812. The work was in four parts, which were printed together the following year. In 1833, a small book of 108 pages, "Rudiments of Music," was published, followed by another in 1842. A plain, little volume, covered with blue paper, also appeared in 1833, at Watervliet, O., "A Selection of Hymns and Poems, For the Use of Believers, by Philos Harmoniae." This lover of harmony was Richard McNemar. The 180 pages are aglow with the religious fervor and quaint conceits of the time, and some of its picturesque, inspiring songs still arouse the old-time enthusiasm at Mount Lebanon. "Millennial Hymns" appeared at Canterbury in 1847. The same society, in 1852, published a collection of selections from masterpieces, for the purpose of study and musical training. The collection of hymns, familiarly known as the "Canterbury Book," "Hymns and Anthems for the Hour of Worship," published in 1892, is a favorite for its spiritual tone and inspirational power. From Mount Lebanon came "Original Inspirational Shaker Music," in two volumes, dated 1884 and 1893. "The simple offering of a simple people," they well illustrate the later developments of a unique system of hymns and songs, evolved from the simple word pictures of the early days, graphic, like the homely language of the time, ever growing in wealth and flexibility of expression, in richness and delicacy of coloring, as minds have become enlarged and enriched by literature, thought and spiritual affiliations. With the thought has developed the music, till later years have evolved some beautiful harmonies. A peculiar charm, a spiritual quality pervades many of them, as elusive to analysis as the "angel look" on the faces of those who produce them.

While dwelling on the details of the preparation of Volume II, for the press, Eldress Anna White awoke one morning repeating rhythmic lines of true poetic feeling. She appealed to her colleague to know whose they were and whence they came. It was finally decided that the lines were to be found on no printed page, but had been given by inspiration for the title page of the book, where they appear:

> "Man is a harp of a thousand strings;"
> Touch the spiritual chord of his heart,
> And lo! with what inspiration he sings,
> Unaided by science, unskilled in art.
> 'Tis the voice of God in his soul that sings,
> And is more than a harp of a thousand strings.

In recent years the question has arisen of introducing instrumental music in worship, but, although it is sometimes employed in the family meetings, the feeling is nearly or quite universal against its regular use in Sabbath services. The free use of piano, organ and other instruments in the family has long been general, and instruction in music holds as prominent a place in the Shaker home as in the private family.

The Gift of Song has not passed with the years, but continues to gladden with its ministrations the hearts of the faithful children of that Mother, whose songs were like angel harmonies when she walked and talked among her children upon the earth. These hymns are marked by sweetness, simplicity and spirituality, a force of appeal which touches strongly all who listen. Many have come by inbreathings from the spirit world, often to one unversed in musical art, but whose soul is attuned to the harmony of holy living. The simplest are often the most effective, accompanied, as they frequently are, by movements of the hands or person. The Kindergarten movements in song, as practised in the schools of today, seem to have had a spirit origin when we compare them with the spiritually vitalized action of the inspirational songs and movements of the Shakers in religious worship.

Songs and their Stories.

Elder Frederick W. Evans, in a morning dream, was impressed by a spirit company of brethren and sisters of the family, and, getting up in the dark, he wrote the words which were set to a tune by one of the sisters.

CHRIST ANGELS.

My heart is in the spirit world,
    My soul is roaming there,
I dwell amid the denizens
    Of that bright world so fair.
Like seasons in this earthly sphere
    The cycles come and go,
Their ceaseless aeons none may see,
    They are not counted so.

Years follow years, the centuries pass,
  And thus earth ages roll,
Unnumbered figures may not tell
  The history of the soul.
Its days are deeds, its years are shown
  By changes in it wrought,
It lives when God's own spirit rules
  The secret springs of thought.

Then, O my soul, immortal, thou
  Shalt never, never die,
While truth to feed thee shall exist
  And love to vivify.
The angels in the inner sphere,
  In age eternal all,
In God they live, in God they move,
  God is their all in all.

They sing to us in accents sweet
  The music of their sphere,
"Arise and stand upon your feet —
  We come, our home is here.
No more shall war, with direful curse
  Stain earth with human gore,
Contending armies fight for right,
  The reign of sin is o'er.

New earth and heavens are coming up,
  The old fast fade away;
The night of antichrist is o'er,
  All hail, the new born day!"
Blest Gospel kindred, firm and strong,
  Cheer up, your zeal renew,
Leave all the errors of the past —
  Christ angels are with you.

Hannah R. Agnew, a seer of remarkable gifts, in a vision of Eldress Antoinette, received the following:

"On, onward, away from the world,
In joyful triumph we're moving;
Keeping the banner of Christ unfurled,
By love our discipleship proving.
Sing, sing with the angels around thee,
Thou beautiful Zion of God;
From near and afar to the isles of the sea,
Thy song of salvation now echos abroad,
And many will come unto thee."

Many years ago, the Canterbury Ministry, visiting at Mount Lebanon, united with the North family in an outdoor meeting, held in "Locust Grove," where a powerful spiritual influence was manifest. A young girl who was present related in after years the thrilling effect of the movements. Of the visiting Ministry, she said, "It seemed as though they had come down from heaven." Returning home, Elder Abraham Perkins paused by the shore of the pond, and, starting a quick song, the whole assembly joined in the dance and continued dancing up the hill to the dwelling. Pausing in the door-yard, they again sang, and "a spiritual influence went out from them that seemed to fill the whole door-yard." Lastly, in the hall of the dwelling-house, which had been consecrated as a House for the Heavenly Father and Mother to dwell in, Elder Abraham sang with intense feeling a song that had been given to him as "a song ·that was never to be written," and which has never been set to time or notes, but is held in the memory as a prophetic message:

"I looked and beheld in the Heavens strange things,
The impress was that which humility brings,
E'en the angels fell prostrate and lowered their wings;

For a moment 'twas silent, then a shadow passed by,
Succeeded by voices, remote, from on high,
Prepare, ye people, the Eternal will come,
He'll fan you, He'll sift you, again and again!"

Some have frequently received songs while asleep, and one sister at Mount Lebanon would often, on awakening, be called upon to listen to her own songs, which had been noted down by her room-mates as she had sung them while asleep. In the early days of the Civil War, before the Emancipation Proclamation had been issued, one thus received prefigured that event. This song was sung in every family of Believers, although without any previous arrangement or understanding, on the occasion of President Lincoln's funeral.

Sometimes healing and song come together in accordant blessing. One thus came to Eldress Mary Ann Gillespie, of the Maine Ministry, when sick and supposed to be upon her death bed. The Central Ministry, from Mount Lebanon, came to visit her and as the revered Heads of the Order entered her room, although she had been unable to speak above a whisper, she suddenly rose up in bed and sang in a clear, full voice, by instant inspiration:

> "Precious Gospel kindred,
> You are mine to love and bless, etc."

One of the sweetest singers of Israel was the pure and beautiful soul who, by attraction of spiritual affinity, rose to the world of immortality in 1898, Eldress Dorothy Durgin, widely known and dearly loved without as well as within the Shaker fold. One dark, stormy night, when the roads were danger filled, she was anxiously awaiting the home-coming of a party of young sisters, who had been detained. While listening for the carriage her anxiety became intense, when, in the silence, she heard the spirit assurance within her soul, sung to a beautiful harmony:

> "Angels are keeping watch, etc."

One, received by Eldress Anna White, during the tedious process of recovery from a severe attack of neuritis, when she was exercised in mind on the necessity of an advance by the whole Order, voices the faith that claims as its own and by obedience to physiological and spiritual laws may attain to the rightful inheritance, long promised and often bestowed upon individuals, of the spiritual Gift of Healing Power.

Among the many endowed with inspirational gifts, none more harmoniously responded in every faculty of being to the divine touch than Sister Martha J. Anderson.

Her spirit was like an Aeolian harp keyed to the airs of the upper spheres. Her imagination, enkindled at the altar of devotion, ever aspired toward the source of purity, harmony and love. She literally gave her life for the welfare of others. In devotion to hand labor, she nobly fulfilled the famous injunction, "Hands to work and hearts to God." Sympathetic as a spirit of love, her benediction rested on everyone in sorrow or soul struggle. A child of nature, electric currents flowed between earth and its flowers and her sunshine-gifted soul. A vigorous thinker and writer, pages of Shaker publications and local papers glow with her gems of thought. Hundreds of her songs enrich the music treasuries of her people, and the echoes of her rare, sweet voice still resound in her beloved home. In one hymn, she embodies the Shaker understanding of

RESURRECTION.

Dying daily, 'tis the conscious
Evolution of the soul,
In a life of endless progress,
As the ages onward roll.
Dying just as seasons, changing,
Leave the forms that pass away,
Higher life new growth unfolding
Smite the old with sure decay.

Dying to the loves of nature,
  Self and selfishness they hold,
In a sphere too cramped and narrow,
  For the being to unfold.
Dying unto worldly honor,
  Glory's vainly boasted name;
Laurel wreath of truth immortal
  Never crowned the sons of fame.

Dying unto bitter envy,
  Jealousy and vain conceit,
Demon spoilers of the blessing
  Shared where peace and union meet.
Dying to life's sordid grasping,
  Love of power and earthly gain,
That would rob a needy brother,
  Heeding not his want and pain.

Dying to a lofty spirit,
  Overbearing, proud and high,
Stooping not with gentle pity
  When the lowly passeth by.
Dying unto false pretences
  Held in pure religion's name,
Cant, hypocrisy and grandeur —
  Silken robes for sin and shame.

Dying, that in resurrection,
  Grand and true the soul may rise,
Noble type of Godlike image
  Wrought through perfect sacrifice.
Life is in the Christian's triumph,
  When from sin and bondage free;
Lo! the prince of darkness cometh
  And can find no place in me.

XX

THE WORKS OF CHRIST

A S in the former advent, to those who brought the searching query from the troubled heart of the imprisoned John, "Art thou he that should come, or do we look for another?" Jesus said, "Go and tell John what things ye have seen and heard, how that the lame walk, the deaf hear, the blind see, the lepers are cleansed, the dead are raised up and the poor have the Gospel preached to them!" so, in the later coming of the Christ in Ann Lee, are found the same confirmatory facts, attesting to her power, by means of the indwelling Divinity, over natural phenomena and sequence of material movement and effect.

Spiritual Gifts.

Jesus said, "Greater things than these shall ye do because I go unto my Father," and "Whatsoever ye shall ask the Father in my name, that will I do." Father James, speaking of the increase of the work of God and prophesying of the beauty of Zion, was wont to say: "But greater power will never be on earth than now is."

As an instance of these

Gifts of Power,

Jemima Blanchard, of Harvard, having a gift of turning, would sometimes go from the Square House to the South

NO. 27. SISTER MARTHA J. ANDERSON.

House, whirling rapidly and passing over fences or whatever came in her way, without touching them or making the least effort to clear them. At times she would be entirely supported by the power without touching any material thing.

Of this same Jemima Blanchard, one who was with her in old age and blindness, and who took down from her lips many remembrances of Mother Ann and the days of the opening of the Gospel, speaking of the impression made on the early Believers by the power and sublimity of the work of Mother Ann and the influence of her spirit, said it was not in her power to portray the vivid idea Jemima would give of the divine influence Mother Ann would shed upon all around, of the beauty of her person, the spiritual grace of her movements. "I have frequently discovered by the expression of Jemima's countenance that she was thinking of Mother Ann, before she uttered a word."

At the Square House were given many strange signs and operations of the Spirit, and Mother Ann sometimes seemed to be laboring to understand them. At one time she was heard to say that she never saw anything like it, but, after a pause, "It is of God, and it is not for me to condemn it."

John Dunlavy wrote this description of scenes at Pleasant Hill, which are but samples of the action in all the societies of Shakers, in the days of these strong manifestations of power:

"Sometimes the hands are raised, palms outwards, and the position shifted with such quickness and velocity as to indicate the lively, sweet and beautiful motions of the heavenly spirits, in all the charms of heavenly beauty, untainted with the flesh. Sometimes the subjects of these operations are taken from the floor, as if their feet were snatched from under them, and they are again caught and supported from falling, as being handled by the most active and powerful agents. Some are whirled off to a distance and others carried to and fro, or in a circle, with indescribable force, and the hands brought together in such a manner as to resemble the report of guns rather than the clapping of hands, or with unspeakable velocity put into an untold variety of motions, waving and clapping together with childlike joy and simplicity.

"They sing in a gift of the Spirit, the most beautiful songs and words. They appear like beautiful spirits moving in their appropriate element — Mother's pure Love, carried in the Power of God, unbodied spirits rather than the inhabitants of the earth."

Within very recent years, two instances are recalled, where brethren, working in the tops of high trees, have, by the breaking of a branch, been precipitated to the ground; but, instead of receiving any harm, have been conscious of being supported, and have felt as though moving gently through the air to the earth. One was conscious of Elder Richard Bushnell holding him in his arms.

Gift of Tongues.

"Ye shall speak with other tongues," and "They spake with other tongues as the Spirit gave them utterance," is the promise and the fulfilment in the days of the apostles; when the gift of the Spirit was restored in the latter days, speaking in unknown languages was one of the marked features and signs of the reality of the coming of the Christ Spirit.

"The sign of the first Gospel degree was the Gift of Tongues. Mother Ann spoke in seventy-two different languages, showing that she was en rapport with representatives of the nations who needed the Gospel in the spirit world. Throughout the sounding of this first testimony, the gift of tongues invariably rested upon those whom the spirit raised up as leaders to preach and minister the Gospel, from Mother Ann to Samuel Johnson and Richard Bushnell, who were greatly gifted in tongues."

The latter, known wherever the Shaker faith has gone as "Elder Richard," who had received a double portion of the anointing of a Savior, was remarkable in his day for this peculiar and convincing power of the Spirit.

The story is well authenticated that the hero of so many legal and literary labors in the early part of the last century, Seth Y. Wells, owed his conversion to a gift of tongues that rested upon a sister, unversed in any language but her own, and a gift of interpretation bestowed upon another.

Seth Y. Wells, then principal of the Hudson Academy, N. Y., was visiting an uncle living in one of the Shaker families at Watervliet. Making a study of the Order, he attended the services, where he heard much plain testimony. At last, one sister began to talk in an unknown tongue. Recognizing the language, and feeling a personal interest in what she was saying, he inquired if anyone knew what that woman was talking about. "Yea," replied another, "she is talking of that journey you are expecting to take." As neither of the sisters knew the language spoken, and as no one but himself knew of his plan to take a journey, he felt assured that a gift of inspiration had been imparted, and he yielded obedience to the divine power which he recognized as existing in the Shaker Order.

Eldress Antoinette Doolittle, in recent days, also had this endowment in a marked degree, often speaking in a language unknown to herself or to her people. She was sometimes given the power of interpretation, to give the meaning of the message which had been given in an unknown tongue.

Origin of the Christmas Gift.

Before the Church left England, the question arose on what day Christmas should be observed. The famous controversy over the New Style or Old Style day was then agitating the minds of the common people of England. When Christmas drew near, in the home at Niskeyuna, Mother Ann, as was her wont in all important matters, set the minds of her people at work on the question as to the date and the manner in which Christmas should be observed.

Elder John Hocknell felt an assurance that it should be observed according to New Style, and in a sacred manner, not as a day of jesting and frivolity. Hannah Hocknell, on the contrary, decided for the date according to Old Style, and that no particular significance should be attached to it.

Accordingly, on the morning of Christmas Day, N. S., Hannah arose and began to dress for a day's work at washing and house-cleaning. For some unaccountable reason, she could not get her shoes on; some peculiar operation prevented her each time she tried. Mother Ann, quick to see a spiritual meaning in everything, said this was a sign, as spoken of in Exodus iii. 5, and in Joshua v. 15, where it reads: "Put off thy shoes from off thy feet, for the place whereon thou standest is holy ground."

She recognized Hannah's cleaning gift in appointing that the labor of the day should be the cleaning of the spiritual house and garments. She also appointed that the day be yearly kept and devoted to spiritual purposes. Father Joseph, in the Gathering into Order, also established it as an abiding ordinance that Christmas should be kept as a special time for confessing and putting away sin, making restitution for wrongs, forgiving offences and restoring peace and union. He taught that this was the fulfilment of the typical law of Yearly Sacrifice by expiation, wherein a similar work was required of the Jews; and that thus we should be enabled to work in unison with the Savior in whom Christ was revealed; that we ought to do this in grateful remembrance of the opening of a door, through the birth of

Jesus, for Christ to usher in the era of salvation. Mother Lucy and Elder Henry, successors to Mother Ann and Father Joseph, confirmed the Christmas Gift.

Gift of Healing.

The promise of the power to heal diseases and to live free from sickness is held by the Church of Mother Ann's founding. Numerous instances are certified to by those who personally knew Mother Ann and the Elders, where a word or a touch from her or from them had released from suffering, cured disease and restored to health and strength. A few of the many have been placed on record. Among them are cases of lameness, hip disease, consumption, acute dyspepsia and stomach troubles, exhaustion, obsession, dislocation of bones, glandular affections and many more.

One instance is related of a leading member at Mount Lebanon, whose child was said to have died. Word was brought to him while at work in the field. After a time he entered the house, took the little girl in his arms, walking up and down the room with her, and life returned.

Zaccheus Stevens, mentioned in connection with the mob at Harvard, was at one time taken very sick at Watervliet and was not expected to recover. He told Mother Ann that important matters at home demanded his attention. She said to him: "Take faith and you will recover. You may set out tomorrow morning, return home and settle your business." This command amazed every one. But Zaccheus obeyed and started promptly on his journey of one hundred and fifty miles, going thirty miles the first day, increasing in strength daily, until he reached home in good health. He afterward said: "I am bold to say that no one ever came under loss through obedience to Mother."

23

The well attested fact, that for several years after the first Gathering into Order, when all were exerting themselves to the utmost in physical and spiritual labors, Believers were almost entirely free from sickness and death, is cited by Elder Calvin Green, as showing that the spirit and life of the Gospel is conducive to health and longevity.

A story was told by Eunice Bathrick, of Harvard, that a man who professed to be a Believer once came to Father Joseph asking permission to call on a world's doctor. Father Joseph, considering the matter, walked up and down the floor, trying to "gather a gift." Finally he replied: "They that have my spirit have no occasion to go to world's doctors, for there is power enough, sufficient to heal soul and body."

The petitioner had not faith simple enough to rise to the occasion, but Ezekiel Morrill, lying the other side of a partition, sick with a serious complaint and supposed to be past cure, thought that he would appropriate Father Joseph's gift and did so. His faith was rewarded. From that time he was restored to perfect health, lived for many years as Elder Brother in the Church at Canterbury, and passed away at an advanced age.

The Healing Gift has always existed in some degree in the church and is still found. It is recorded of Issachar Bates that, on his solitary tramp of nearly eight hundred miles from Mount Lebanon to Union Village, bearing the funds for the home of the new society, his left foot and ankle became very much swollen and extremely painful. He could not sleep nor wear his shoe. He was in much distress of mind. Then came a question to his heart: "Where is your faith"? "I said abruptly, Faith! I should as soon think of asking to have my leg cured if the bone was broken." A voice whispered, "Whatsoever ye shall ask the Father in my name, it shall be done!" "I cannot describe my feelings, but it seemed to me that I gave my whole soul into the name of Christ, and asked. In a moment I realized a change, and it was all over; my foot was as well as ever. And how to express my thanks I could not tell; but I put on my shoe and ran nearly three miles, singing as well as I could while on the race. People stared at me as I passed them on the road, and no doubt they thought I was a crazy man; but I did not care for that, I was so overjoyed that I had been healed."

In the year 1807, word was one day brought to the North family that a widow, Lucy Brown, living in the family of John Vining, on Hammond mountain, was very sick and wanted Ruth Johnson, an able doctress, to come to her. The next day word was sent that Lucy would die, and Isaac Crouch, the Church physician, was requested to come, with two sisters for watchers. The North Family Elder, Calvin Green, had a strong impression to go with them.

Entering the house, they found the sick woman in bed, scarcely able to breathe. She said: "I am glad to see you, Calvin. I have heard that you have the gift of healing for all that have faith in you."

He replied, "I have had such a gift for myself." Taking hold of her right hand, he felt a strong flow of power. Lifting her gently by the hand, she rose up in bed, "trembling like a leaf in a gentle breeze." The Elder assured her that if she would have faith she would be healed. Anna Alden, one of the watchers sent from the North Family, was immediately seized with strong power and began to speak in an unknown tongue. Lucy was operated upon with increasing force, began to shake violently, the fever left her and she felt relieved.

For thirty-six hours she had been unable to retain any food. Now she arose, was led down to the kitchen and partook of a hearty meal.

The same Elder performed a still more remarkable cure upon a sister at Hancock. Joanna Brewster, mother of the Brewster family, was in a decline and was expected to die of consumption. "I do not feel willing to die yet! I want to live and do more good," were her words. Seeing that she had faith in spiritual aid, Elder Calvin felt the strong responding influence in himself and gave it out to her with much power, telling her to take faith, be prudent, and she would recover. She replied, "I feel healed!" She was soon entirely restored, and lived for more than a half century after that, vigorous physically and mentally till the age of ninety and over.

In 1816, a poor family in Hancock were left fatherless, and the Justice of the Peace brought the widow and six children to the Lebanon Shakers. They were taken in. The youngest child, two years old, had never walked, was covered with sores from head to foot and could not be touched without screaming.

Elder Calvin felt a strong impression that she could be healed. Sitting down beside the mother, the little one reached out from her mother's lap toward him. He took her and gently stroked the sore places on her head, neck and arm, the child turning that he might touch them. He put her down, with the words that she would recover, and left her. Forty-eight hours after this occurrence she got up and began to walk for the first time in her life. On examining her, the mother found the sores entirely healed.

This family of girls grew up to become good Shakers, occupying positions of trust and responsibility. One of them, Marilla Fairbanks, was Eldress for many years in the Second Family, while her sister, Samantha, was in the Ministry at the time of her decease.

A brother of fervent spirit but of delicate health, utterly unaccustomed to severe manual labor, one morning appealed to Elder Frederick W. Evans to release him from the day's work, which happened to be felling trees upon the mountain. He felt unable to do the work. The usually fatherly Elder surprised even himself by inquiring in an apparently cold, unfeeling manner, "What is the matter with you?" and then saying, abruptly, almost sternly, "Go to work with your brethren! Strength will be given you." The brother meekly obeyed, and in his obedience was blessed with a gift of strength. He did with ease a hard day's work, felt no harm therefrom and from that time enjoyed better health and increased strength.

Before the families at Mount Lebanon had united for one Sabbath service in common, a meeting of the whole society was held in the meeting-house, which, from some failure of the heating apparatus was very cold. Elder Daniel Boler remarked, with great fervor, that if they had come in the gift and power of God it was his belief that no harm would come to anyone from the cold.

Eldress Antoinette was subject to severe attacks of quinsy sore throat, and that night she was taken very ill with all the symptoms of a severe attack. The next day she was to start with a company of sisters for New York. This plan was given up. After retiring, she thought, "If what Elder Daniel said is true, I ought to be all right; I should not be affected by the cold." Her head and neck were seized with shaking, her head thrown back and forth and from side to side on the pillow, and her neck and chest agitated. The soreness and pain departed, she slept quietly and in the morning she was entirely restored, went to New York according to plan and accomplished her mission.

At one time a sister in the North Family at Mount Lebanon had sprained or otherwise injured her ankle, so that she could not walk without the aid of a crutch. She hobbled into the meeting-room, on Saturday evening, to the family meeting. Eldress Antoinette, in the course of the meeting, fixed her eyes upon the lame sister and, calling her by name, told her to come to her. Without hesitation, the sister started to obey, although it was an apparent impossibility. Her faith and obedience were rewarded as were the same acts of the cripple by the beautiful gate of the Temple at Jerusalem, in the days of Peter and John. She arose and walked to her Eldress, and was completely restored.

Preeminent, among those who are firm believers in the continuance of the healing power in the Church of Mother Ann, is Eldress Anna White, of Mount Lebanon. Many a testimony has she borne that, if the avenues of the soul were kept open to the touch of the spirit world, Believers would have no call for doctors and medicine. If physiological laws were observed and the laws of true spiritual life were adhered to, vital currents from the higher spheres would keep pure and active both bodily and spiritual forces, and death would be a natural and painless passing from one side to the other of the thin veil of separation between matter and spirit.

In her own experience, she has repeatedly exemplified her belief in the practical action of spirit force on the physical being.

In a severe attack of facial neuralgia, weary of the futile efforts of her attendants, she tore the compresses from her face and threw them aside. Instantly a kiss fell upon her cheek, she recognized the presence of a loved, departed sister, Eldress Mary Ann Gillespie. The excruciating pain departed and complete cure followed.

During the intense heat of the summer of 1901, the atmospheric pressure on the brain caused such prostration that one day she seemed hovering on the verge of the unseen world. There came to her two spirits, Eldress Antoinette Doolittle and Sister Martha J. Anderson, each giving her a remedy to take. She tasted of the medicine, drinking it as if it were material substance. The flush of returning life swept through her veins and vigor returned.

During the winter of 1901-2, an injury to the left arm, from a fall some weeks before, formed the centre of a severe attack of nervous exhaustion, the result of long overwork and heavy burden-bearing. Acute inflammation of the nerve developed and intense suffering followed. Hot water packing afforded some relief from the agonizing paroxysms of pain, but the worn out system was in a state of exhaustion scarcely less alarming and the arm was powerless. Repeated healing ministrations were given through one and another organism, but, in spite of scientific massage, electricity and medicine, the injured nerve remained obstinate, the elbow could not be bent nor the hand raised beyond a certain point.

Almost by accident, a group of sisters formed a circle about her, one evening, and, joining hands with her, united their hearts in a concentrated appeal to the spirit world for aid. It came. The circle was continued for successive evenings. More and more positive manifestations of spirit presence and power were felt and heard. The current at times pulsing through the clasping hands was like a strong charge from a battery.

One evening, sitting thus, one sister was operated upon by a spirit who gave utterance to a vigorous and hopeful testimony to the continuance of the work and the permanence of the faith so dear to every one present. "Eldress Mary!" was exclaimed, in recognition. Then the power passed to another, who recognized the same presence. A healing hand was passed slowly over the form and head of the invalid. A sweet, old song of inspired and inspiring faith was sung. Eldress Anna herself was then seized by a powerful influence. Her muscles grew tense; her arms were moved, the helpless fingers tightened in a firm clasp on the hand that had been gently holding them, the lame arm was stretched and shaken, then drawn out to the circle. "Touch every hand in the circle!" was heard, and when the electric current was complete a commanding voice, that of a strong man, spoke through her lips: "Use your arm! Bend your arm! Bend your arm!" At the same time the arm was bent and shaken with great violence, yet without pain. A moment before, to have saved her own life or another's she could not have moved the hand within two feet of her face. A very slight attempt, by an experienced and trained nurse to flex the joint had produced but a day of increased suffering. Now the hand went with ease to her face, stroked it all over, to her head and all over that, and, as limber as ever, answered the impulse of her will as promptly and easily as of old. Nights of sweet and restful sleep followed. The stiffness did not return; the overtaxed nerves were repeatedly affected by gentle influences from the recognized touch and presence of loved and familiar spirit friends, and the healing process was continued.

It is prophesied by inspired leaders among the Shakers that the Gift of Healing will be the sign of the Second Gospel Testimony. "When the Spirit begins to raise up the leaders of the new faith, they will be endowed with the Gift of Healing in a preeminent manner. This will be both as a sign and as a ministration of intrinsic good. A sign that the Gospel has increased, progressed from faith to faith, that health of body is hereafter to be conjoined with health of soul."

XXI

VISION AND PROPHECY

THE opening heavens that bent over Ann Lee's child life were never closed, the views of angels that hovered about her in early years never passed away. In mature life the world of spirit was as real to her as the world of sense. Prophetic insight and open vision were marked features of the daily life and conversation of Mother Ann, the first Elders and their early followers. Mother Ann and Father William frequently said, "Where I see one soul in the body, I see a thousand in the world of spirits." Mother Ann often spoke of seeing angels. Once, after a night of great suffering, she told a sister that she had been supported and comforted by visions, in which she had seen the glory of God about her pillow like the colors of the rainbow. Twelve angels came into the room, six on one side and six on the other, in the form of a heart. Once at Watervliet she sat in her chair from early morning till afternoon, exercised by the power of God, singing in unknown tongues, seemingly entirely abstracted from her surroundings. After she came to herself, she said to the people: "The way of God will grow straighter and straighter, so straight that if you go one hair's breadth out of the way you will suffer loss. I felt myself walking with Christ in groves and valleys as really as if he had been here on earth." She often spoke of walking with Jesus in beautiful places. Nor did she alone see the spiritual presence, whose union with her spirit had accomplished the redemptive work. Nathan Farrington, who lived in the western part of New Lebanon, has recorded a vision that he experienced while gathering Indian corn in his field. He was carried in spirit to the spot, five miles distant, where now stands the Shaker meeting-house. Looking up at the eastern mountain, he saw it bare of trees. Near the summit he saw Jesus with Mother Ann by his side, their faces toward the west. Side by side, they walked down the mountain, to within a few rods of where he stood, when they disappeared. Nathan found himself again in his cornfield. He soon after made the journey to Harvard, where Mother Ann and the Elders were then laboring, and related the vision to Mother Ann. She said: "I own your vision; it is so, it really is, and it is a great vision of God." Nathan said that he thought it was given him as an anchor to his soul. She replied, "Ah, truly it is, and it will hold you when all else fails."

Several instances are on record of followers of Mother Ann, who, before her advent in their vicinity, had seen her face in vision, in connection with some more or less striking spiritual perception. One which seems to contain a hint of the modern composite photograph, which has played so large a part in sociological research, was related by one of the early Believers, Lois Burch, who, with her companion, Josiah, united with the society at Hancock, and, being possessed of ample means, dedicated their wealth to the use of the society. The narrator of the vision passed to the spirit world in the year 1820, at the age of eighty-three. The vision occurred before the opening of the Gospel in America. She says: "Not long before I heard the Gospel I was sitting in a room by myself, when suddenly a great light appeared and I saw angels come forward in that light. Then I saw Christ Jesus appear, and by his side was walking a woman. In the woman's face I seemed to see the faces of the saints from the foundation of the world to the end of time, yet her face was in size like the face of an ordinary woman. I never saw that woman until I saw the face of Mother Ann. When I related my vision to her, she said: 'Lois, that is a great vision of God. I have seen just such an one.' "

Story of Gilbert Avery.

Gilbert Avery, father of Elder Giles B. Avery and brother-in-law òf Elder Richard Bushnell, had some remarkable experiences in answer to prayer. Elder Giles tells the story that his father's two eldest children, by a former marriage, were placed at Enfield, Conn. The boy, Gilbert, left the Shakers at the age of twenty-one and traveled through the South and West, working on farms and teaching school winters. "My father," he says, "was employed at chair making. One day, while standing at his work-bench, he distinctly heard a spirit voice call him by name, requesting him to kneel and pray for his son Gilbert. He replied aloud: 'What can I do for him? I provided him a good home, and he has left it; I know not where he is or that he is living on the earth; I have not heard from him in fifteen years.' But the spirit visitant was not to be put off in this wise, and insisted that greater efforts on the part of Gilbert should be made in prayer for his son. His reply was, 'What shall I pray for?' The answer came, 'Pray that he may return to his Gospel home, he does not belong outside and cannot find there a home.' Then said Father Gilbert to the spirit: 'If it is my duty to pray for my son, give me an evidence in some manner.' 'What evidence do you desire?' said the spirit. 'Restore to me my hearing,' said Gilbert, he being quite deaf. Instantly his hearing was restored and so remained through life. He immediately knelt and prayed for his son, pursuant to the will of the spirit missionary.

"On the third day after this incident, while crossing the street, near the Church Trustees' office, I met my brother Gilbert, with his valise in his hand. We passed compliments, and I inquired, 'Where do you hail from?' 'Kalamazoo, Mich.' 'When did you leave there?' 'About three o'clock, three days since,' said he, and continued, 'I was teaching school, when suddenly the impulse came over me that I must return to my Shaker home. Before this I had no destire to return, although I had never felt that I had a home since I left Believers. I now seek the union I have lost. Will you intercede for a privilege for me in Elder Richard Bushnell's family here at Mount Lebanon?'

"I replied, 'I will not!' 'Why?' queried he. 'Because it would not be honorable,' I said, 'but if you want a privilege in a Shaker community, go to the society where you lost it, and apply for admittance.'

" 'Will you intercede for me there?' I answered, 'I will,' and did so. The next day we both went to Canaan, where our father resided. He met his son kindly and cordially. The interesting fact was made manifest that an hour after Gilbert had knelt in prayer, according to the request of the spirit, my brother was impressed to leave his school and return to his friends in the East, and in two hours after the prayer of his father he was on his homeward course." At this date (1904) the son, Gilbert Avery, is still living, at the age of ninety-six years, his faculties in remarkable preservation, his handwriting clear and plain as print, his erect, vigorous form and marvelous activity a wonder to all who see him. He talks with enthusiasm of his early adventures, enjoys his daily walk and takes part in the tasks of the family, where he has been a member for over a half century. He often delights visitors by reciting from memory "Gray's Elegy," as well as other poems and songs.

Not often is the sight of a spirit guide so clear and distinct as in the following tale of

A Child's Vision.

The present Head of the Central Ministry is Eldress Harriet Bullard. Coming to the North Family when a little child, her life of seventy-nine years has for the greater part been spent in the peaceful but strenuous spiritual course of the Gospel. Her pure, serene face seems to wear a halo— the outflow of her saintly spirit. In company with her sister, Marcia, now passed to the spirit land, she early embraced the faith. Their mother had died. Father and brothers made determined efforts to secure the girls, who quietly persisted in their choice of home and faith. Both were mediums, and often in childhood Harriet has lain in trance for days at a time, watched over by her Elders, revealing by her unconscious words the heavenly scenes through which her spirit was passing.

At one time a report came to the family that their relatives were coming to take Harriet and Marcia, "dead or alive." In care of a Shaker brother, the girls were allowed to go over the mountain to the neighboring society in Massachusetts. When the danger was over, they started to return, but lost their way. After wandering about for some time, they were met by an old man, with long, white hair, in whom they realized the presence of a spirit friend, sent for their protection. He said to them: "My name is the Ancient of Days. Follow me, and I will lead you aright." They obeyed, the spirit guided them in safety to the right road, and, when they had reached familiar scenes, vanished from their sight.

Another story is told that is full of interest to those who know the beautiful life of this Shaker Eldress. When a little girl, she had at one time the care of a dark corner closet, into which people seldom looked. One day, being in haste, she brushed it carelessly, thinking, "It does not matter if it is not clean, no one ever looks in here." Just then, in one corner, her clairvoyant eyes saw a bright light, and, as she looked, an eye appeared. It came to her at once as a lesson and a token that the angels saw all that she did, whether in the dark or in the light, and from that time it became her fixed practice to do all her work, even in the dark, well enough for the angels to see.

The Assassination of President Lincoln

was witnessed in the visions of the night, by Sister Cecelia De Vere, of Mount Lebanon,.who says: "The night after the announcement of the taking of Richmond, I dreamed that I was at a theatre, a splendid place, remarkable for its drapery of flags and brilliant lighting. At the back of the stage was a transparent curtain, on which negro faces were faintly traced. A man seemed to walk on the air out of one of the boxes; a flag flew after him, but he trampled on the end of it and disappeared. In a moment there was a wild commotion, such that the whole assembly swayed like people in anguish. I shared the intensity, but knew not the meaning. When I looked at the stage, four ropes were hanging from the ceiling, and distinctly through the tumult that prevailed was whispered, "For the great crime they are to be executed before the people, when the hour strikes." My terror at being compelled to witness so fearful a scene was just then relieved by the morning signal that awakens us from sleep in our quiet home. The dream, however, so burdened me that when it was related it made a deep impression on all who heard it. Eleven days after, the news of the assassination reached Mount Lebanon."

Very often, those who depart make their presence known to friends at a distance by songs or personal ministrations.

NO. 28.   ELDRESS ANTOINETTE DOOLITTLE.

The Departure of Eldress Antoinette Doolittle

on the last night of the year 1886, was the same night made known to Eldress Matilda Butler, of Union Village, O., who thus tells the story:

"I retired as usual and fell asleep and dreamed that some one I had never met before came into our room and very kindly requested me to attend a funeral, or two, in fact. I answered, 'At what time?' My visitor replied, 'At two o'clock, Sabbath afternoon.' I then said, 'How shall I go?' 'We will take you,' was the reply.

"Without more ceremony, I prepared myself and followed my visitor down stairs and out of the house, where a beautiful carriage was standing. I noticed some sisters who were in before me. They only recognized me by a simple bow and a sweet smile. The place where I was taken was all new to me. I cannot remember any of the songs that were sung, nor can I recall anything that was spoken. But all was so solemn, and such a feeling of resignation and sweet calm, that I shed tears with the rest of the company.

"The power of the meeting filled me full, and with these impressions, I awoke, to find myself in bed at home. The clock in our room struck one. I still kept the feeling on me and could not get it off. It seemed to me that my mysterious dream had something to do with the Mother Church at Mount Lebanon. In the morning I told the dream, but the feeling did not leave me, and all day Saturday, and Sabbath day the same, until about half past four o'clock Sabbath afternoon, while passing through the hall, I found myself singing a new song.

"The impression came with the song that it was from the departed, whose spirits had left our earth plane. I sang the song to our sisters. Many of them felt the inspiration. I give the song as I received it:

"Angels, archangels and seraphim sing,
   Glory to God the Most High,
Our spirits are triumphing o'er earthly things,
   The power of His love draweth nigh,
Sing glory, glory,
   Join in the chorus, ye justified throng,
Sing glory, glory,
   Honor and praise to Him doth belong."

A curious coincidence lies in the fact that on the Friday evening, the 31st of December, Eldress Antoinette passed away at eight o'clock, and a sister of the same society also passed away the same evening, and both funeral services were held on the Sabbath, one in the morning, the other at two in the afternoon.

Visions and prophecies relative to the future of the Shaker Church have been common all along the course of its history, and while many have spoken in general terms of blessing and glory attending its work among men, there have from the early days been frequent and sometimes very explicit warnings of a time of decline, of testing, which should try the souls of the faithful, to be followed by a new, more glorious opening of the Gospel.

To Job Bishop, Mother Ann once said: "Though a young man, you are called now to go and preach a purer Gospel than Saint Paul preached; for this day requires a confession of every known sin and a full cross against the flesh, with all its affections and lusts." Among her prophetic utterances were these: "This Gospel will go to the end of the world, and it will be propagated not so much by preaching as by the good works of the people." "The time will come when the knowledge of the Lord will cover the earth, as the waters cover the sea, and a nation will be born in a day." In 1841, among the prophetic messages received from her was this: "God hath now raised up the Order of inspired messengers with divine gifts, never to cease among His chosen people. Though they may, in a great measure, be withdrawn for a time, that the children of Zion may be proved and thereby manifest what use and improvement they make of these heavenly blessings, and that the faithful and unfaithful may appear as they are, yet they shall be revived and spring up and operate in various times and manners, so long as the Divine Spirit has a work to do with the children of men."

In 1827, there came from Canada to Union Village, two by the name of Daniel Merton and Jason Shepherd. In the same year, after a three days' fast, Daniel made this prediction concerning

The Future of the Shaker Church.

"At the present time, the Church is in great peace and prosperity, and it seems as if nothing could disturb her tranquility. But a change will come over her, many will *prove unfaithful and drop out of her ranks.* Sorrow and adversity will visit her, and desolation and defection will be such that even the most devoted and faithful will begin to forebode the utter annihilation of the Church. But this destruction will not take place, for after she has reached the lowest level of her adversity she will arise and move to a higher culmination of glory than at any previous period—to the highest reachable in that day." In the trance into which he was thrown, a spirit of sadness came over him. He seemed caught up, as were the prophets of old. Looking up, he exclaimed: "They are going! They are going! 'Twould seem they'd all go, but they'll not. There'll be some left!" For a time animation seemed suspended. Then a new scene burst upon his vision. He arose, and, clapping his hands, exclaimed: "They come! They come! From the east and the west and the north and the south! 'Twould seem the whole world would come!" Both were in a transport of joy.

On Mount Pisgah.

Strangely thrilling is it, in these latter days, when old prophecies of Zion's decline are finding their fulfilment, as,

24

one by one, her white-haired saints wave their farewells, letting fall their mantles from receding chariots that bear them away to the ever increasing hosts beyond, to catch their vibrant shouts of hope and cheer!

Ere they depart, all, like Moses, ascend to Pisgah's top, and to each is given a vision of the time to come, an outlook, far and wide, over lands as yet unconquered, realms as yet unseen by the weary travelers at Pisgah's foot.

"Smaller and smaller shall you grow, fewer and fewer, till a child in its mother's arms can count the remnant," is the echo of a prophetic word that repeats itself again and again, as years go by, and the ever diminishing numbers awaken the frequent comment, "Shakers are dying out!"

As the time draws nearer when that lowest point shall be reached, the faithful and true-hearted lift their eyes in joy to the distant "hills whence cometh their help." For the correspondent prophecy, like the others given to Zion, they feel will not fail. A new opening of the Gospel—a far grander and more universal revelation of these and other sacred truths will come. The faithful remnant shall become the germ of a new, far reaching life and the glory of the latter days shall outshine the brightest that went before.

Two strong-hearted friends, both enkindled with prophetic fire, the one within, the other without the Order, thus beheld in recent

Accordant Visions.

Amanda Deyo, the well-known preacher and reformer, whose prophetic gaze looks ever to the hights where mankind shall at length breathe the pure airs of Universal Peace, writes thus, under date of November 13, 1902, to Mount Lebanon:

"In spirit I have felt so impressed with the beautiful life God has in store for us in the great future. Last Sabbath I was led to speak of the community to which you belong. Through the week a beautiful dream came to me. I was with you all in your mountain home. Old things were passed away, a new heaven and a new earth seemed about us. You were no longer an isolated community, but the heads of colleges were centered with you. Your ideas were leading.

"The land was no longer suffering for caretakers, but from all directions were coming the workers, desirous to learn that beautiful care of the soil that shall make it blossom as the rose. No more selfish grasping of estate, but only held for the good of all! I seemed to be with you, and how beautiful you all looked, as you received into your fold the fresh young life — all anxious to help you and to learn that wonderful way of Christ! I saw the tables so bountifully spread, and poor, hungry, tired ones of earth being ministered unto, never more looking upon work as a curse, but, equally divided, no one was burdened; no one was dreading an old age, forsaken and in poverty, but amid peace and plenty and abounding love. I saw the ever widening circle of God's dear children coming to the mountain home.

"As long as life lasts that wonderful vision will remain with me."

The reply by Eldress Anna White contained these passages:

"Where there is no vision the people perish. We think some of the leaders of our host, drawn by your heartfelt pictures of the life and mission in whose interest they still live and work, opened your spirit sight to show you things to come. The vision has a significance, a meaning, slowly unfolding as we travel on toward its fulfilment.

"It is an ideal view of an ideal Home, that Millennial Home, of which we have a foretaste here and now; where we fear neither poverty nor riches, where old age has lost its terrors and where, in the heart of a loving family of brothers and sisters, we are 'never forgotten, never forsaken.'

"Before us, as behind us, lie prosperous homes and gladsome labor; woman, redeemed from the curse—broadened in mind, trained in intellect, cultivated in taste, skilled in judgment, no longer slave or toy, or cast out as the off-scouring of the earth, but standing where God placed her, when 'in His own image,' He created man and woman. Then shall the land be redeemed—the earth shall again be free to all as the ocean and the air are free. Then shall each live for all and all for each, and the brother and sister love, which every pure child heart believes in and enjoys, before passion has sullied the soul with its poisoned breath, which the first Christians felt for each other and which has ever actuated the hearts that have felt a baptism of the Christ Spirit,— this pure, spiritual love shall become the bond and seal to unite the whole, crystallizing all the blended elements into one Unit of Life. The vision shall yet be fulfilled.

"A similar view of the possibilities before us, would we but be true to our Gospel call, came to us a few months since.

"We saw our Home a centre of intellectual and spiritual power. We saw our people, our beloved people, children of our Mother, sons and daughters of God, arisen to their rightful place as Leaders of Humanity, in the van of an advancing host, the redeemed, the great harvest from the fields of earth, who were gathering into our midst; our vacant dwellings busy with life's manifold interests, the loom and the cook stove of the old time replaced by the finer equipments of the new; our lonely fields alive with toilers accomplishing, in a grander way than of old, the work of feeding the hungry of the earth.

"We saw our younger brothers and sisters also redeemed. Our hills and pastures no longer echoed with cries of sorrow and despair — the cattle on a thousand hills were roaming free as air, nothing to hurt nor harm; lambs and calves and colts frolicked fearlessly beside their mothers, whose eyes no longer bore the animal's look of dread, anxiety and unutterable sadness. Man's hand no longer bound in unwilling servitude the least or weakest of his fellow beings, forcing them to an unnatural development for his own selfish pleasure, imposing a life of suffering and a death of torture to increase his comfort and pamper his appetite. Powers of earth and air, not the brute strength of animals, gave the farmer the force needed for his work; and, freed from the necessity for tyranny and usurpation, no longer a driver of slaves, man stood erect in natural, though long forgotten tenderness and justice, the acknowledged leader and trusted protector of the animal creation. The stamp of cruelty and greed had left his face; his features were open, manly and true.

"Before the advancing host of humanity, sprang up forests of noble trees, whose branches showered down nuts for food, as of old the manna fell about Israel's host. Orchards and vineyards yielded luscious fruits, grain fields goldened in the sun and the whole earth laughed in plenty.

"The soil had become pure; diseases — blotch and blight and scab and scar — had disappeared from grain and fruit and vegetable. Sickness and pain had flown; doctors had spilled their useless drugs upon the ground and were raising food, or teaching scientific truth to men, instead of filling graveyards with their bodies. Pure diet had made pure men and women. Schools were centres of intellectual life,— eager, active minds, no longer clogged by the waste from heavy, unnatural foods, mastered the arts and sciences of life in one-half the time, with one-quarter of the effort now required."

Meeting a Spirit Army.

In the summer of 1902, Sister Matilda Reed, cousin of Eldress Polly Reed, whose story was so graphically told by Elder Calvin Green, passed to the spirit land from the Church Family, at Mount Lebanon. A member of the society since early childhood, an Eldress in the Family for many years, she had been active and devoted during the greater part of the nineteenth century. The morning after her departure, Eldress Anna White was going on an errand to the Church office. She says: "I was enjoying the morning walk, with mind intent on duty, and felt nothing uncommon until I had passed the large elm tree, where the two roads merge into one. Here a flood of life met me. I heard the tread of myriad feet; there were whole congregations, like armies. It was like meeting a great mountain. The street was alive; the air was buoyant with voices. An army with banners was surging to and fro. Among the hosts were faces that I knew. I recognized Eldress Betsey Bates, Eldress Ann Taylor, Eldress Polly Reed, Sisters Prudence Morrell, Eliza Sharp, Rachel Sampson, Mary Ann Mantle, Sarah Bates, Jane Blanchard, Elder Daniel Crossman, Elder Daniel Boler and many others. I felt their greeting, and all the while I was saying, 'What does this mean?'

"Entering the office, I said to the Sisters: 'Do you know how many are treading our streets to-day?' Sister Emma Neale replied, at once, 'Yea, I should think so! Sister Matilda will have a heavenly escort.'"

The Heavenly Escort.

I was walking along the highway,
  In the morning, calm and still;
The sunshine brightened the village,
  The mountain and wood-crowned hill.
And bird songs flooded the silence,
  A melody glad and free,
Joy danced in the lowly flower,
  And gleamed in the tall elm tree.

Through the summer morning's glory
  I heard the sound of feet,
A mighty host was treading
  Our lonely village street,—
Faces and forms familiar
  In days long passed away,
When last I had looked upon them,
  They were feeble, bent and gray.

Now, fresh in eternal beauty,
  Glad with eternal youth,
They trod with the joy of victor,
  In the strength of eternal truth.
The ancients of our city,
  The heroes of mob and strife,
Once more trod the scenes of conquest
  Where they offered up their life.

And many the forms and faces
  Whose hands I had clasped in the years,
Whose blessing had brightened my journey,
  Whose passing had left me tears;
The hosts of our own true kindred,
  The great and the good of yore,
Were treading the well known highway,
  Were thronging our street once more.

"What is it?" I asked. Unpausing,
  The mighty host swept on.
In the dawn of the glorious morning
  Our beautiful sister had gone;
Her Heavenly Escort had met me,
  In my walk in the early day,
The gladness and cheer of their greeting
  I shall bear on life's lengthening way.

Not feeble nor few in number,
  But strong as Assyrian band,
They overflow from the earth life,
  And crowding the spirit land,
Pour back in militant thousands,
  To carry the warfare on;
To help and support the struggling,
  To cheer when a victory's won.

They wait to gather the faithful,
  They watch the erring to win,
They join in our song's sweet cadence,
  They shield us from harm and sin.
They open our minds in vision
  To gather the angels' thought,
Our hands they strengthen in action
  Till their will in deed is wrought.

They've many a message to give us,
  They've work for us yet to do,
There are depths of renunciation,
  And hights to attain unto;
Yea, onward steps to be taken,
  And victories yet to be won,—
Our cause is a cause of triumph,
  Our mission is but begun.

Up, then, to the work! ye faithful,
  Hear the message the angels bring,
Nor dream that the day is declining
  When the birds of morning sing.

Our street of wonderful record,
 By mob hunted heroes wrought,
Shall echo to further conquests
 Of Truth enkindled thought.

Be pure, as our Mothers were pure,
 Be true, as our Fathers were true,
Rid hearts and homes of weakness
 False pride would conceal from view.
Cleanse lips for the Testimony,
 That our hands may the Standard bear;
And our hearts, a sacred Altar
 For the ancient Fires, prepare.

Leila S. Taylor.

NO. 29. ELDER FREDERICK W. EVANS.

XXII

A LOOK INTO THE FUTURE

I N the movements of events, the trend of thought and reformatory action, many Shakers see the beginning of the fulfilment of a series of prophetic visions recounted, more than a score of years ago, by that politico-religious seer, Elder F. W. Evans:

"The old Heaven and Earth — united Church and State — are fast passing away, dissolving, melting with fervent heat, the fire of Spiritual Truth. Out of the material of the old, earthly, civil governments, a civil government will rise, is even now arising, in which right, not might, will predominate.

A New Earth.

"It will be purely secular, a genuine Republic. Men and women will be citizens. All citizens will be freeholders. They will possess and inherit the land by right of birth. Wars will cease with the end of the old monarchical, theological earth. The meek will inherit the earth and the nations neither learn nor practise war any more. Every man and woman will literally sit under their own vine and fig tree, and none to make them afraid, as violence or destruction shall no more be heard nor felt in the land. Neither shall anyone say, I am sick. The Lord their God shall, by revelation and true science, take all sickness away from the midst of the people. No doctors, drugs nor poisons. The same power exercised in the first Christian dispensation of healing all manner of diseases, and saying,— 'Go and sin no more,' physiologically, will be again revealed from the spirit spheres. The people of God, when God, as Father-Mother, walks and dwells with them, will leave off contention ere it is begun, and by prevention forestall sickness

(377)

"In the New Earth, sexuality will be used only for reproduction; eating, for strength not gluttony; drinking for thirst not drunkenness. Property, being the result of honest toil, as those who will not work will not be allowed to eat, will be for the good of all, the young and the old. There will be no more sorrów nor crying, no more pain, no more death, for the people will neither hurt nor harm any sentient thing. He that killeth an ox will be as he that slayeth a man — a murderer. All will have adopted the bloodless diet."

A New Heaven.

"Out of the material of the old, ecclesiastical governmental organizations, a new, spiritual religious organization, or order, will arise, in which truth, not authority for the truth, will be the ruling power. God's people will be a willing people. Their belief will be the result of evidence.

"The separation of the New Heaven from the New Earth will be as perfect as the separation between soul and body: — matter being the object of the bodily senses, spiritual substance the object of the soul sense. A Second Pentecostal Church will arise in which, as in the First, will be a baptism of the Holy Christ Spirit,— generative lusts will give place to Celibacy. People will become eunuchs for the Kingdom of Heaven's sake. Blessed are the pure in heart for they shall see God. Not only will they not fight but they will love their enemies.

"The New Heavens and the New Earth — Church and State Governments — will co-exist like the sun and moon, distinct, yet acting and re-acting upon each other, while they move independently, yet harmoniously, each in its own orbit. The lust of property becomes extinct when no one says this is mine, that is thine, and each seeks another's wealth, not his own. When, in honor, each prefers his brother, selfish ambition will not exist. Simplicity in dress and plainness of speech will exterminate envy and pride, and he who would be great will be servant to the household of faith."

"This Testimony," or Shakerism, says Elder Giles B. Avery, "through which is being formed the New Heavens, is the focal light of all the concentrated rays of Divine illumination that have beamed upon humanity's pathway. It is the bundle of nerves that feels for lost humanity in every situation and bears ministratión to his necessities. It is the perfect work of righteousness, illustrating the love, mercy and goodness of our Heavenly Father-Mother. It is a power, ministered by angels, that is turning upside down the old earth and old heavens orders of the natural man. It is an epistle, written in the characters of the children of God, to be seen and read of all men. It is a surgeon that amputates from the body of the Church every incurably diseased member. It is the good Samaritan physician that ministers to the healing of the soul. If accepted and obeyed, this Christian Testimony is a present power of salvation from sin. It destroys the old crooked man or woman of sin, makes a New Creature, an inhabitant of a New Creation."

Because of the needs of humanity, for the benefit of thousands whose lives are now uncentered, purposeless, Shakerism utters

A Call for Men and Women —

honest, true-hearted, desiring purity, strength, brotherhood and sisterhood, the attainment of self-control, contentment, spiritual happiness, willing to work for soul development, for the good of others, for the uplifting of humanity— those who will confess their sins, and depart therefrom.

What Will it Amount To?

This Yankee-like query meets every new idea, wherever presented. Significant of the times! Value, worth, virtue, the old Latin word, *vir*—a man—at the root of it all. The price of a man, his effort and soul, the portion of him that is put into an enterprise—by that is it measured, valued, the return estimated and a balance struck.

Shakerism, which is but another name for advanced Christianity, calls for the whole being. It takes a whole man or woman to be a Shaker. For it means to be cut off—to come to the end of the world in one's self. It means to leave kindred, home and people; to renounce worldly ambition and preferment; to renounce politics,

to cast no party vote, to hold no political office in
nation, state or city. It means to surrender one's whole
life — time, talent, will; to give up one's own way; to
work earnestly through all of life and have nothing of
one's own to show, save character—the progress made in
the work of redemption. It means what Jesus meant when
he said: "I am among you as one that serveth;" "I came
not to do mine own will, but the will of my Father which
is in heaven;" "If I, your Lord and Master, have washed
your feet, ye ought also to wash one another's feet."

What return for this outlay of self, the vir, the man?
What does it amount to in the life balance? A man, a
woman, may not care for dollars, or gear, or lands, or
shouting thousands, or swinging caps, or whatever coin
men pay for use or tickled fancy, may not even prize a
mighty mausoleum or monument; but a man, a woman,
wants to know, or should want to know, what energy is to
be set in motion in world mechanism, before the whole
stress of one's being is given in any one direction. If I become a Shaker, what is it to signify, wherever my life
force is spent? It is a fair question, and should be fairly
answered.

The beautiful ideals of Shakerism are woven into the
world's best life. The great houses stand ready to become
once more the centre of hopeful, communistic activity. The
vast acres, gathered at such cost of toil, fenced with boulders dug by strong hands from the hillsides, the mighty
barns, reared of stones that once whitened the broad, green
fields, all await the new inflow from earth's earnest seekers
after simplicity and the rich gifts of labor. They will
abide, as they have already stood for a century and a quarter, object lessons of thrift, integrity and noble ideals.

Shakers may see the manifestations of the living Christ
today in the hearts of men and women, turning to Him as

flowers turn to the sun, their faces following its course. "Where is the Christ, that I may worship Him?" is on a million lips. Where is the Christ today? Not in the churches. Hungering and thirsting men and women found that out long ago, and left them vacant! Not in the heavens. Space and distance have left void the old-time heaven. Where is Christ? Where can He be, but in humanity? Where, in humanity, save in one, if there be one man or woman, redeemed from sin, cleansed from pollution, preserved from defilement, alive, instinct in every fibre of being, with the godliness, the help, sympathy, tenderness, salvation, the Divine love and energy that thrilled and saved men and women in Jesus and in Ann Lee? Do you, Shaker brother, Shaker sister, know any such? Then you know where Christ is found. Have you not something, then, to give these starving millions? Perhaps the harvest hour has not yet struck. In Syria, the traveler, Thompson, tells us, no man may gather the olive harvest, even from his own trees, until a certain day. Proclamation is made by the Governor of each little town and city, that on a certain date the gathering of the olives will begin. When the proclamation goes forth to shake the trees, there can be no postponement. When thus the time has been declared, all go forth from the villages into the orchards, whatever the cold or storm.

The harvest even now is ripening. Do you realize how many are heart-hungry for purity? How many hundreds live in a marriage that is not legalized fornication, but true union of the spirit, leaving the wife free to her own person? Do you realize how many women, and men also, are longing and striving, keeping the body free from sensual taint? To whom, to what, is this cry for purity made? Is there in the world a life, prepared for over one hundred years, suited for such souls, where their secret aspirations and solitary efforts might meet response and association with those whose constant experience proves the blessedness, the holy joy, the health of body, soul and spirit, found in continence and purity — a Christlike union of man's and woman's spiritual being? Has the Shaker aught to offer here?

Do you hear the cries of the weary, the burdened, the anxious;—of those who toil and struggle against the fearful odds of modern combinations, competitions and trade rivalries; men and women who long to be generous, unselfish, helpful to brother men and sister women, but who have no opportunity; who must fight for a chance to live; driven from the earth by land monopolists; driven from air and light by monopolists of sky and space; the whole of existence a struggle for breath, for food, raiment, for mere existence? The world is full of such! Have one hundred and thirty years given Shakers anything for this world crisis? True, they are somewhat pressed. Some of their industries have been taken from them, and their lands are heavily taxed. But not a Shaker in America today is worried over the question, What shall I eat? What shall I drink? What shall I wear? Their bread is certain and their water sure. They work serenely, they lie down and sleep peacefully, and no dreams or bogies of want or Wall Street disturb their hours of slumber. Has not a century and a quarter of cheerful, helpful communistic life in brotherhood and sisterhood given them something to offer? Look at Shaker homes—clean, sweet, comfort-full; tables loaded with vegetables, fruits, breads, dainties of many kinds, all the product of earth bounty and the offering of skilled and loving hands; foods well cooked, well served, abundant, pure, wholesome and nutritious, free as the air of the hills to all who will work according to strength and ability. The broad acres could support one hundred where they now feed one.

Do you see the thousands of anxious faces in the streets; those who, in silent dread, are watching the sure approach, not of death, but of old age and its forerunner, the years when, the dead-line of desirability passed, with force unabated and strength unscathed, with judgment and experience of more value than ever, they must be thrust aside to make room for the nerve-filled young athletes, swarming every gate of opportunity? If old age, in its neglect and loneliness, is pathetic, the unwhispered sorrow of ante-age is tragic.

Have Shakers any dead-line of usefulness? Have they any room for the old folks? "There are no old folks among us; we are all young together!" was the answer given to the question, "What do you do with your old people?" It is more than a trick of speech. The absence of anxiety and foreboding has banished old age. The tender love and sympathy, the sincere respect and affection in which are held the ripening saints, whose years have been spent in unselfish devotion to others, in obedience to God's laws for the body and the soul, whose halos of heavenly light are already reflecting from their whitening locks, change the blight of old age to the glory of the harvest. Even in extreme age, place and opportunity, a chance to be helpful and useful—that greatest boon to age and weakness—is provided. The old are never thrust aside, out of the home interests. Noting the serenity, cheerfulness, content, comfort and happiness of the aged Shakers, visitors often affirm that nothing like it is found anywhere else in the world. Had Shakerism done nothing else, the blessing it has bestowed upon its aged adherents, some declare, would be accomplishment enough.

Where am I going? What does life mean? these
millions are asking. Where are my loved ones? Have
they become but dust beneath my feet? Are they gone
from my love forever, into nothingness? Will old age
and weakness and disease blot out all the sweetness of life
for me? Shall I endure it all, or shall I go, despairingly,
by my own hand, into silence? Men and women are asking thus, and they are going, thousands yearly, by suicidal
hands. Has Shakerism any answer?

What of its knowledge of eternal verities? What have
Shakers to tell of the "open door" that has led them, and
will lead others, into a present consciousness of immortality, eternal life; into salvation that keeps the temper true,
the heart clean, the imagination pure, the eyes alight with the
joy of holy thoughts and pure affections? What have they
to tell of a life linked to the life beyond, of the presence of
loved ones from that life, demonstrating their active, intelligent, loving participation in the daily interests, their healing, beneficent influences on body and soul, their revealings
of the future?

The peaceful, joy-filled faces of the Shakers, Believers
in the Gospel of Love, Purity and Peace, charm unuttera-
bly the hearts of many. Out of the whirling world currents come, now and then, one and another, drawn by a
power they cannot name. When, in spite of rebellion against
the unaccustomed restraints, of unadaptation to communistic demands, the new-comer gains an insight into the
spiritual meanings, a hold on the life principle, the charm
of this new life seldom fails to win and bind, until the struggle with selfhood becomes the choice of life and the fire of
the Gospel is eagerly sought to burn out from the soul all
that is unlike the Christ seen embodied in the holier, more
developed souls, by whom one is surrounded. The love of
Christlikeness in others grows to the love of Christ, and

desire turns to earnest effort for the development of that spirit in one's self.

What Has Shakerism for You?

New life takes on new forms. Never does the spirit of a new age attire itself in just the garments of the old; never does the thought of today clothe itself in just the dress of yesterday. Scripture exposition may not appeal to you. You may not care for Ezekiel's Vision, or Daniel's Days of Prophecy, or for a whole apocalyptic menagerie of beasts, with horns and eyes. You do care for the needs, to you, of body and soul; for freedom to live and work and be paid a fair price, not alone in the world's coin, but in the satisfaction of knowing that you are doing something to better world conditions, to benefit and uplift your fellow-beings. You do care to know that your life force is being spent in a way to help yourself and others to think deeper, see farther, live better, to "enter into living peace." You want to find a life with practical issues, in which, grasping more than food and raiment, your energies be not spent in "marking time," but may take hold of eternal life. All this the Shaker life offers to those who embrace it. It means today just what it meant in 1792—the best that Heaven has to offer Earth.

The world is but now beginning to ring with the reverberations of the Divine messages that came, in still, small voice, through the Shaker revelations of one hundred and thirty years ago. Shakers have been working out, demonstrating in their microcosmic societies, the principles revealed by the Christ Spirit, embodied in Jesus the Anointed, in Ann the Anointed.

Is the Brotherhood of Man more than a dream?
Shakerism has proved it a fact.
Is Communism possible?
25

Shakerism has proved it a glorious success, if only its essential elements are regarded. What of the Rights of Labor?

The Rights of Labor are never infringed by Monopoly or Capital, for, among Shakers, all work for each and each works for all.

Is Sexual Equality natural or desirable?

Ann Lee first declared and maintained Woman's Freedom and Equality, suffered for it at the hands of a raging and envenomed public, embodied it in spirit and letter in the organization that is founded upon her teachings. The principle of freedom to man and woman alike has, for over a century, made the Shaker Sister the freest woman in the world—the free woman in Christ—and a sweeter, happier, more womanly woman does not exist.

But does not this life blunt, wither and destroy the maternal nature, the mother instinct? Let the host of spiritual mothers, embodiments of the Divine Maternal Spirit, unstained by passion and unmarred by impurity, reveal to the world, for the first time, the meaning of true motherhood— more tender, more divine, as spiritual pangs are harder to bear than physical, as the spiritual being underlies and overtowers the natural.

Social purity is the cornerstone of the Church founded by Mother Ann—the only church today that demands and lives it, banishing from its doors all, of whatever name or office, who infringe that law.

She took the initiative in freedom of speech and religious toleration, and her people have ever been the most free and untrammeled in the one, most catholic and universal in the other.

Medical freedom has always been their practice, and healing by spirit touch and mental control has from the first distinguished this faith, although skilled physicians and simple remedies are employed.

Animal protection in all its many phases was forestalled by Mother Ann's first lessons—justice and kindness to all the brute creation. No man could be a Christian, was her teaching, and abuse his dumb, defenceless animals.

Child protection?

Let the happy homes of thousands of defenceless children for a century and a quarter answer.

Peace and non-resistance were the basic pillars of her life temple.

Temperance in eating and in drinking was another.

Health food and sanitation were, from the first, her study and that of her colleagues.

The widening vistas of the modern spiritualistic philosophy are outgoings from the life that started in spirit manifestation in 1758.

Is personal freedom possible? I cannot lose my individuality. Are you free as you are? Are you in any degree bound by your appetites, your passions, your self-will? Are you at all in bondage to the opinions of your neighbors, to the customs and notions of society, however harmful or absurd? These do not trammel the true Shaker. Free, by self-effort and spiritual power flowing into his soul from the order of God; cleansed by his faith, in the purifying fires of God's love, from the one, he is wholly free, by the separating force of his institutions, from the other.

In the freedom of the community is found opportunity for every form of ability, for every grade of genius. Each finds his own peculiar gifts needed and valued by the rest; and, in the recognition of his worth, the communist finds, perhaps for the first time in his life, a chance to work along

the lines of his best endowments, feeling that the results
are of value and are prized by those about him. Here is
opportunity for natural taste and talent to develop. Re-
striction only falls, where it should always fall, on whatever
is for undue self-pleasing, or against the welfare and comfort of others. The principles of communistic life make
necessary that the development of the ideal yield in unselfish
precedence to the demands of daily living, the common
needs of the family and home.

What of literature, art, music—must I abandon these?
Here is the most noble freedom of all. What do you desire, license to roam through every miasmatic swamp or
deadly fen of putrid imaginations? Then will you find true
love for your soul's health forbidding. But do you want
to breathe pure airs of lofty ideals? Do you want the
breadth and hight of God-enkindled thought? Is it the
expression of absolute harmony for which your soul yearns?
Then, with those whose lives are attuned to God and truth,
will you find freedom and encouragement, not only to enjoy
the works of masters, but yourself to create, if touched by
the creative spirit of beauty, truth and harmony. The
noblest conceptions in literature, art and music are yet to
come, from intellects clarified by spirituality, from lives
attuned to purity, holiness and love. In this development
of the æsthetic, as well as the intellectual nature, the principles of Shakerism open the noblest of opportunities and
invite to the grandest efforts.

The system that by its principle of being is in connection with the centre of essential light, beauty and harmony,
open to constant inflow therefrom, can but expand. A
cathedral of Milan could not have been guessed from its
foundation stones; the world of today could not have been
read from the phenomena of the Mesozoic Age; nor from
the accomplishments of Shakerism in its primal epoch, its

era of foundation laying, can its later evolutions be foreseen. Sufficient to know that it holds the great substratal principles of truth—purity, harmony, eternal growth. Then, from the knowledge of what God has wrought in nature, enter into intelligent, sympathetic and responsive receptivity, and place yourself in the line of highest ultimate development.

Are Shakers Dying Out?

Yea! dying out and up. Men and women die — advance, go to higher planes, to spheres of greater radius than earth, where we hear of them actively engaged along the same lines as on earth—the spread of truth among humanity.

Is Shakerism Dying?

Nay! not unless God and Christ and eternal verities are failing.

Thought, spiritual life, move in spirals; each great spiral returning on itself, yet ever higher, ever onward. Progression is the law of life. Always at the passing of the old and the coming of the new is a period of apparent decline, as between the harvest of one year and the leafage of the next. As in physical nature, so in spiritual life, organizations obey the tidal law of ebb and flood, the spiral law of retrogression and fresh advance.

Hepworth Dixon, the English lecturer and writer, has much to say about Shaker ideas, affirming that they have modified the religious thought of America. He says: "One man with ideas may be worth a whole Parliament, nay, a whole nation without them. The Shakers may not be scholars and men of genius. In appearance, they are often very simple; but they are men with ideas, and capable of sacrifice. No one can look into the heart of American society without seeing that these Shaker unions have a power upon men beyond that of mere numbers. If a poll-tax were decreed, they might pay into the exchequer less than many of the sects, but their influence on American thought is out of all comparison with that of such sects. The Shakers have a genius, a faith, an organization, which are not only strange, but seductive; which have been tried in the fire of persecution and are hostile to society as it stands.

"A Shaker village is not only a new church, but a new nation." The church is based on these grand ideas: the kingdom of heaven has come; Christ has actually appeared again upon earth; the personal rule of God is restored. In the wake of these ideas, and dependent upon them, are many more. Mount Lebanon is the centre of a system which has a distinct genius, a strong organization, a distinctive life of its own through which it would appear to be helping to shape and guide in no small measure the spiritual career of the United States of America."

Said a Shaker after sixty-two years of experience in the Order: — "It is of all cases and places by far the best experience for developing one's individuality. We have an excellent opportunity for bringing every shaky, unstable principle to the altar of self-sacrifice, so that when we are through with it all, we find that all that is in our heaven and earth, that can be shaken, has been shaken and shaken to pieces, and that which could not and cannot be shaken remains. At this stage of our experience, we find ourselves in possession of a completely rounded out individuality."

Rich with thought suggestion is that brief remark of Father Joseph, remembered and recorded by Jemima Blanchard of Harvard. In answer to a question as to what the increasing work of the church should be, he said: "The

NO. 30.   ELDRESS HARRIET BULLARD.   HEAD OF THE CENTRAL
MINISTRY.

work of God in the church is a gradual coming down and so it will continue through time."

One who wears beautifully the glory of her many years, a true exponent of the principles nobly taught and lived, in all positions of trust and responsibility, writes thus of

"The Beauty of My Shaker Faith.

"My call to be a Believer is something more than a casual circumstance. I feel its force and realize its holiness. As a woman in the sphere of nature, I realize how enslaved I should be to the fashions and life that gratify the merely animal, the object and slave of man's passions. As a sister in the spiritual family of Christ, I am relieved from earthly servitude, and am a free being — free to live and be as pure as the heavens, with companions who are also pure. I have the association of brethren, upon whom I can depend for my spiritual and physical protection,— who are not seeking the spoliation of the angel virtue in woman. We, as their sisters, are enabled to be their ministers of comfort and love. The reciprocity of gentleness and sweet companionship between brethren and sisters, who are true and well tried, may find an equal illustration in the heavens, but no other condition on earth yields an equal joy. I realize every day of my life the beauty of my Gospel faith. Living in pure virginity, apart from the excitements of a worldly life; with the privilege of confessing and forsaking the mistakes of the past and of feeling my attachment and relation to the spirits in the heavenly world. My whole being is under the guidance and ministration of the superior world. I love its discipline. I am happy in my call to an entire consecration of soul and body to a cause so noble; and though many rebel against the call of God, I know that the discipline of a Shaker life is of God and that its principles can never fail. I have tasted the bread and waters of a regenerated and eternal life, and to every sincere seeker after truth, I send greeting, and a welcome to share with me."

ELDRESS HARRIET BULLARD, 1872.

Said Elder Evans:

"If I believed that what we have now was the whole of the Gospel, it would confound me at once; but, believing as I do that we are now in the decadence of the first degree of the seventh cycle, that the fact of the Christ Anointing in Woman, a virgin life, revelation, non-resistance and a Visible Lead to receive confession of sins and obedience, were the prominent principles of this first degree — and that in each successive degree other important principles will be added, I abide my time. The existing cycle becomes the seed of the succeeding one. The new cycle will surpass the old and supplant it, as the work of Jesus supplanted that of John. Woman must be a potent factor in founding the second cycle as she was in founding the first. The Order is eternal, by reason of the absolutely true principles that are the foundation of the society organizations. These principles will remain, others will be added."

When, where and in what key, the call will be sounded to usher in

The New Age,

we may not say; but that it will soon sound, perhaps is even now sounding, the prophetic teachings of the past, the trend of present events and the currents of thought within the Shaker Order and in the outer world, lead us to believe.

The truths inherent in Shakerism are the underlying truths of God-life in all ages. The mission of the Shaker is to illustrate and teach these principles of truth, these laws of light and freedom.

When the materialism of the age just passing shall have rubbed the clay from its world-blinded eyes, it will see men—divine truths—as trees walking. It sees them now; for this is just the state of humanity today, in Europe and America. A little more light, another stage of advance and the world of spiritual truth will unfold as eyes open to see, and then, the Christ-embodying man, woman, church, organization, will receive, assist and instruct the awakened soul of humanity. This is the mission of Shakerism and this the work of the Shaker.

A new age of spirituality is at hand, and the conditions now existing in embryonic form in the old time Shaker communities will develop, in a manner perhaps as startling to Shakers as to the world. They will receive, protect and develop the principles that for over one hundred years have been implanted in human hearts, have been germinated, nurtured and brought forth to light and air, by the spirit hands of hosts of true Believers beyond the veil of mortality. Undying are these life principles for they are truth.

Conditions suited to the needs of the new age will develop and take on form. The Shaker faith and the Shaker life, will, from its elastic nature, be ready to receive the impress of newly revealed truth and expand in new forms.

Souls harvested from earth conditions will anew, as of old, find in Shaker faith and practice their true home. Under conditions such as are found only in the Shaker Religious Community, can the lofty ideals of purest minds and most humanitarian thought find full scope and culture. As mankind progresses in evolution toward pure spirituality, more and more will individuals find in advancing Shakerism, the physical, intellectual, social and spiritual necessities of being met and satisfied.

In the life of these communities, many antiquated features are changing with the changing time, to fit the demands of a new day. The time will doubtless come, when the society and not the family will be the unit of community organization; when separate business interests will be united and wider cooperation, resulting from fresh baptisms of love by the Christ Spirit, will impart new life and vigor. Were the principle of concentration, which has in some cases merged together families and societies, to be generally applied, it might be better for the Order and for the world in which it is a centre of truth. In the religious, as in the scientific and business world, the day of individual interests, of small holdings, has passed, the age of concentration and conservation of force has dawned—beginning of a world-wide realization of God's great law of cooperation. One or two strong centres would mean more power, broader and more useful living.

As changes occur in the outer world, in material, industrial and social conditions, as "brawn gives place to brain" and spiritual forces come into ascendency, as earth can support more of her children and increased knowledge lengthens the span of life, just in proportion will grow the necessity of provision for humanity's flower and ripened fruit—for those who shall be free to live the higher spiritual life. Purity, self-denial, practical brotherhood and sisterhood call for men and women of health, high purpose, activity and consecration. Such, in ever increasing numbers, will gather into communistic, religious homes, where divinely affiliated action shall work out divinely inspired purpose in noblest effort for humanity, along divinely directed lines.

All that ripened humanity demands is found in the principles underlying these communities, principles existing in the Gospel of Mother Ann, among those "harvested from the world."

A student and worker in humanitarian fields, after a stay of several weeks at Mount Lebanon, wrote thus to "Brotherhood," a London periodical:—"The spiritual wave—the religion of the future, for which the times are preparing—will gather into itself not only the *living* among Shakers, but the true-hearted everywhere, under all creeds and forms. And then the Shaker homes will become restful and vital centres for a *world movement* which will strike at the root of all evils in church and state and bring the kingdom of heaven nearer to this struggling world."

In the September sunshine float myriads of tiny, fairy ships, air drifted on their unknown course. What are they? Seeds of trees and plants, floating off to root and spring up next year. Thus is it with the seeds of truth! Principles lived by this Order for one hundred and thirty years are being scattered over the earth. Here and there are found living centres of truths whose preaching once brought stoning and imprisonment. Never have men and women been so imbued with the principles of Shakerism as now.

Essential Shakerism can never die, for it holds within itself principles which the developed life of humanity demands to have embodied in practical daily living.

XXIII

A MESSAGE TO SHAKERS

FOR many years progressive leaders and thinkers in all
societies and families have felt that spiritual and
temporal advance, true Gospel Union, demand a
deeper Communism, a wider cooperation in family
and society relations. The total absence of creed and formal constitution, the deeply grounded principle of spiritual
influx and advancing revelation make possible, in the
Shaker Order, a continuous progress which shall wisely
conserve all essential elements, and progress without revolution marks the evolving history of the Order.

It has long been felt that the future success, if not the
continued life of the organization lies in a firmer grasp
and more radical application of that primal order of a
United Interest—a true Communism based on Gospel Love
and Harmony; and that, while the Covenant provides the
most perfect system of government known to man, in details of application, it should broaden with the broadening
spirit of the age, the growing intellectuality and self-gov-
erning power of the individual. As March buds in their
swelling push off the dry leaves left by December winds,
thus in Shakerism, the pulse of the Spirit is ever replacing
old forms by new growth and beauty. Let the new life
pulse and the old excrescence drop to earth where it belongs! Never in the history of Shakerism has there been
such opportunity for increase and power as now. The
world is astir with the impulse and quickening of this Gos-

(396)

NO. 31.   ELDRESS ANNA WHITE.

pel of purity, equality and brotherhood. Never have people turned as now they are turning, with eager, inquiring thought, to seek in the principles of Shakerism the key that shall unlock the mystery of life. Let Shakers arise in the joy and strength of their faith and minister its spirit and its power!

Other religious organizations have failed because the people that composed their constituent parts have been recreant to principles, have drifted away from the truth entrusted to them. The religious history of humanity is strewn with wrecks, as were the desert trails across western prairies in the days of the emigrant wagon,—bleached and crackling bones alone whitening on the sands; thus are strewn along the sands of time the blanching remnants of spiritual revelations, wrecked by unfaithfulness, untruth, or lack of courage.

The Shaker Covenant, strong though it is, may be weakened by indifference to its obligations and laxity in its enforcement. No power of medicine can cure the blood-taint in the human organism, caused by neglect and viola-tion of physical law in the ancestral line; no more can later mendings repair the devitalized and poisoned spiritual or-ganism, when dishonesty and supine selfishness and greed have overborne truth and rectitude. Herein lies the weight of dread, anxiety and responsibility for future generations, that is resting heavily today on the hearts of all clear-sighted thinkers in the Shaker Order.

The life current must touch every part of the organism continuously. The Shaker may change his style of coat, may alter the cut of her gown or cease to wear a cap, and no harm be done. Vital harm may be done by retaining either, at outlay of time and thought, by effort of soul and sense, merely to preserve old forms and customs, when the time is crying out in vain for action; for spontaneous,.

out-reaching sympathy here, aid there, cooperation yonder. Do cap and broad brimmed hat stand for separation from the wórld, for pure integrity of soul, and does altered dress express, in terms of milliner and tailor, a spiritual weakening of stalwart principles, a compromise with worldliness? Then, in truth, is it a vital matter and firm should be the resistance to encroachment on the forms of by-gone days until by labor in soul-gardening, true spiritual life attains maturity. The sheltering fence about the frail sapling may not safely be removed; but the strong young tree, in its vigorous growth, is hampered by its presence.

Are you, my Shaker sister, keeping your phylacteries broad and white in cap band and kerchief, — and neglecting to spur on women and children in your neighborhood or among your guests, to preserve the lives of birds and to drop feathers from their head gear? Are you strenuous to preserve intact all good old careful ways of handling pottery and cleaning floors, and do you still, despite the quickening consciences of thousands in the outside world, persist in living on the dead carcasses of animals,—do you still slay, or permit others to slay for you, loading your table with the forms of your dependent fellow-beings? Are the smothered shrieks ascending from helpless living animals, and, we are told, from friendless human criminal and pauper, bound beneath the vivisector's knife, and are you silent? Does the cry of them go up to heaven and is your ear deaf? Then are you failing to hear the call that sounds so plainly on the ears of thousands who have never heard of Ann Lee, but whose convictions, fast hardening into principles, were voiced and set in motion by the same Christ Spirit that inspired Ann Lee.

Are you, my Shaker brother, true to the ancient faith, seeking first the Kingdom of God and His righteousness, --not the righteousness of the world, with its low standard of morality and honesty? Are you, for the sake of society or family gain, seeking investments, whose inner workings are contrary to that life principle of the true Shaker—the Golden Rule? By such investments are you linking your people with the unjust stewardship of the monopolist? Do you even exact usury of your own spiritual brother of the "United Society?" Are you defiling your hands, your homes, your altars, with the forbidden spoils of the conquered cities of worldly life? Because the broad green leaf of the tobacco plant is so easily transformed into the bank bill, do you slight the oft-repeated injunction of Mother Ann, speaking in the name and through the endowment of the Divine Mother? Then are you a violator of your sacred charge, your profit will turn in your hands to loss and all the people must suffer with you. Has the glamour of Wall Street blinded the eyes of any to the pure light of that Highway cast up for the ransomed of the Lord to walk in? Let us

Turn the Battle to the Gate!

In his later years, Elder Evans often gave public testimony to the effect that confession of sin was essential, not only for the individual, but for the Order. "When, in the advancing light of truth," he would say, "we come to a knowledge of our sins as an Order, it is our duty publicly to confess those sins. Are we dumb dogs, that dare not bark against the sins of our own institution?" Shakers have not been blind to errors of judgment in those whose hearts have been loyal to the cause; neither have they been blind to those graver errors of laxity in observing covenantal obligations and compromise in maintaining fundamental principles, by those who have heeded not the exhortation, "Seek ye first the Kingdom of God and His righteousness." With however great reluctance the truth may be spoken, in the face of present conditions,—conditions largely due to this moral remissness, loyalty to the cause demands that the facts be told by Shakers themselves.

Not Infallible.

Human nature is the same, yesterday and today, — exposed to imminent dangers, open to manifest advantages. Happy that man of Shaker faith who sees his errors, realizes his sins and is willing to rectify them by honest confession and repentance; who seeks his union with those whose sole desire is to be known as he is known, and whose every transaction is open to the light. No loss, financial or spiritual, can move him from his high station. His friends with reason trust him implicitly, he is honored and reverenced by all. Yet, this man, with all his attainment, is not infallible. There comes a change, a turn in the tide of affairs, his platform is weakened, doubt and fear crowd in to displace faith and hope. Then it is that he needs the help of strong hands and brave hearts; but pride, fear and specious reasoning come in; too far shaken to accept the aid of Elders and brethren, he goes down and dismay and death follow in his track.

Every one who is unfaithful to his inner light is unfaithful to his brother man. Some Shaker societies, through individual representatives, have been untrue to their covenant, unfaithful in their practise of the fundamental principles of the Order. Set to practise community, cooperation, from the vital principle of Divine Love,—they have separated themselves into distinctive interests of society and family, and, in an only wider selfishness than that of the natural man, have sunk into rivalry and competition. In this way have they robbed their fellowmen, not alone by sharing in monopolistic financial operations, but by depriving them of that high, spiritual standard, that Light to lighten the world, that was set upon Mount Zion. As with individuals, so with organizations. The organization is but a composite individual, and, from that composite nature, is more exposed than the individuals of which it is made up. In every Shaker society,. Ministry, Elders, Trustees and Deacons do, by the Covenant, agree to build each other up in the faith of the Order. That faith is to avoid debt, to "owe no man anything but to love one another," to submit implicitly all business transactions and whatever is for the interest of the family to the leading authority, vested in the Ministry. They, in turn, advise, instruct and give decision, not, however, before attaining a thorough knowledge of details and relations and ascertaining the minds of others in positions of trust. "Do the Ministry not err?" is often asked. "Do they not make serious mistakes, and do they not come under the same penalty for so doing as lay members?" "When one member suffers all the members suffer with it." To err is human. The Ministry are not infallible; only the Christ Spirit is that, and, though appointed to receive the anointing of the Christ Spirit, they are not beyond being touched, as was Jesus, Elder Brother of many brethren, with the feeling of others' infirmities. Neither can they always be unaffected by the pressure of strong personal influence from individuals, by the spirit of the time, the atmosphere of the age. It is a close distinction to draw the line demarking the human judgment from the divine wisdom residing in the individuals that compose the Order.

Notwithstanding our explicit teaching of the purest life and the loftiest conceptions of right, the societies have suffered through certain members, some by defalcations and others by grossest mismanagement. Why is this, when rules and orders are given for the safety and protection of all? Simply because those rules and orders have not been obeyed. Where so little coercion exists, where so much responsibility rests on individual loyalty, one person, taking advantage of the trust reposed in him, by signing a document, or by secret, ill-judged investments, may deluge a whole society with debt. This has been frequently done. At the present time, societies east and west suffer from the violation of this most weighty and all-important order in the covenant. What penalty is suffered? Does a public reprimand ensue? As a rule, such betrayers of trust are removed from official position, but in this regard, our Order falls far behind, in discipline, the custom of other religious organizations. In the Quaker societies, from which our Order sprang, such a delinquent is visited by a committee appointed by the Meeting, his case must pass the ordeal of the several Meetings, and only after labors and repentance can he be reinstated in confidence and union. If he fails to satisfy his peers, he is disowned. In the Salvation Army, a violation of fundamental principle, in an officer, is punished at once by remanding him to the ranks. He must, by confession and repentance, by "doing the first works," reinstate himself in the confidence and respect of his fellows.

Shakers, out of charity, sympathy for the individual, from tender consideration of age or imbecility, have held such delinquents in union and, as far as possible, have condoned their misdeeds. By this laxity, that high standard of truth, entrusted to our Order, towering above all other standards, reared in times of adversity and poverty, when persecution and suffering were the portion of Believers, has, by compromise, by undue thirst for power or popularity, fallen, and we are left to bite the dust, or, in other words, to reap the fruits of disobedience.

Shakers, through suffering and sorrow, must learn the lesson that has been so fully taught in other circles and on other planes of life, that it is both unwise and unsafe to entrust unlimited power in the hands of one person, thereby placing him in the direct path of that direful foe, temptation. If through that come sin and disaster, then all are sharers in that disaster and in that sin.

All this arises from the supremacy of material interests over the spiritual life. In the early days, Ministry and Elders were withdrawn from temporal responsibilities and held themselves strictly in the line of spiritual influx. They were the fountain of spiritual supply, the power centre of spiritual force. For many years, increasingly, as numbers have diminished, have places of temporal care and responsibility fallen back upon the hands of these Spiritual Leaders, and these places are being filled by Ministry and Elders. A vessel can be no more than full. When temporal burdens of this nature must be borne, the spiritual gift, of necessity, depreciates.

In our present condition, we have no reason to doubt the efficacy of the principles that have stood for one hundred and thirty years. In all of our societies are noble members, in whom faith and courage are still aglow. Like the exiled Parsees, in ancient times, who, through their long and wearisome journey, guarded the sacred flame that had come down to them from the spiritual world, to light again their altars in the new land of their adoption, — these faith-lighted hearts in our own time are guarding this sacred flame, the testimony of truth from the heavenly world, until such time as the Spirit shall lead to those new altars, in a people prepared to accept and carry forward unto fuller and more glorious expression those special revelations of truth, the first cycle of whose manifestation has been here recorded.

"Gather My Saints Together."

Gathering out treasures of wisdom from past experience, adapting our organic life and habits to the present age, in government more largely representative, under a new Pentecostal baptism, the love of brother and sister will lead to industrial cooperation and spiritual unity. In union there is strength. Thirteen little separate States, in 1787, amounted to zero in the world's great sum of power; welded together by the Constitution, the thirteen zeros became a unit, whose potency has grown in one hundred years to the first rank in the order of nations. Fifteen societies, separate, each from each, families within each society forming still smaller integrate particles, can no longer hold their own in domestic, business and spiritual efficiency. For the future of this noble inheritance, for the love of Truth, we should unite our forces.

Has not the day arrived when that grand, divinely ordained theocracy, which unites the spiritual man of earth to the heavens and to God, may, without endangering the structure, readjust its temporal relations? When the method of theocratic control in all the details of life, a system brought forth in an adolescent age of mingled subservience and rebellion, may give place to the broader freedom that belongs to men and women who have attained intellectual maturity? Let not the spiritual connection be lost! The eternal principles of right, justice and purity, the foundation of our Order, laid in the nation's childhood and youth, are as grand, as broad, as enduring, now. But the man and woman of today, free of thought, trained in judgment, holding the world as a standing place for the lever that shall move a universe, cannot be bound and shackled in swaddling clothes.

Again, from the realms of spiritual thought rings out the message, "No man can come to Me, except the Father which hath sent Me, draw him." No one can enter this Spiritual Church and take on its covenantal relationships, without renunciation of the old. They may be attracted by certain laws of the Church and seek to find access through them, but, unless baptized into the very life essence of the Gospel in all its phases of cooperation, practical communism, increasing revelation, a virgin life, peace and non-resistance, it will be but an attempt, a fruitless expenditure of time and talent. It is recognized that prepared, spiritually unfolded men and women are the only ones to whom this Order is of permanent use. Give to such, the faithful, covenant-keeping members, a voice in all affairs of financial and temporal import. Grant them the intellectual freedom their development requires. Fit Shakerism to humanity today, as the Fathers and Mothers of the past fitted it to their age and time. Make it possible for the noblest man, the most broad-minded woman to fit himself, herself, to the simple, lofty, spiritual life of Shakerism.

Let Shakers keep their birthright of leadership, in the van of human progress. Let Truth and Steadfastness, those two bright "angels by the mast," guide the Gospel Ship safely to the port of opportunity and world-wide service. Let Shakers seek the shrine where still abides the Divine Spirit and then go forth to seek the quickened spirits in the outer realm.

Through a return to first principles,—a foundation that cannot be shaken,—and building thereon a character above all censure, through consolidation and consecration alone, can genuine, essential Shakerism restore the depleted ranks, usher in the new cycle of increasing truth and holiness to this, the only Virgin Church on earth, founded upon principles of Eternal Truth.

"The mighty God, even the Lord, hath spoken;— Gather my saints together unto Me; those that have made a convenant with Me by sacrifice; And call upon Me in the day of trouble: I will deliver thee and thou shalt glorify Me," O thou Virgin Church of the New Creation!

Our Watchers.

Ye spirits of the Mighty, great in faith,
That hover yet upon these mountain hights,
And brood above this valley;
Ye who once against a world of scorn,—
Scorn and contempt, and bitter, persecuting hate,—
Stood like Truth, unmoved, unbent;
Ye men and women, plain of garb and speech,
Exact, sincere, true to your heavenly vision;
Ye who jested not, nor swerved
One hair's breadth from conviction;
Ye who centered in your souls
Throbbing life currents of the Infinite,—
Love, Sacrifice, Devotion, Faith;
Ye who endured and triumphed,—
Watch and wait, leave us not yet!
Your trailing robes, your echoing songs,
Your warnings and your beckonings divine,
We need, we feel them still.
Stand not aloof on hill tops far,
But here, amid our gardens and our fields,—
Here, in our rooms and halls, kitchens and barns —
Pass and repass; touch us in passing.
And may weak wills grow strong,
Eyes lose their world glitter,
Faithless hearts their ache, as we
Touch, haply unknowing,
But your garments' hem!

LEILA S. TAYLOR.

INDEX.